Palgrave Studies in Compromise after Conflict

Series Editor
John D. Brewer
Queen's University Belfast
Belfast, UK

This series aims to bring together in one series scholars from around the world who are researching the dynamics of post-conflict transformation in societies emerging from communal conflict and collective violence. The series welcomes studies of particular transitional societies emerging from conflict, comparative work that is cross-national, and theoretical and conceptual contributions that focus on some of the key processes in post-conflict transformation. The series is purposely interdisciplinary and addresses the range of issues involved in compromise, reconciliation and societal healing. It focuses on interpersonal and institutional questions, and the connections between them.

More information about this series at
http://www.palgrave.com/gp/series/14641

Linda Asquith

Rebuilding Lives After Genocide

Migration, Adaptation and Acculturation

palgrave
macmillan

Linda Asquith
Leeds Beckett University
LEEDS, West Yorkshire, UK

Palgrave Studies in Compromise after Conflict
ISBN 978-3-030-14073-1 ISBN 978-3-030-14074-8 (eBook)
https://doi.org/10.1007/978-3-030-14074-8

Library of Congress Control Number: 2019934751

This Palgrave Macmillan imprint is published by the registered company Springer Nature Switzerland AG.
The registered company address is: Gewerbestrasse 11, 6330 Cham, Switzerland

For my family: Phil, Rebecca, Bethany and Rochelle, you make my life brighter and more joyful.

For Lydia: We've come a long way since sitting in that criminology lecture together.

Acknowledgements

I owe a huge debt of thanks to Dr Graham Gibbs and Dr Gráinne McMahon for their support, guidance and advice during the research for this book.

The survivors in this study gave their time and stories willingly, and fed and watered me as I trekked around the UK. My heartfelt thanks go to every participant for giving me their time. I hope I do your stories justice.

General Editor's Introduction

'Compromise' is a much-used, but little understood, term. There is a sense in which it describes a set of feelings (the so-called spirit of compromise) that involve reciprocity, representing the agreement to make mutual concessions towards each other from now on: no matter what we did to each other in the past, we will act towards each other in the future differently as set out in the agreement between us. The compromise settlement can be a spit and a handshake, much beloved in folk lore, or a legally binding statute with hundreds of clauses.

As such, it is clear that compromise enters into conflict transformation at two distinct phases. The first is during the conflict resolution process itself, where compromise represents a willingness amongst parties to negotiate a peace agreement that represents a second-best preference in which they give up their first preference (victory) in order to cut a deal. A great deal of literature has been produced in peace studies and international relations on the dynamics of the negotiation process and the institutional and governance structures necessary to consolidate the agreement afterwards. Just as important, however, is compromise in the second phase, when compromise is part of post-conflict reconstruction, in which protagonists come to learn to live together despite their former enmity and in face of the atrocities perpetrated during the conflict itself.

In the first phase, compromise describes reciprocal agreements between parties to the negotiations in order to make political concessions sufficient to end conflict; in the second phase, compromise involves victims and perpetrators developing ways of living together in which concessions are made as part of shared social life. The first phase is about compromises between political groups and the state in the process of state-building (or rebuilding) after the political upheavals of communal conflict; the second is about compromises between individuals and communities in the process of social healing after the cultural trauma provoked by the conflict.

This book series primarily concerns itself with the second process, the often messy and difficult job of reconciliation, restoration and repair in social and cultural relations following communal conflict. Communal conflicts and civil wars tend to suffer from the narcissism of minor differences, to coin Freud's phrase, leaving little to be split halfway and compromise on, and thus are usually especially bitter. The series therefore addresses itself to the meaning, manufacture and management of compromise in one of its most difficult settings. The book series is cross-national and cross-disciplinary, with attention paid to interpersonal reconciliation at the level of everyday life, as well as culturally between social groups, and the many sorts of institutional, interpersonal, psychological, sociological, anthropological and cultural factors that assist and inhibit societal healing in all post-conflict societies, historically and in the present. It focuses on what compromise means when people have to come to terms with past enmity and the memories of the conflict itself, and relate to former protagonists in ways that consolidate the wider political agreement.

This sort of focus has special resonance and significance, for peace agreements are usually very fragile. Societies emerging out of conflict are subject to ongoing violence from spoiler groups who are reluctant to give up on first preferences, constant threats from the outbreak of renewed violence, institutional instability, weakened economies, and a wealth of problems around transitional justice, memory, truth recovery and victimhood, amongst others. Not surprisingly, therefore, reconciliation and healing in social and cultural relations is difficult to achieve, not least because interpersonal compromise between erstwhile enemies is difficult.

Lay discourse picks up on the ambivalent nature of compromise after conflict. It is talked about in common sense in one of two ways, in which compromise is either a virtue or a vice, taking its place among the angels or in Hades. One form of lay discourse likens concessions to former protagonists with the idea of restoration of broken relationships and societal and cultural reconciliation, in which there is a sense of becoming (or returning) to wholeness and completeness. The other form of lay discourse invokes ideas of appeasement, of being *compromised* by the concessions, which constitute a form of surrender and reproduce (or disguise) continued brokenness and division. People feel they continue to be beaten by the sticks which the concessions have allowed others to keep; with restoration, however, weapons are turned truly in ploughshares. Lay discourse suggests, therefore, that these are issues that the Palgrave Studies in Compromise After Conflict series must begin to problematise, so that the process of societal healing is better understood and can be assisted and facilitated by public policy and intervention.

This new volume is an exciting edition to the series given its focus on the everyday life experience of migration to Great Britain. It is exciting for two reasons. First, it gives a glimpse from direct, first-hand data of the everyday experiences of survivors of genocide who had relocated to Great Britain, something which is under-reported and both new and novel compared to other treatments of genocide. Second, it uses sociological ideas to help understand these everyday life experiences, particularly the work of the late and sadly missed Pierre Bourdieu. Bourdieu's work is encompassing and is popularly applied in areas such as education, religion and civil society. Linda Asquith's application of Bourdieu's conceptual map and ideas to survivors of genocide is pioneering.

Asquith's sample of survivors is small, as most opportunity samples amongst hard-to-access groups inevitably are. It is significant that they are all survivors who have integrated into British society in different ways and to different degrees. While this distinguishes them from many forced migrants in Britain's contemporary Brexit climate, with the legitimacy this has given to public expressions of intolerance, and to hate speech and far-right extremism, amongst other things, it makes the sample relevant to the themes of this series, by showing how tolerance, compromise, healing, social reintegration and the like are possible after genocide. New lives can be recreated after involuntary relocation.

As series editor I am particularly enthusiastic about this volume for it fits into two bigger themes that have been pushed in the series and as part of broader work by other writers and me in the series. The first is the application of the sociological imagination to the study of peace processes in an attempt to rescue the field from political scientists, international relations experts, and human rights and transitional justice specialists. The use of ideas by Asquith from social capital theory, and in particular Bourdieu, is part of this attempt to reshape the field and to develop the sociology of peace. Second, there is now a growing literature, including contributions from the series, on the everyday life of peace-building. International relations has discovered the notion of everyday life but treats it unsociologically. Some books in the series have given sociological insight into the everyday life experiences of victims of conflict in Northern Ireland, South Africa and Sri Lanka (Brewer, Hayes, Teeney, Dudgeon, Mueller-Hirth and Wijesinghe, *The Sociology of Everyday Life Peacebuilding*) and into the everyday life experiences of displaced peoples returning to their former homeland in Bosnia (Sivac-Bryant, *Re-Making Kozarac*). In other words, Asquith's discovery of the everyday life of people surviving genocide is part of a bigger discovery of the sociology of everyday life of people emerging out of conflict.

In all these ways, Asquith's book makes both empirical and conceptual advances. It is an impressive empirical analysis of a very hard-to-access group, and the wealth of material offers ethnographic richness to our understanding of genocide survivors' everyday lives. Its advances are also conceptual, not only by adding significantly to our knowledge about the aftermath of genocide, but also in the application of Bourdieu's work to develop further the sociology of everyday life peace-building. As series editor, I warmly welcome this new volume to the series.

Belfast, UK
January 2019

John D. Brewer

Contents

About the Author

Linda Asquith is the course director for the BA (Hons) Criminology course at Leeds Beckett University. Her research focuses on the 'life afterwards'—for victims, offenders and those who have experienced wrongful convictions.

1

Introduction

The last four decades have seen a marked surge of interest in genocide studies. This surge, led by scholars such as Adam Jones, Henry Huttenbach, Alex Alvarez and Phil Clark, has illuminated previously unconsidered areas of study, such as the Holocaust's place in a continuum of genocide (Huttenbach 1988), the challenge of transitional justice after genocide (Clark 2010), gender and genocide (Jones 2012), climate change as genocide (Alvarez 2017) and genocide as a state crime (Alvarez 2001). This interest has partly been driven by the increase in the number of states which are willing to use genocidal violence in order to gain power, for example, the conflict in the former Yugoslavia and the gassing of the Kurds in Iraq (Totten and Parsons 2012). It has also been driven by new developments in technology that have resulted in the news about such events being heard more widely and more quickly; consider those who have used Twitter and other social media sites to inform the world what has been happening in Syria. Whilst a considerable amount of literature has been published that relates specifically to the Holocaust, especially by scholars such as Dan Stone (2018), studies of other genocides are also developing significant literature bases as a result of the work of people such as Philip Gourevitch (1999, 2014) and Elizabeth Neuffer (2002) on

L. Asquith, *Rebuilding Lives After Genocide*, Palgrave Studies in Compromise after Conflict, https://doi.org/10.1007/978-3-030-14074-8_1

Rwanda and Bosnia, respectively, and Alexander Hinton (2005) on Cambodia. These and other studies have shed light on how genocide occurs (Bauman 1989; Shaw 2003; Straus 2006), the stages of genocide (Stanton 2019) and how the perpetrators are dealt with following genocide (Clark 2010; Arendt 2006; Karstedt 2018). Despite this burgeoning field of interest, however, little attention has been paid to what happens to genocide survivors *after* genocide, especially those who migrate to a different country.

In the main, studies that examine genocide come from a historical or psychological viewpoint, either chronicling the historical events that happened or concerning themselves with the motivations of perpetrators or bystanders. Until recently, the crime of genocide has been virtually ignored by all of the social sciences, with sociology largely ignoring genocide until the late 1970s (Fein 1990; Owens et al. 2013). Kaufman (1996) suggests that this neglect was due to epistemological limitations such as dispassion and value neutrality that the scientific method places upon sociology and sociological discourse. Fein (1990) suggests that there may have been some reluctance to study genocide due to the disciplinary and psychological barriers of the researchers but also that sociologists may have had concerns about upsetting or further traumatising survivors of genocide. Indeed, Gerson and Wolf suggest that sociology is marked by a "profound silence" in relation to the Holocaust. "Few sociologists, regardless of their religious or cultural identity, have focused their academic work on the Holocaust or post-Holocaust life" (2007, 3).

This lack of focus is also problematic in relation to migration, and Hoffman (1989) suggests that migration is a strangely ignored aspect of studies on the Holocaust. Migrants can carry with them a particular set of vulnerabilities and disadvantages. These vulnerabilities or disadvantages can interact with the other social statuses that they occupy, such as the vulnerability of being a 'victim' of torture in their home country, but being seen as an immigration 'offender' in the UK (McDonald and Erez 2007). Equally, qualifications which are not recognised in the host country are a disadvantage to the migrant (McDonald and Erez 2007).

Criminology, as a newer discipline, has focused until recently on 'volume' and 'traditional' crime such as burglary and individual rape and murder offences, and there is a growing recognition of the importance of the life afterwards in relation to offenders' desistance of such crimes (Maruna 2017). Furthermore, victims' recovery from 'traditional' crime has a significant literature base, particularly in relation to burglary (Maguire 1980; Coupe and Griffiths 1999) and gender-based crimes such as rape and sexual violence (Westmarland 2015). However, many victimological approaches are not appropriate for the study of genocide survivors; for example, positivistic approaches which consider the role of victims in their own victimisation (e.g. Amir 1971) would be wholly inappropriate for the study of genocide survivors. Equally, approaches that examine the routine behaviours of either offenders or victims are also inappropriate as these again seek to examine the behaviour of victims and consider who is most likely to be victimised. Both approaches are problematic because those who experience genocide have been targeted because of their identity (i.e. who they are, or whom they are thought to be). Therefore, the theories and concepts of such approaches would not aid our understanding of the experiences of genocide survivors in any meaningful way.

Using a different approach, some authors, such as Alex Alvarez (Alvarez 2001) and Dave Kauzlarich and others (Rothe and Kauzlarich 2014), have applied a criminological lens to the study of genocide, with Rothe and Kauzlarich, in particular, considering the victims of genocide. This research tends to come under the umbrella of what has become known as 'Supranational Criminology', dealing with not only genocide but crimes against humanity, people trafficking and state crimes. This interest, whilst positive, has been focused on the victims of genocide (i.e. those who died) and the event itself rather than those who survived and their life afterwards. These analyses of genocide have focused on attempting to explain the occurrence, timing or severity of genocide and mass killing (Owens et al. 2013) or defining the act of genocide (Straus 2001), the individual cases of genocide and why they happened (Bauman 1989; Browning 1998; Des Forges 1999) and how the aftermath is managed in relation to justice (Clark 2009, 2010). Arguably, this has been at the expense of survivors of genocide who often remain the subjects of research only in terms of the psychological effects of genocide, such as post-traumatic stress disorder (PTSD) (Kellerman 2001).

Focusing on only the psychological effects of trauma ignores the wider context which may well influence how people react to trauma (Schwartz Lee 1988). Therefore, it is important that the life afterwards be examined from a sociological point of view as, whilst psychology can aid understanding of the individual pathology of the survivor, a sociological approach can uncover further knowledge and understanding of how the individual sees himself/herself in society and how society responds to the individual. Meierhenrich (2007) suggests that 'cultural trauma' operates alongside psychological trauma, with the concept of cultural trauma recognising the collective manifestation of trauma and underlining the distinction between individual experiences of trauma and the processes and mechanisms which are involved in the social construction of trauma. In discussing the genocide in Rwanda, Meierhenrich argues that "the trauma of the genocide was not simply inherent in the events of 1994, but to a large extent created in its aftermath, when it was subject to manipulation by social actors" (2007, 559). For that reason, an exploration of the wider context in relation to genocide survival is essential. More specifically, sociological theory can illuminate the processes by which survivors of genocide re-establish their lives and resettle into new communities. Often, survivors who migrate to the UK arrive with nothing except the clothes they are wearing, and on their own with no or little social network available to them. Furthermore, many survivors come from countries which are linguistically and culturally very different to the UK (Kushner 1999); therefore, as forced migrants, they arrive into a wholly new culture with no preparation. Yet despite this, the vast majority of survivors appear to rebuild and recover remarkably well. Ayalon et al. (2007) acknowledge that there has been little attempt to understand how and why the majority of Holocaust survivors were able to rebuild these adaptive lives and this can be applied to genocide survivors more broadly.

Furthermore, approaches that consider how social structures can affect the recovery of genocide survivors, and those that examine the responses of the state or powerful bodies to victims, could illuminate genocide survivors' experiences. In particular, those which consider how individuals recover and rebuild their lives using social networks, and where power lies within those networks, could aid understanding of the process of the re-establishment of life following genocide. Hence, the idea of social capital—that is, the ability of the individual to draw upon those resources available through his/her social network—has value. There are three key thinkers on social capital: Robert Putnam, James Coleman and Pierre Bourdieu. Putnam's and Coleman's perspectives share many similarities and are concerned with social capital and community, and the nature of networks in communities and how they facilitate the success or otherwise of a community. In this context, success is seen as low crime rates, high educational performance and high economic productivity. However, as the issues of language acquisition, cultural and structural acculturation, and 'ways of talking' (i.e. the different ways in which stories are told) may be just as important for re-establishing lives after genocide as those strong social networks, it is argued that Pierre Bourdieu's ideas of field, habitus and social capital may be useful as a lens through which to understand genocide survivors' experiences.

Bourdieu's concept of 'field' (Bourdieu 1993) allows for an exploration of how survivors create networks to begin with, how they may struggle for dominance in certain networks and why this struggle for dominance is important. Bourdieu's 'habitus' (Bourdieu 1977) is the individual's way of being and his/her understanding of his/her place in the world and how to act in it. Both of these concepts are the building blocks of Bourdieu's theory of social capital (Bourdieu 1986), which is the idea that the varying resources available to an individual affect how and in what ways she/he achieves in life, for example, socially, career-wise and educationally. Individuals also have varying amounts of 'cultural' capital, that is, for example, the ability to speak a language, play a sport, or hold specific educational qualifications. If those cultural resources are recognised by the wider society, they can be drawn upon in order to access social capital and build social networks, which can then be used to gain, for example, a better social position or improved employment opportunities. Bourdieu's theory is concerned, therefore, with the individual and the wider culture and community. Bourdieu suggests that those individuals whose cultural (and therefore social) capital is not recognised will struggle to 'better themselves' and instead remain fixed in their particular social class and status with no opportunity to move up (Bourdieu and Passeron 1990). Therefore, Bourdieu's ideas illustrate the potential challenges of a lack of social capital, which is important in understanding the post-genocide experiences of survivors. In applying the sociological imagination to the post-genocide life of migrants, this volume contributes to the growing intellectual debate and discussion in sociological approaches to peace as seen in this series of monographs. This series illustrates the value of sociology in exploring post-conflict situations, both from a geographical and, in this volume, from an individual approach.

Defining 'Genocide'

'Genocide' is a contested concept, and as such, it is important to define what is meant by the term in the context of this research, in order to justify the inclusion of the cases of genocide considered in this project. Genocide as a concept has existed since at least biblical times (e.g. the killing of all firstborn children in Egypt, described in the book of Exodus, or Herod's massacre of the infants in the Gospel of Matthew). It is almost universally accepted as being a crime with only very limited defence or mitigation; it is not possible to commit genocide accidentally or with good intentions, unlike other, more common domestic crimes (Amnesty International 1997).

However, the *word* 'genocide' has only existed since 1944, when the lawyer Raphael Lemkin coined the term in his text *Axis Rule in Occupied Europe* (Lemkin 1944). Lemkin defined the term in reference to the Nazi atrocities he saw committed against the Jews and other minority groups. Lemkin spent his formative years in Bezwodene, in Eastern Poland, and trained to be a lawyer before escaping from Poland in 1939 and moving to the US via Sweden. He had been shocked by the massacre of the Anatolian Armenians during the First World War and in particular the inability of the Allies to prosecute effectively the Turks who had perpetrated the violence. Gigliotti and Lang suggest that "Lemkin had been concerned with what he saw as a lack in both national and international law—their common failure to protect the rights *of* groups *as* groups" (2005: 389; emphasis added). This led Lemkin to argue and campaign for an international law that would protect ethnic and religious groups from destruction. He acknowledged that to achieve such a law, it was likely that there would be a need to limit state sovereignty (Lemkin

1944), an idea which most other legal scholars of the time rejected, as this would imply that states could no longer be wholly self-governing.

While in America, Lemkin extrapolated from his own experiences in Poland, studying the decrees of the Nazi government and considering the jurisprudence of the German occupation. From this, it appears that Lemkin saw at the time what others only saw later: the systematic extermination of the Jewish people as the *essence* of the Nazi occupation of Eastern Europe rather than a by-product of it. Lemkin defined genocide as "a coordinated plan of different actions aiming at the destruction of essential foundations of the life of national groups, with the aim of annihilating the groups themselves" (Lemkin 1944, 79). He campaigned relentlessly to have this concept of genocide recognised by the international legal community, and his recommendations were finally acknowledged in 1948, with the creation of the Convention on the Prevention and Punishment of the Crime of Genocide, which entered into force on 12 January 1951. However, Stuart Stein argues that there is only a tenuous relationship between Lemkin's view of genocide and the final version as defined by the Convention. He argues that in terms of detail and emphasis, none of the measures in the Convention requires the "coordinated plan" of Lemkin's definition, or the development of death camps (Stein 2002, 43). Both of these are qualities of the Holocaust: the 'coordinated plan' of the Nazis to make Europe 'Judenfrei' (free of Jews) (Gilbert 1987) and the 'elaborate system' of concentration and death camps in Eastern Europe (Stein 2002). Equally, the definition of genocide stated in Article II does not "represent an 'elaborate, almost scientific, system developed to an extent never before achieved by any nation'" (Stein 2002, 43). The notion of a scientific basis in genocide and the formulation of a coordinated plan are clear markers of the Nazi government's method of genocide, as they are seen throughout the Nazi government's policies and procedures, outlined specifically in the minutes of the Wannsee Conference of 1942 wherein the "final solution to the Jewish problem" was described (Roseman 2003). It is therefore evident that Lemkin's definition of genocide is deeply rooted in his conceptual understanding of the Holocaust and the definition could be seen as Lemkin's symptomatic response to a particularly problematic situation (Powell 2007, 543). Consequently, defining genocide at this point had to take on the features of the Holocaust, as there was no conceptual precedent for understanding how to treat the perpetrators of genocide or what made these actions any different from other war crimes such as crimes against humanity (Claughton 1949).

Whether the Convention on the Prevention and Punishment of the Crime of Genocide bears any hallmarks of Lemkin's definition or not, it is recognised that Lemkin's persistence led to its creation and it is argued that the Convention is Lemkin's great legacy (Levene 2000). The Convention defines genocide as follows:

> any of the following acts committed with intent to destroy, in whole or in part, a national, ethnical, racial or religious group, as such:
> Killing members of a group;
> Causing serious bodily or mental harm to members of the group;
> Deliberately inflicting on the group conditions of life calculated to bring about its physical destruction in whole or in part;
> Imposing measures intended to prevent births within the group;
> Forcibly transferring children of the group to another group. (UN 1948)

Whilst the Convention was created in 1948, it was not used to prosecute genocide suspects until 1993, when the UN Security Council formed the International Criminal Tribunal for the former Yugoslavia. This was in response to the genocide which occurred there following "serious violations of international humanitarian law committed in the territory of the former Yugoslavia … and as a response to the threat to international peace and security posed by those serious violations" (UN Security Council Report of the Secretary-General 1993, 3).

It is the killing of a group which is the ultimate aim of genocide, but that is not the only means of group destruction; that lies in annihilating the group's way of life, social networks and values of the community, effectively destroying the real or perceived social power of the community (Gerson and Wolf 2007). In Eastern Europe, there are any number of towns where synagogues no longer exist or are used as libraries, swimming pools or coffee houses, where restaurants serve 'Jewish style' food rather than being authentically Kosher and where cemeteries go untended because the individuals who *would* have tended the graves of their relatives were never born, their family lines halted by the genocide. Lemkin's definition recognises this social aspect of genocide, and it is, therefore, the definition that is utilised within this book in order to select cases of survivors. It recognises the sociological meaning of the physical, psychological and social destruction of a people and their way of life, going beyond the simple act of killing a large number of people. Lemkin's definition is wider than the one contained within the UN Convention, and it acknowledges the link between genocide and armed conflict, which many other definitions do not. Utilising this definition allows the inclusion of Bosnian survivors from outside Srebrenica as well as including the more well-known and accepted genocides of the Holocaust and Rwanda. Moreover, it also facilitates the inclusion of more recent cases such as Darfur where legal arguments are still ongoing as to whether events in Southern Sudan are genocidal or not (United to End Genocide 2018).

This clarification is important, as whether an event is genocidal or not is often disputed; for example, debates continue about whether the mass murder of the Armenian people by the Ottoman government in 1915 can be classed as genocide or whether it should be classed as a 'crime against humanity' instead (Adalian 2009). Equally, the International Criminal Court has recognised only the massacre of 7000 boys and men in Srebrenica in 1995 as genocide, with other acts in Bosnia being defined as 'crimes against humanity' or 'war crimes' (Mennecke 2013). This book argues that cases where men are removed forcibly from their families into concentration camps on starvation rations, as happened in Bosnia (Mennecke 2013), are genocidal, as this prevents births in the targeted ethnic group. It is important to clarify an appropriate definition of genocide as once genocide has been identified as such, it follows that such acts are seen as crimes, which therefore produce victims. Thus, there are implications of such definitions, and it is this status of 'victim' that is now considered.

Defining 'Victims'

As genocide is a crime under international law, it is fair to assume that those who experience genocide are victims of crime. However, those who experience genocide and survive are rarely considered victims. For example, those who survived the Holocaust were initially termed 'displaced persons', whether they had been in Auschwitz in 1945 or had escaped to neighbouring countries during the war (Bridgman 1990; Shephard 2010). Slowly the countries of Western Europe, Australasia and the Americas began to see these 'displaced persons' as a new pool of labour, so those who had experienced the Holocaust were seen as potential workers, but still not victims (Shephard 2010).

The term 'victim' is not a neutral, value-free word (McGarry and Walklate 2015), and Hope (2007, 63) argues that there is no "objective, impartial nor universally applicable way of defining who is or who is not a 'victim'" and many consider victims to "have something of the uncomfortable 'other' about them" (Rock 2007, 41). The victim 'label' may be something that some individuals do not wish to have, as it indicates their difference from the wider, non-victimised group. The notion of the 'victim' is problematic because it challenges beliefs in a fair and just world, where only people who deserve it are victimised (Rock 2007). When individuals are victimised, they may see themselves in a different light and redefine their identity. Therefore, a 'victim' is an identity and a social construct dependent on "an array of witnesses, police, prosecutors, defence counsel, jurors, the mass media and others who may not always deal with the individual case but who will nevertheless shape the larger interpretative environment in which it is lodged" (Rock 2002, 14). Consequently, being or becoming a 'victim' depends on not only the experience of a crime by an individual or group but also others' perceptions and understandings of that event, which in turn is informed by their own personal experiences and understandings of the world.

Those with the power to label individuals as victims may not do so "because the individual presents some characteristics—whether biological or circumstantial—which conflict with the values they hold" (Miers 2000, 81). For example, an individual may not recognise another as a victim because she/he does not recognise the original 'victimising' act as a crime; if there is no crime, then there can be no victim. Furthermore, some who experience crime may themselves reject the label of victim, because they may see themselves not as victims, but survivors. Some may feel that the term 'victim' has negative connotations, with a victim being seen as helpless, passive, shameful and weak (Lamb 1999; Spalek 2006).

This concept of 'victim' is a particularly feminine one which may go some way towards explaining why men particularly resist the 'victim' label, as the feminine nature of the victim label may threaten a man's masculinity (Spalek 2006). Furthermore, Weiss and Borges suggest that due to socialisation and sex-role learning, a male-dominated society tends to "establish and perpetuate the woman as a legitimate object for victimisation" (1973 cited in Fattah 1979, 206). As a result, men stereotypically see women as defenceless, weak and needing rescuing from victimisation. Consequently, it could be argued that there is a societal expectation that women should be victims, and men should not be. In order to resolve this, a new non-victim identity needs to be devised.

Lamb (1999) proposes a 'survivor' rather than 'victim' identity, which implies that the person was possibly an active resister and that whatever the individual did during their victimising experience, she/he did to survive. Linden agrees with Lamb's concept, suggesting that "a victim is one who is acted upon; a survivor is an active subject" (Linden 1993, 89). This, therefore, reduces ideas of passivity and helplessness and indicates a more positive, active individual. Eva Schloss, in her biography about her Holocaust experiences, said that at the end of the war

> I decided I would not be a victim, no matter what happened to me. I would never let myself have that mentality—it was almost like accepting the role of utter helplessness that the Nazis had wanted to instil in us. I wasn't helpless. I was a survivor. (Schloss 2013, 158)

Yet the term 'survivor', like victim, is also a socially constructed identity and, as such, is a problematic concept. For example, those who survived the atom bombs in Hiroshima and Nagasaki do not use the term 'survivor' as it is felt disrespectful to those who did not survive. Instead, they are referred to as '*hibakusha*', which means 'explosion affected people' (Tatara 1998). Similarly, the concept of a 'genocide survivor' is problematic as an individual is a genocide survivor by the mere virtue of the fact that she/he managed to avoid being killed, and not always through any specific survival ability. Whilst some will have actively fought to stay alive, others may have fled to safer areas, still surviving, but their actions may not be seen in the same light as those who resisted by fighting. This seems to suggest that there may even be a form of hierarchy within genocide survivor groups.

Understandings of persecution are shaped by individual experiences before, during and after the persecuting event, being interpreted and reinterpreted over the course of a lifetime. It follows that genocide survivors' narratives are constructed and reconstructed in the light of the present and represent genocide as lived experience, with individuals perhaps becoming survivors as they begin to talk about their experience. What will be considered in this book is how these identities of victim or survivor develop from experiences of persecution, how a genocide 'victim' becomes a 'survivor' (Linden 1993).

The Focus of This Book

This book makes the argument that those who survive genocide have qualitatively different experiences than others who experience forced migration. David Kauzlarich, in his study of the victims of genocide, argues that those who are targeted for genocide lack social power. The targeting of individuals is facilitated by removal of their rights as individuals combined with a gradual dehumanisation of the group and the reduction (and destruction) of their existing social power (Kauzlarich et al. 2001). Indeed, those who experience state crimes such as genocide are usually the least socially powerful, with large power differences existing between the victim and the victimiser (Kauzlarich et al. 2001). Furthermore, the difference between those who experience forced migration and those who experience genocide lies in genocide survivors' experiences of being targeted because of their identity. Therefore, recovery and rebuilding goes beyond the 'usual' psychological recovery such as managing the effects of PTSD, but is in fact also about reconstructing or redefining their identity (Cohen 2001; Stein 2007). This reconstruction often occurs in an unfamiliar society alongside living with the recent memories of being targeted. Leslie Hardman was the Jewish chaplain tasked with dealing with the survivors at Bergen-Belsen following the British liberation of the camp in 1945. In his opinion, the inmates of the camp had been "subjected not only to a deliberate extermination of themselves as a people but to a disintegration of their souls. They have become, not outcasts of society, but outcasts of life" (Hardman and Goodman 1958, 19). Indeed, Grossman (2003) states that immediately after the Second World War, the consensus about Holocaust survivors was that they were human debris, at best to be rehabilitated and resocialised into good citizens, and, at worst, they were asocial and beyond redemption. Therefore, those who survived have to rebuild every aspect of their lives, including their identity, and as such, genocide survivors are a very specific group who warrant special attention. In being both victims of crime and migrants, the study of genocide survivors warrants an interdisciplinary approach, drawing on sociological and criminological ideas alongside theories of migration and integration.

Methods, Methodology and Ethics

Genocide is a problematic area to research. Perpetrators often deny their involvement in genocide or simply vanish following the genocide. Victims are often initially too traumatised to tell of their experiences and bystanders often seek to shift the blame of their inaction onto others. Because of this, original data on genocide and mass killing are often rare. Owens et al. (2013) argue that because of this, researchers need to be flexible and creative as well as analytically rigorous in order to advance scholarship in this area.

Within qualitative research there has been an expectation that researchers 'bracket off' their personal experiences, values and culture (Etherington 2004). In addition, an assumption within many methodologies and methods that the researcher, methods and data are all separate identities (Mauthner and Doucet 2007) and that subjectivity is a contaminant which should be avoided by approaching studies with an objective rigour (Etherington 2004). Wincup (2001, 18) notes that confessional or personal accounts are often presented separately from the research, adding to the myth that "personal feelings do not influence the research to any great extent and do not taint the final product". Yet as Ahern (2007, 130) notes: "It is not possible for qualitative researchers to be totally objective because total objectivity is not humanly possible". Furthermore, by attempting to be objective there is a risk that I may have viewed my interviewees merely as data providers, rather than individuals who have their own story to tell. However, it is noted here that objectivity and subjectivity are not polar opposites; they can serve each other, a point which Bourdieu (1992) acknowledges. Reflexivity channels the dualism of the subjectivity/objectivity debate and creates a conceptual space where we can acknowledge the blurred boundaries of our research (Etherington 2004). Indeed, researchers are part of the social world they study and "methods of data analysis are not simply neutral techniques because they carry the epistemological, ontological and theoretical assumptions of the researchers who developed them" (Mauthner and Doucet 2007, 92). The inductive approach demands that qualitative researchers go into the field without a fixed idea of what may develop and as a result our experiences and identities shape the stances we take in our research (Kleinman and Copp 1993). Therefore, we should be aware of and reflect on our varying roles: "We must consider who we are and what we believe when we do fieldwork. Otherwise we might not see how we shape the story" (Kleinman and Copp 1993, 13).

Pierre Bourdieu's main project was to fuse structural and phenomenological approaches into a coherent, epistemologically grounded mode of social enquiry that could be used to explain almost any phenomena (Wacquant 1989). In Bourdieu's view, one of the key errors in social sciences is an uncontrolled relation to the object that results in the projection of this relation into the object. He argues that sociologists rarely objectivise themselves and fail to recognise that what they are talking about is not the object but their relation to the object (Wacquant 1989). However, as well as reflecting on the usual categories of race, gender and age, a truly reflexive practitioner, according to Bourdieu (Wacquant 1989), also reflects on their position in the universe of cultural production in the academic field. That is, in order to be truly reflexive, I needed to consider not only my status as a white, middle-aged female but also my role as a researcher and the implications of that upon my practice. I needed to be aware of what I injected into my perception of the cases discussed in this book, and in particular, I needed to reflect on the power of the academic world and how my role within it may have changed my perception of my participants and, hence, my interpretation of their stories. As someone researching into the life of genocide survivors, I had to not only tell the truth of this world, but also show that this 'survivor world' is one which is the site of ongoing struggles in which people fight to have their stories heard.

In considering my relation to my object, I acknowledged that I am not a survivor, nor am I related to any survivors of mass trauma. My role therefore in terms of the academic production of knowledge was one of an outsider to these participants and therefore whilst I did not bring any emotional understanding of what it meant to be a survivor to this project, nor did I bring any biases linked to any previous experiences related to genocide.

Hence, it was important that I reflected on my personal history, my presuppositions and my own status in terms of gender, class, ethnicity and culture in order to recognise my position, acknowledging that how knowledge is acquired and interpreted is relevant to the claims made within research. Without engaging in a reflexive process, I ran the risk of imposing my own ontological structure onto the participants' narratives. Conversely, by viewing the relationship between researcher and participant as one which is consultative and collaborating, a sense of power, involvement and agency could be encouraged in the participants (Etherington 2004). Moreover, Bourdieu also argues for intellectuals to engage in reflexive practice in order to free themselves from "their illusions—and first of all from the illusion that they do not have any, especially about themselves" (Bourdieu 1992, 195). Hence, reflexivity is the ability and capacity of the researcher to acknowledge how their own status and experiences inform the research process and outcomes (Etherington 2004). In being reflexive, the researcher adds validity and rigour by being honest about the contexts in which data are located (Etherington 2004). Rather than arguing that the voices of respondents speak on their own, this research recognises that I, as the researcher, have made choices as to how these voices are interpreted and which elements of transcripts to use as evidence (Mauthner and Doucet 2007).

Furthermore, as Reinharz (1992, 26) notes, "every aspect of a researcher's identity can impede or enhance empathy", and as such, it is important that I reflected on my own position to understand not only my own responses to participants, but also my participants' responses to me. As Hallowell, Lawton and Gregory (2005, 42) note, all research involves emotional work (both our own and our participants) and our research interactions "are influenced by who we are, what we are, where we are and how we appear to others". In order to be reflexive, we need to be aware of our personal, social and cultural contexts and how these impact on how we interpret the world (Etherington 2004).

In being reflexive, I needed to ask myself about my own positioning and in particular, whose side was I on (Reinharz 1992)? Did I want participants to tell their stories because there would be some benefit to them or the wider community, or was I merely seeking data because it would benefit my career and me? In reflecting on my own status and culture, I was aware that I shared very little, if any, similarities with my participants. I have not experienced genocide or the loss of large numbers of my family. I am not black, or from an ethnic minority, and I am Christian, rather than Jewish or Muslim. This meant that many of the survivors I interviewed would see me as an 'outsider'. However, interviews are bound up with complex structural positions between the interviewer and interviewee, in terms of the ability to control the interview and the over-interpretation of data. "The recipients of intimate details about one's life are most likely to be either those standing in a very intimate relation to oneself, or those who are socially remote (Lee 1993, 113). Hence, my initial remoteness may not have been the problem I had been concerned about. Certain elements, such as the fact that I am a parent, I did share with the vast majority of the participants and this provided common ground to aid discussions relating to parenting, and how our own childhood experiences affected our parenting styles. In particular, my gendered role as a mother facilitated some survivors opening up to me about their own experiences of being a mother and how they were perceived as mothers as well as genocide survivors. It appeared that some of the survivors I interviewed saw my parental status as something that gave me some status beyond that of researcher; I was not simply an 'ivory tower' academic, but in their understanding a mother with a demanding job. This appeared to reassure some of the survivors that I interviewed that I would at least in part understand some of their life experiences. Hence, my status for the interviews was one of 'outsider' (Reinharz 1992; Hallowell et al. 2005) with occasional forays into the 'insider' role where my personal culture or experiences aligned with the interviewees.

The research takes the position of a respect for individual autonomy, obligations to others and informed consent. To this end, participants had the right to request that their data was not anonymised and their real identity be included. This was in accordance with the following ethical guidelines:

> Paragraph 23 of the British Educational Research Association's ethical guidelines states that "researchers must also recognise participants' rights to be identified with any publication of their original works or other inputs, if they so wish" (BERA 2004). The Social Research Association's ethical guidelines state: "Some subjects may wish their identities to be disclosed in order to maintain 'ownership' of the data (Grinyer 2002) and, while the researcher has a responsibility to present the potential disadvantages of removing anonymity, they cannot be held responsible for subjects who choose to disclose their identities themselves" (SRA 2003, 40). In addition, it is noted that there have been a number of studies of genocide survivors where actual identities have been used, such as Jean Hatzfeld's *Into the Quick of Life*, which documents 14 survivors' stories of the Rwandan genocide (Hatzfeld 2005b). Hatzfeld has also completed a study of ten convicted killers who had been involved in Rwandan genocide, again using actual identities (Hatzfeld 2005a). Fergal Keane's commentary on reporting the genocide also uses actual identities (Keane 1996), as does Martin Gilbert's 'The Boys', which is a study of 732 concentration camp survivors (Gilbert 1997). However, the right to be identified with your own data for genocide goes beyond ethical guidelines as genocide survivors have had specific experiences that may affect their need to be identified with their data.

Specific Experiences of Survivors of Genocide

Genocide dehumanises, as noted by Fein (1990). The process of genocide is one which removes victims' rights to the point where they are eventually denied the right to life; for example, the Nazi treatment of Jews went from laws aimed at limiting freedom of movement to a policy of mass murder (Arad et al. 1999). Due to the nature of the cataloguing and then targeting of populations, by being tattooed, the wearing of an armband or the requirement to carry an identity card, some survivors may have denied their identity in an attempt to survive. By ensuring that all participants had the option of retaining their real identity, the research did not repeat any process of dehumanisation. Moreover, the process of anonymising interview data is a representational strategy which has political, historical and psychological consequences for researchers, as well as their respondents (Linden 1993). If these consequences are not considered, there could be negative impacts on all involved in the research process.

Genocide survivors are unusual by their very definition; they survived where the majority did not. The survivor population in the UK is a small one; for example, there are approximately 1000 survivors of the Rwandan genocide living in the UK (ONS 2015). It is worth noting that some participants may not be anonymous to begin with, due to their stories having already been published, or participants may have a story that is particularly unusual. Participants may have followed a very unusual route to get to the UK, and this alone may make them identifiable. By removing these details, I would have also lost much of the richness of the data. I wanted to ensure that I was truthful with my participants, that they understood that my best efforts to preserve their anonymity might not be enough because their story was so well known. However, participants also had the right to remain anonymous within the constraints highlighted above. In this case, a culturally appropriate pseudonym was allocated to the case.

As with all ethically sound research, informed consent was gained from all participants prior to any research taking place. This was done by posting or emailing the information sheet and consent form to the participant prior to the interview, then going through the form at the start of the meeting and providing an opportunity for all participants to ask questions prior to the interview. It was made clear prior to, during and after the interview that the participant could withdraw at any time. Further to this, participants were also sent a copy of their interview transcript so they could read their words and decide at that point whether they wanted to remain anonymous or have their true name associated with their transcript. This also gave participants a further opportunity, should they wish, to withdraw from the research or stipulate the data they wished to be included in the research. This is based on Anne Grinyer's comments following her experiences researching young adults with cancer. She argues that by allowing participants to see their words in print, researchers are giving them the ability to make a more informed judgement and thus maximising the likelihood of participants' wishes being fulfilled (Grinyer 2002). Pseudonyms were initially assigned to all data with the provision that these pseudonyms could be removed once the participants had seen their interview transcripts and could then make an informed decision as to their anonymity.

The testimonies in this book are taken from both interviews with survivors and published testimonies from four different genocides: Rwanda, the Holocaust, Bosnia and Darfur. Published testimonies were included alongside interviews for a number of reasons. First, it was recognised that the Holocaust survivors interviewed were children/young adults during the Second World War, and as such, testimonies of people who were adults at that time were included. Furthermore, the biography of a Darfuri survivor was also included to provide consideration of a more recent genocide. It would not have been appropriate to interview survivors from this genocide as their English acquisition may be limited, and the trauma may still be too recent for those survivors to talk about (see the appendix for a contextual summary of each individual included in this research).

Structural Overview

Chapter 2 provides an overview of the literature relating to social capital, focusing on Pierre Bourdieu and underpinning concepts of field and habitus. Following this, Chap. 3 considers the interrelationship between migration, integration and social capital, and this chapter finishes by considering how Bourdieu's ideas aid understanding of the experience of migration. Chapter 4 explores survivors' experiences of the immediate effects of migration and genocide. Chapter 5 considers the more medium-term effects of migration and the beginnings of resettlement, exploring survivors' experiences of employment, education and the development of culture. Chapter 6 explores how survivors develop a linguistic habitus to talk about their experiences, and briefly considers the effect of collective memory upon genocide survivor testimony, as well as investigating how and why survivors begin talking about their experiences following genocide. Chapter 7 draws together and concludes the findings and discusses the key theoretical points and policy recommendations.

References

Adalian, R. P. (2009). The Armenian Genocide. In S. Totten & W. S. Parsons (Eds.), *Centuries of Genocide* (pp. 55–92). London: Routledge.

Ahern, K. (2007). Ten Tips for Reflexive Bracketing. In A. Bryman (Ed.), *Sage Benchmarks in Social Research Methods: Qualitative Research 2 Issues of Representation and Reflexivity2* (pp. 130–135). London: Sage Publications.

Alvarez, A. (2001). *Governments, Citizens, and Genocide: A Comparative and Interdisciplinary Approach*. Bloomington: Indiana University Press.

Alvarez, A. (2017). *Unstable Ground: Climate Change, Conflict and Genocide*. London: Rowman and Littlefield.

Amir, M. (1971). *Patterns in Forcible Rape*. Chicago: University of Chicago Press.

Amnesty International. (1997). *The Quest for International Justice: Defining the Crimes and Defences for the International Criminal Court*. Report [online]. Retrieved December 1, 2018, from https://www.amnesty.org/download/Documents/164000/ior400061997en.pdf.

Arad, Y., Gutman, Y., & Margaliot, A. (1999). *Documents on the Holocaust; Jerusalem; Yad Vashem* (8th ed.). Jerusalem: Yad Vashem.

Arendt, H. (2006). *Eichmann in Jerusalem*. London: Penguin.

Ayalon, L., Perry, C., Arean, P., & Horowitz, M. (2007). Making Sense of the Past - Perspectives on Resilience among Holocaust Survivors. *Journal of Loss and Trauma, 12*(3), 281–293.

Bauman, Z. (1989). *Modernity and the Holocaust*. New York: Cornell University Press.

Bourdieu, P. (1977). *Outline of a Theory of Practice, Cambridge Studies in Social and Cultural Anthropology*. Cambridge: Cambridge University Press.

Bourdieu, P. (1986). The Forms of Capital. In J. G. Richardson (Ed.), *Handbook of Theory and Research for the Sociology of Education* (pp. 241–258). London: Greenwood Press.

Bourdieu, P. (1992). *The Rules of Art: Genesis and Structure of the Literary Field.* Stanford: Stanford University Press.

Bourdieu, P. (1993). *The Field of Cultural Production.* Cambridge: Polity Press.

Bourdieu, P., & Passeron, J. C. (1990). *Reproduction in Education, Society and Culture* (2nd ed.). London: Sage Publications.

Bridgman, J. (1990). *The End of the Holocaust: The Liberation of the Camps.* London: B.T. Batsford.

British Education Research Association (BERA). (2004). *Revised Ethical Guidelines for Educational Research.* Nottingham: BERA.

Browning, C. R. (1998). *The Path to Genocide: Essays on Launching the Final Solution.* Cambridge: Cambridge University Press.

Clark, P. (2009). *After Genocide: Transitional Justice, Post-Conflict Resolution and Reconciliation in Rwanda and Beyond.* London: Columbia University Press.

Clark, P. (2010). *The Gacaca Courts and Post-Genocide Justice and Reconciliation in Rwanda.* Cambridge: Cambridge University Press.

Claughton, R. (1949). The Crime of Genocide. *American Journal of Economical Sociology, 8*(4), 351–365.

Cohen, S. (2001). *States of Denial: Knowing about Atrocities and Suffering.* Cambridge: Polity Press.

Coupe, T., & Griffiths, M. (1999). The Influence of Police Actions on Victim Satisfaction in Burglary Investigations. *International Journal of the Sociology of Law, 27*(4), 413–431.

Des Forges, A. (1999). *Leave None to Tell the Story: Genocide in Rwanda.* New York: Human Rights Watch.

Etherington, K. (2004). *Becoming a Reflexive Researcher.* London: Jessica Kingsley Publishers.

Fattah, E. (1979). Some Recent Theoretical Developments in Victimology. *Victimology: An International Journal, 4*(2), 198–213.

Fein, H. (1990). Genocide: A Sociological Perspective. In A. L. Hinton (Ed.), *Genocide: An Anthropological Reader.* Oxford: Blackwell.

Gerson, J. M., & Wolf, D. L. (2007). *Sociology Confronts the Holocaust.* London: Duke University Press.

Gigliotti, S., & Lang, B. (Eds.). (2005). *The Holocaust: A Reader.* Oxford: Oxford University Press.

Gilbert, M. (1987). *The Holocaust: The Jewish Tragedy.* London: HarperCollins.

Gilbert, M. (1997). *The Boys: Triumph over Adversity.* London: Phoenix.

Gourevitch, P. (1999). *We Wish to Inform You that Tomorrow We Will Be Killed with Our Families.* New York: Picador.

Gourevitch, P. (2014). Remembering in Rwanda. *The New Yorker*, April 21. Retrieved December 27, 2018, from https://www.newyorker.com/magazine/2014/04/21/remembering-in-rwanda.

Grinyer, A. (2002). The Anonymity of Research Participants: Assumptions, Ethics and Practicalities. *Social Research Update*, Issue 36.

Grossman, A. (2003). Gendered Perceptions and Self Perceptions of Memory and Revenge: Jewish Displaced Persons in Occupied Postwar Germany as Victims, Villains and Survivors. In J. T. Baumel & T. Cohen (Eds.), *Gender, Place and Memory in the Modern Jewish Experience*. London: Vallentine Mitchell.

Hallowell, N., Lawton, J., & Gregory, S. (2005). *Reflections on Research: The Realities of Doing Research in the Social Sciences*. Maidenhead: Open University Press.

Hardman, L., & Goodman, C. (1958). *The Survivors: The Story of the Belsen Remnant*. London: Vallentine Mitchell.

Hatzfeld, J. (2005a). *A Time for Machetes*. London: Serpent's Tail.

Hatzfeld, J. (2005b). *Into the Quick of Life*. London: Serpent's Tail.

Hinton, A. L. (2005). *Why Did They Kill? Cambodia in the Shadow of Genocide*. California: University of California Press.

Hoffman, E. (1989). *Lost in Translation: Life in a New Language*. London: Vintage.

Hope, T. (2007). Theory and Method: The Social Epidemiology of Crime Victims. In S. Walklate (Ed.), *Handbook of Victims and Victimology*. Cullompton: Willan Publishers.

Huttenbach, H. R. (1988). Locating the Holocaust on the Genocide Spectrum: Towards a Methodology of Definition and Categorisation. *Holocaust and Genocide Studies, 3*(3), 289–303.

Jones, A. (2012). *New Directions in Genocide Research*. London: Routledge.

Karstedt, S. (2018). "I Would Prefer to Be Famous" Comparative Perspectives on the Re-entry of War Criminals Sentenced at Nuremberg and the Hague. *International Criminal Justice Review, 28*(4), 372–390.

Kaufman, D. R. (1996). The Holocaust and Sociological Inquiry: A Feminist Analysis. *Contemporary Jewry, 17*(1), 6–17.

Kauzlarich, D., Matthews, R. A., & Miller, W. J. (2001). Toward a Victimology of State Crime. *Critical Criminology, 10*(3), 173–194.

Keane, F. (1996). *Season of Blood: A Rwandan Journey*. London: Penguin.

Kellerman, N. (2001). Psychopathology in Children of Holocaust Survivors: A Review of the Research Literature. *Israeli Journal of Psychiatry and Related Sciences, 38*(1), 36–46.

Kleinman, S., & Copp, M. (1993). *Emotions and Fieldwork*. London: Sage Publications.

Kushner, T. (1999). *Refugees in an Age of Genocide*. London: Frank Cass.
Lamb, S. (1999). Constructing the Victim. In S. Lamb (Ed.), *New Versions of Victims: Feminists Struggle with the Concept* (pp. 121–137). New York.
Lee, R. M. (1993). *Doing Research on Sensitive Topics*. London: Sage Publications.
Lemkin, R. (1944). *Axis Rule in Occupied Europe*. Washington: Carnegie.
Levene, M. (2000). Why Is the Twentieth Century the Century of Genocide? *Journal of World History, 11*(2), 305–336.
Linden, R. R. (1993). *Making Stories Making Selves*. Columbus: Ohio State University Press.
Maguire, M. (1980). The Impact of Burglary upon Victims. *British Journal of Criminology, 20*(3), 261–275.
Maruna, S. (2017). Desistance as a Social Movement. *Irish Probation Journal, 14*, 5–20.
Mauthner, N., & Doucet, A. (2007). Reflexive Accounts and Accounts of Reflexivity in Qualitative Data Analysis. In A. Bryman (Ed.), *Sage Benchmarks in Social Research Methods: Qualitative Research 2 Issues of Representation and Reflexivity* (pp. 91–109). London: Sage Publications.
McDonald, W. F., & Erez, E. (2007). Immigrants as Victims: A Framework. *International Review of Victimology, 14*, 1–10.
McGarry, R., & Walklate, S. (2015). *Victims*. London: Routledge.
Meierhenrich, J. (2007). The Trauma of Genocide. *Journal of Genocide Research, 9*(4), 549–573.
Mennecke, M. (2013). Genocidal Violence in the Former Yugoslavia: Bosnia Herzegovina and Kosovo. In S. Totten & W. Parsons (Eds.), *Centuries of Genocide Essays and Eyewitness Accounts* (4th ed., pp. 477–512). London: Routledge.
Miers, D. (2000). Taking the Law into Their Own Hands: Victims as Offenders. In A. Crawford & J. Goodey (Eds.), *Integrating a Victim Perspective within Criminal Justice*. Hants: Dartmouth Publishing Company.
Neuffer, E. (2002). *The Key to My Neighbour's House: Seeking Justice in Bosnia and Rwanda*. New York: Picador.
Office for National Statistics. (2015, August). *Population by Country of Birth and Nationality Report*. London: Office for National Statistics.
Owens, P. B., Su, Y., & Snow, D. A. (2013). Social Scientific Inquiry into Genocide and Mass Killing: From Unitary Outcome to Complex Processes. *Annual Review of Sociology, 39*(4), 69–84.
Powell, C. (2007). What Do Genocides Kill? A Relational Conception of Genocide. *Journal of Genocide Research, 9*(4), 527–547.

Reinharz, S. (1992). *Feminist Methods in Social Research*. Oxford: Oxford University Press.
Rock, P. (2002). On Becoming a Victim. In P. Rock (Ed.), *New Visions of Crime Victims* (pp. 1–22). Oxford: Hart Publishing.
Rock, P. (2007). Theoretical Perspectives on Victimisation. In S. Walklate (Ed.), *Handbook of Victims and Victimology*. Cullompton: Willan Publishers.
Roseman, M. (2003). *The Villa, the Lake, the Meeting*. London: Penguin.
Rothe, D. L., & Kauzlarich, D. (2014). *Towards a Victimology of State Crime*. London: Routledge.
Schloss, E. (2013). *After Auschwitz*. London: Hodder & Stoughton.
Schwartz Lee, B. (1988). Holocaust Survivors and Internal Strengths. *Journal of Humanistic Psychology, 28*(1), 67–96.
Shaw, M. (2003). *War and Genocide*. Cambridge: Polity Press.
Shephard, B. (2010). *The Long Road Home*. London: Bodley Head.
Spalek, B. (2006). *Crime Victims: Theory, Policy & Practice*. Hampshire: Palgrave Macmillan.
SRA. (2003). *Ethical Guidelines*. London: SRA.
Stanton, G. (2019). *10 Stages of Genocide*. Retrieved January 2, 2019, from http://genocidewatch.org/genocide/tenstagesofgenocide.html.
Stein, S. (2002). Geno- and Other Cides: A Cautionary Note on Knowledge Accumulation. *Journal of Genocide Research, 4*(1), 39–63.
Stein, A. (2007). Trauma Stories, Identity Work and the Politics of Recognition. In J. Gerson & D. Wolf (Eds.), *Sociology Confronts the Holocaust* (pp. 84–91). London: Duke University Press.
Stone, D. (2018). "Somehow the Pathetic Dumb Suffering of These Elderly People Moves Me More than Anything": Caring for Elderly Holocaust Survivors in the Immediate Postwar Years. *Holocaust and Genocide Studies, 32*(3), 384–403.
Straus, S. (2001). Contested Meanings and Conflicting Imperatives: A Conceptual Analysis of Genocide. *Journal of Genocide Research, 3*(3), 349–375.
Straus, S. (2006). *The Order of Genocide*. New York: Cornell University Press.
Tatara, M. (1998). The Second Generation of Hibakusha, Atomic Bomb Survivors. In Y. Danieli (Ed.), *International Handbook of Multigenerational Legacies of Trauma* (pp. 141–146). New York: Springer.
Totten, S., & Parsons, W. (2012). *Centuries of Genocide: Essays and Eyewitness Accounts*. London: Routledge.
UN. (1993). *UN Security Council Report of the Secretary General*. Retrieved May 27, 2013, from http://www.icty.org/x/file/LegalLibrary/Statute/statute_re808_1993_en.pdf.

UN General Assembly. (1948). *Convention on the Prevention and Punishment of the Crime of Genocide*, December 9, United Nations, Treaty Series, vol. 78, p. 277.

United to End Genocide. (2018). *South Sudan*. Retrieved December 12, 2018, from http://endgenocide.org/conflict-areas/south-sudan/.

Wacquant, L. J. D. (1989). Towards a Reflexive Society: A Workshop with Pierre Bourdieu. *Sociological Theory, 7*(1), 26–63.

Westmarland, N. (2015). *Violence against Women: Criminological Perspectives on Men's Violence*. London: Routledge.

Wincup, E. (2001). Feminist Research with Women Awaiting Trial: The Effects on Participants in the Qualitative Research Process. In K. Gilbert (Ed.), *The Emotional Nature of Qualitative Research* (pp. 17–36). London: CRC Press.

2

Bourdieu and Social Capital

In their study of victims of genocide, Kauzlarich et al. (2001) argued that those who are targeted in genocide lack social power. The targeting of individuals in genocide is facilitated by the removal of their rights as individuals, combined with a gradual dehumanisation of the group and a progressive reduction and destruction of social networks (Jones 2016). In addition, victims of state crimes such as genocide are usually the least socially powerful because large power differentials exist between the victim and the victimiser (Kauzlarich et al. 2001). By highlighting the process by which people are targeted by genocidal killers, Kauzlarich's analysis adds much to our understanding of the effects of genocide.

Kauzlarich et al. (2001) do not clearly define what they mean by social power, but when discussing people who lack social power, they refer to individuals lacking resources, being typified into groups, and power being unevenly distributed between groups. These ideas conform to the concept of social capital which, in its basic understanding, is the idea that 'relationships matter' (Field 2008, 1). By building relationships and ensuring they continue over time, individuals can use the networks these relationships create to aid them in a variety of ways throughout their lives. Given that genocide survivors who have migrated have, for the

L. Asquith, *Rebuilding Lives After Genocide*, Palgrave Studies in Compromise after Conflict, https://doi.org/10.1007/978-3-030-14074-8_2

most part, had to rebuild their families, relationships and networks from scratch, it is appropriate to use these ideas to understand how survivors rebuild and recover. Kauzlarich et al.'s (2001) assertion that genocide victims lack social power (and thus capital) suggests that genocide survivors need to rebuild this power/capital once they have arrived in a new country. Hence, this chapter discusses the different variants of social capital and their applicability to genocide survivors.

There are two schools of thought in relation to the concept of social capital: Pierre Bourdieu's ideas developed from a European perspective, while James Coleman's and Robert Putnam's theories emerged from the American School of Sociology. These backgrounds have had a significant impact on the direction of their discussions on social capital. Both Coleman and Putnam scholars focused on how social capital aids progression in society, drawing on notions of the 'American Dream', whereas Bourdieu's European-based focus was on how social capital may be restricted to those of a certain class as a result of the structures within society that bind people to particular class groups.

Whilst investigating educational attainment in the ghettos of America, James Coleman argued that social capital was not limited to those with power, as poor people and marginalised communities could also utilise social capital in order to improve their opportunities (Coleman 1990). This concept of social capital involves the expectation of reciprocity: that what an individual gives to a community or group will be paid back when they need to access something within that specific group. By going beyond the individual and involving wider networks, Coleman draws out the role of trust and shared values in communities (Coleman 1990); hence, social capital is something that groups, rather than individuals, hold. In rooting his ideas in the framework of rational choice and arguing that people make choices that maximise their personal advantage, Coleman developed a worldview that suggested that society is a result of aggregating individual behaviours and preferences. He saw social capital as a useful resource that was available to individuals because of their relationships with others, arguing that social capital is a public good that benefited everyone in the social structure; and hence, it is a public rather than a private resource. As a result of this, Coleman suggested that there were certain forms of structures that were more likely to facilitate social capital than others, and he particularly identified the family as the key to social capital (Coleman 1994). Many genocide survivors arrive in the UK with no family, and consequently, this way of developing social capital would, in Coleman's eyes, be denied them, at least in the short to medium term. Importantly, Coleman argued that the destruction of the family has led to an erosion of social capital and that artificial structures which replace the family are significantly weaker in terms of aiding individuals in developing social capital (Coleman 1994). The strength of any ties is based on a combination of the amount of time, the emotional intensity and intimacy, and the reciprocity which characterise the tie (Granovetter 1973), and as such, stronger ties are those which are between people who have a strong emotional link and spend a significant amount of time together.

Coleman's overemphasis on strong ties failed to acknowledge the value of weak ties fully, wherein a chance encounter may lead to a job offer or insider knowledge that could aid the development of an individual's social capital. As already mentioned, many survivors arrive in the UK without family or close friends and would, according to Coleman, have weaker social capital and should experience greater difficulty in rebuilding their lives (Portes 1998). Moreover, those survivors who have a family should have less difficulty and should be able to rebuild their lives with fewer problems. However, if weak ties *are* valuable to new arrivals, then survivors should be able to utilise those weak ties by making use of chance encounters and acquaintances in order to aid their resettlement and integration in the UK.

Also working in the American sociological tradition, Putnam (1995) decried the breakdown of civic engagement and associational life, arguing that this breakdown was the result of the significant changes in social structure such as women's role changes following the war and the introduction of the home computer, as well as the rise in television viewing and ownership. These changes, he argued, had led to individuals leading isolated lives wherein they 'bowled alone' rather than joining leagues (Putnam 1995). Putnam used the bowling metaphor in order to highlight that individuals were engaging in fewer 'associational' activities which previously brought relative strangers together and fostered general values of reciprocity and trust, resulting in the development of social capital (Putnam 1995). In discussing this, he identified activities such as voting, membership of the scouts and reading a newspaper as 'associational' and therefore likely to lead to associations with others that would prove beneficial. He defined social capital as "the features of social life—networks, norms and trust—that enable participants to act together more effectively to pursue shared objectives" (Putnam 1996, 56). In defining social capital in this way, Putnam points out the importance of trust and reciprocity in societal norms that therefore develop social capital.

After refining his definition to explain social capital as "connections among individuals—social networks and the norms of reciprocity and trustworthiness that arise from them" (Putnam 2000, 19), Putnam then introduced two different forms of social capital: bridging and bonding. Bridging social capital is inclusive, in that it brings together those from different social divisions and acts as "sociological WD40" that greases the wheels for reciprocity. Bonding is exclusive; it reinforces identities and maintains homogeneity and is "sociological superglue" which helps maintain group loyalty (Putnam 2000, 22). Consequently, social capital for Putnam is functional, but his focus is at a societal level rather than an individual one. As a result, it is an individual's lack of participation in societal civic groups which causes the collapse of civic society, resulting in a decline in social capital, rather than an individual's position in society controlling their access to opportunities (Putnam 2000).

However, critics such as Hall (1999) have pointed out that whilst a decline in participation may be occurring in the US, Europe has a vibrant participatory movement, including such things as involvement in trade unions, cooperatives and committees. As such, it may be that Putnam's assessment of social capital within the US is correct, but this assessment cannot be applied to the same degree to the UK or Europe. In addition, Foley and Edwards (1996) argue that Putnam underestimates newer forms of organisations and specifically political associations such as social movements. Moreover, Putnam (1996) appears to present social capital as a cure-all for all manner of social ills, presenting community as a wholly benevolent good, rather than recognising that social networks can also produce conflict and distrust, as well as trust as a result of perceptions of in-group and out-group status (Foley and Edwards 1996). Indeed, Putnam begins with the effects of social capital and focuses on the way that social capital is responsible for these effects, leading to what is an effectively circular argument (Haynes 2009); one which Portes (1998) suggests explains nothing, as social capital is equated with the resources that are acquired through it. Finally, in seeing social capital as the product of long-term processes, Putnam has a romanticised view of the community which fails to recognise the role of human agency and the state (Misztal 2000). Most importantly, Putnam (1995, 1996) sees social capital as a resource which communities hold, and which functions at a societal level, rather than at an individual one.

Bourdieu and Social Capital

Bourdieu first began utilising the concept of social capital in the 1970s when he suggested that culture was both dynamic and structured (Bourdieu 1977b). He wholly disagreed with the concept of rational action and argued instead that humans can only ever act in certain ways as a result of the conditions imposed upon them by broader societal structures (Bourdieu and Passeron 1990). Thus, culture is a choice constrained by the wider field. The concept of social capital gradually developed, firstly as an analogy linked with a range of other forms of capital such as economic capital (financial capability) and cultural capital (knowledge and skills relating to cultural abilities) (Bourdieu 1977b). Later, Bourdieu developed his idea into his eventual definition of social capital, which is:

> the aggregate of the actual or potential resources which are linked to possession of a durable network of more or less institutionalised relationships of mutual acquaintance and recognition—or in other words, to membership in a group which provides each of its members with the backing of the collectivity-owned capital, a 'credential' which entitles them to credit, in the various senses of the word. (Bourdieu 1986, 248–249)

Bourdieu argued that economic capital underpinned both social and cultural capital, but social exchanges were not simply reducible to mere economic explanations (Bourdieu 1986). He saw cultural capital as the consumption of certain cultural forms that marked people out as members of a particular class (Bourdieu 1984). As a result, cultural capital has three underpinning 'capitals'. First is the embodied capital, which is also known as the 'habitus', which is the bodily manifestation of an individual's class—how an individual behaves in certain situations illustrates the class to which they belong. Second is the objectified capital, which relates to the marks of cultural consumption such as books, art and musical instruments and, again, illustrates the class to which an individual belongs. For example, possession of an expensive harp or cello would indicate a different class to the possession of a cheap recorder or guitar. Finally, Bourdieu (1986) argues that individuals hold institutionalised (cultural) capital in the form of educational qualifications. These are qualifications that are recognised by the wider society, not just for the actual qualification, but what it says about the holder of the qualification. This can be as simple as where the qualification came from, with qualifications from certain institutions being perceived as more valid than those from 'lesser' institutions. Thus, it is not just that an individual attended school or university, but rather the location and reputation of that institution.

Bourdieu's conception of social capital is shaped by the material, cultural and symbolic status of the individual and her/his family, status in the community, economic situation and engagement in certain forms of cultural activity. Therefore, the volume of social capital that an individual holds depends upon the size of his/her network and the cultural and economic capital that is possessed by the members of the network. Bourdieu's social capital is an "asset used by elite groups—particularly those who had limited financial capital, such as the French nobility—in their jockeying for position" (Field 2008, 44). Bourdieu's ideas acknowledge the primacy and importance of economic capital but also argue that social capital is not reducible to economic capital; it is not just being able to *afford* to do something, but also knowing *how* to do something. Being able to afford a musical instrument is not enough to develop social capital in Bourdieuian terms. An individual must be able to play the instrument in order to develop or utilise their social capital. However, Bourdieu does recognise that in some situations, economic capital aids the development of other types of capital (Bourdieu 1986). For example, if an individual has the knowledge of how to play a musical instrument, but cannot afford that instrument, then she/he still cannot use that cultural capital to develop their social capital. Social capital is therefore transmitted and accumulated in ways which reinforce social inequality and reproduce privilege (Edwards 2004). This is because engagement in those 'elite' activities (in Bourdieuian terms) such as attending 'high culture' events, playing a musical instrument and attending certain sporting events is limited to a certain group who have the economic capital and existing social capital which has been passed down through generations of the same family.

A key aspect of Bourdieu's ideas is that both cultural and social capital functions by being exchangeable; social and cultural capital can be accumulated and exchanged in the same way as economic capital (Bourdieu 1986). Effectively, social capital is the idea that one's family and associates are assets that can be utilised in a crisis, or to gain materially. However, social capital is not just used for financial purposes; rather, it denotes the mobilisation of people through connections, social networks and group membership and explains how people utilise their economic and cultural capital through the connections they make with others (Bourdieu 1986). Bourdieu further suggests that social capital (and therefore power) is symbolically and culturally created, and is legitimised through the interplay of agency and structure (Bourdieu 1989). Social capital functions in a symbolic way; it is economic or cultural capital that has been recognised and acknowledged by the wider network. For example, Bourdieu argues that a high school diploma is a piece of universally recognised and guaranteed symbolic capital which is acceptable in all markets, suggesting that it is an official recognition of an official identity (Bourdieu 1989).

There have been several criticisms of Bourdieu's ideas, however, not least that he views social capital as the preserve of the elites, with his model being rooted in a static model of social hierarchy, despite his attempts to acknowledge agency (Field 2008). Moreover, Bourdieu's social capital is rooted in a view that is slightly old-fashioned and individualistic, with families subservient to the father as head of the household and the appreciation of Bach or jazz in the cultural field (Field 2008). Equally, in seeing social capital as a preserve of the privileged, Bourdieu suggests that social capital is wholly positive for those individuals who are part of the group, but the lack of social capital is problematic for those who are not in the group as it serves to reproduce and strengthen inequalities. There is no consideration of the idea that non-elite, less powerful groups might also find benefit in their social ties (Field 2008). Bourdieu's (1986) concept of social capital is somewhat circular; privileged individuals maintain their position by utilising their connections with other privileged people, and as a result, this view is a starkly polarised one, effectively allowing only a dark side for the oppressed and a bright side for the privileged.

However, Halsey, Heath, and Ridge (1980) found that the expansion of education did provide for some upward mobility, as individuals were not reproducing or maintaining cultural capital, rather they were creating it (Goldthorpe and Jackson 2007). However, they also found that whilst class differences may have narrowed and individuals may hold the same qualifications, those children with families with greater social and economic capital are better able to exploit them (Goldthorpe and Jackson 2007).

Habitus

Bourdieu devised the concepts of habitus and field to aid his thinking on the topic of human relations, and they underpin the concept of social capital. The habitus is, for Bourdieu, embodied capital, that is, the dispositions which guide an individual's tastes and behaviours (Bourdieu 1986). It is defined as:

> neither the result of free will, nor determined by structures, but created by a kind of interplay between the two over time: dispositions that are both shaped by past events and structures, and that shape current practices and structures and also, importantly, that condition our very perceptions of these. (Bourdieu 1984, 170)

Bourdieu devised the concept from his early discussions of the habitats of humans in his book *The Inheritors* (Bourdieu 1979) and formally defined it in his key text 'Reproduction in education, society and culture' (Bourdieu and Passeron 1990). Despite the name, habitus is more than an individual's habits. It is developed through socialisation processes and determines dispositions that shape people in society (Navarro 2006), and refers to an individual's encoded beliefs or dispositions. It is formed through "one's experiences, one's position and movement through the social world [...] embodied through history and memory" (Aguilar and Sen 2009, 431). Habitus, then, is the *way* people do things. It is relational and mediates between objective structures such as educational systems and subjective practices such as the way people behave in school (Oliver and O'Reilly 2010). Created by a relationship between free will and social structure, habitus is made up of socially learned dispositions that are partially unconscious ways of acting, taken for granted by the individual, which structure values and ways of thinking (Maton 2008). It is developed through the process of socialisation, and as such, aspirations are developed according to what is, and is not, possible within the confines of the habitus. Hence, Bourdieu saw the habitus as an aspect of cultural capital and a visible manifestation of an individual's class and background (Wacquant 1989). It is this structuring of ways of behaving and thinking that illustrates how the habitus allows inequality to persist, as individual behaviours are unconsciously passed on. Furthermore, individuals are under what Bourdieu calls an 'illusio' wherein agents are caught up in the game and have an unthinking commitment to the logic, values and capital of that game (Bourdieu 1992). The rules and structure of a habitus can only function as habitus as long as individuals remain under this illusion and forget the original meaning of acts and words. Webb et al. (2002) give the example of the terminology 'the Dark Ages', which is used regularly by historians without consideration of the meaning of such terminology. The Dark Ages were so called by some to describe the cultural eclipse and encroaching Islamic military forces extinguishing the light of the Roman Empire. However, the original use of the term by Caesar Baronio, cardinal and church historian, was to refer to the lack of surviving sources from the tenth and eleventh centuries. This has political and cultural implications in today's society that mean individuals should reconsider their use of the term, but because of the unthinking nature of much use of language, the use of the term persists. Thus, for Bourdieu, individuals' ambitions are constrained by their habitus through this 'illusio', which is informed by the societal structure (Bourdieu 1993).

Habitus is an internalisation of externality, as individuals internalise the ways of behaving in a particular society, fitting in through their 'ways of being' and feeling at home in the world (Webb et al. 2002). When a habitus becomes conscious, it becomes an externalisation of internality, as internal habits and schema no longer fit into the external society so become visible. More simply, habitus is the way that society becomes deposited within persons in the form of lasting dispositions and propensities to act or think in determinate ways (Wacquant 1996). It is structured by previous life experiences, and it helps shape future practices; thus, dispositions generate perceptions (Maton 2008). These dispositions are durable and transferable, and as such, the habitus does not change quickly but does evolve rather than being set in stone. The habitus is essentially an unconscious process but becomes conscious when an individual is exposed to radically different ideas and ideologies, or when habitus no longer fits the existing context (Bourdieu and Passeron 1990). Equally, they can change through exposure to new external forces, unexpected events, or over a long period of time (Navarro 2006).

The habitus tolerates events such as social upheavals because there is a continuity of meaning which permeates cultures and is usually promoted by the state (Webb et al. 2002). For example, an individual may move job, and whilst they may move into a very different area of work, there are still societal expectations about what working should be like: the commute to work, the lunch break or the payment for a certain amount of work. Some of these expectations are promoted by the state in the form of a minimum wage, a right to a break and the more pragmatic idea that it is better to work than be unemployed. Thus, whilst there may have been changes in an individual's life, there are enough familiar themes to ensure that the habitus does not become disturbed. Bourdieu (1984) does suggest that the habitus can tolerate change, but not without severe disruption to the individual as a result of the habitus becoming conscious.

A key way of transmitting habitus is through family; an individual's class location structures his/her cultural and leisure participation, restricting or widening their leisure choices (Maton 2008). Firstly, material constraints are imposed in terms of how much money and time families have available. Secondly, where an individual lives and car ownership is relevant, as both play an important role in facilitating or limiting access to activities and facilities (Maton 2008). A lower-income family may not be able to access certain sports or musical groups because of their location, or because they cannot afford the relevant equipment to facilitate their involvement in the group. Therefore, a family will not have the habitus of some 'more exclusive' pastimes such as polo, or harp playing. Finally, an individual's class position may impose invisible restraints by "systematically structuring people's access to the necessary cultural competences" (Murdock 2000, 137).

Therefore, it is not just the ability to afford a particular activity, but having the cultural knowledge to partake in activities; for example, sports such as table tennis and football have no marked class difference for those who participate, whereas other sports such as lacrosse or horse riding are only popular in upper/middle classes, and as such, access to these sports is limited to those who possess the economic and cultural capital and habitus to 'fit in' with the groups who engage in these sports. For football, all that is required (initially) is the ability to run and kick a ball. Polo requires the possession of a horse and the cultural knowledge that goes along with horse ownership, plus the required economic capital. However, despite the fact that football is relatively 'open access', when it comes to engaging in the sport, dominant classes rarely take part in actually playing football. Instead, they take on the ownership or sponsorship of teams, thus engaging in the sport but in a different way that only dominant, economically buoyant classes can do. This is an argument that can increasingly be applied to those who support football teams, particularly in the premier league, where a season ticket may cost as much as £950 for a Premier League team such as Manchester United. Those who are in the dominant class appear so because their habitus is immediately adjusted to the inherent requirements of the 'game', requirements which are both social and cultural (Bourdieu and Wacquant 1992). Therefore, their difference is asserted without them consciously seeking to do so (Bourdieu 1988). Overall, then, habitus is how the personal plays a role in the social; our dispositions underpin actions which in turn contribute to social structures (Maton 2008) and interact closely with several types of capital.

Linguistic Habitus

Bourdieu uses linguistics to illustrate how the habitus works in practice. He criticises structural linguistics, arguing language itself is a medium of power relations; language is a code and a system of norms which regulate practices (Bourdieu 1991). Linguistic habitus is a subset of habitus as a whole, as it is a set of dispositions that develop as individuals learn to speak in certain situations. Whilst everyone has the ability to speak, not everyone is able to compel others to listen. Hence language reflects dispositions that are acquired by an individual as they engage in social interactions (Bourdieu 1991). Language is, therefore, the literal embodiment of an individual's cultural capital. Bourdieu (1991) argues that grammar is not the only way that people produce meaning linguistically; speech is not just about its execution. It is also done by saying the appropriate thing at the appropriate moment, showing an understanding of the language games which go on within a conversation (Wacquant 1989). Accents highlight difference or similarity between agents, but also communicate information about the social circumstances of an individual. Language signifies levels of wealth and authority and has a function beyond communication. It indicates information about the individual via their expressive style which takes on a social value (Bourdieu 1991).

Every linguistic interaction between different groups is constrained by the structural relations between the groups, their grasp of the language and the power imbalance within the field. In addition, other factors such as gender, age and ethnicity also impact at this point, suggesting that 'linguistic communism' is a fallacy and access to and participation in language is unequal (Bourdieu 1991). This leads to the presumption that some people have linguistic monopolies, just as others have economic or cultural monopolies. The market determines the price or value of linguistic products; therefore, the content of speech is shaped by its estimated value and therefore linguistic production is inevitably affected by the anticipation of how the market will respond. Bourdieu (1991) argues that official discourse imposes a point of view which everyone has to recognise if she/he is to be seen as legitimate. This can result in discourse and speech being silenced or at the very least censored in some way, depending on its perceived significance in the field (Wacquant 1989). Bourdieu recognises that this domination produces conflicts between symbolic powers which aim at imposing their vision on groups and questions how the spokespersons for groups come to be "invested with the full power to act and to speak in the name of the group which he or she produces by the magic of the slogan, the watchword or the command and by his mere existence as an incarnation of the collective" (Bourdieu 1989, 23).

Topper (2001) argues that those who do not have the full power to act and speak have three alternative options. Firstly, they could contest the legitimacy of dominant language by refusing to recognise it, and secondly, they could try to euphemise expressions by putting them in forms that are acceptable to the market. These options are both usually ineffectual as linguistic dominance and competency goes beyond grammar and includes the way that an individual's accent, pronunciation and comportment are inscribed on the body: the bodily hexis (Bourdieu 1977a). The body is, for Bourdieu, the site of incorporated history, wherein experiences are transformed into permanent dispositions (Bourdieu 1977a), and, as such, irrelevant of *what* is spoken, it is the manner of delivery which is important. The final and most common option is to simply withdraw from these domains, where the agent feels that their speech has no linguistic competency (Bourdieu 1991). Bourdieu suggests that when individuals talk, they anticipate the likely profit of their speech that determines what it is permissible and not permissible to say. There may be a fourth option of an agent finding space in their private life where their linguistic products are legitimised, but this is never the same as having a formal recognition by the dominant agents or class in that field (Bourdieu 1991). Individuals learn the value of their speech through reinforcement and repudiations, producing a linguistic sense of place (Bourdieu 1991). It is this 'sense of place' that controls the degree of constraint that a field will bring to bear on the construction of discourse. This imposes silence on some narratives but allows others the liberties of "language that is securely established" (Bourdieu 1991, 508).

Field

The second of Bourdieu's underpinning concepts is 'field', where a field is a "structured space of social positions which are also a structure of power relations. The various 'positions' within this space are occupied either by agents or institutions, and the relations between the positions determines, at any given time, the structure of the field" (Topper 2001, 39). Field is a geographical/mathematical metaphor for how individuals are arranged in society (Aguilar and Sen 2009) where fields are essentially networks in which people compete for resources contained within that field. For Bourdieu, to think in terms of a field is to think relationally (Wacquant 1989), and by thinking relationally, it is argued that the connections and disconnections between people can be seen. Relations exist in the social world, and a field is a network of relations between objectively defined positions. It is these positions which impose external restrictions upon their occupants, dependent upon the distribution of power within that field (Bourdieu 1993). There are limits to a field, and those limits are seen when social or cultural capital is no longer recognised. That is, where an individual's specific knowledge or skills does not bring her/him any benefit (Bourdieu 1993). For example, the ability to play the piano is useful in a field that requires musicians but would be deemed to have significantly less, if any, value in a field of athletes or engineers.

Through the use of the field concept, Bourdieu (1993) suggests that the world is structurally differentiated and stratified, with an individual's position in that field being governed by the volume and type of capital she/he possesses, which in turn structures that individual's options and strategies. Fields are governed by specific laws of functioning that determine the conditions of entry into the field, for example, social connections, professional qualifications, and economic capital, and also by specific relations of force within it (Topper 2001). Each field has a boundary, often marked by 'institutionalised' barriers to entry; these boundaries can be detected by identifying the point at which the effects of the field cease (Wacquant 1989). Thomson (2008) uses the metaphor of a football game to illustrate the interrelationship between habitus and field. In the game, players have set positions, and there are specific rules and skills within the game. In addition, the physical condition of the field has an effect on the players and their capacity to play to the best of their ability. This analogy illustrates how field functions, and how positions within the social field are occupied by agents who face limitations on their behaviour both by the rules of the game and by the condition of the field. It also introduces the idea of a field having boundaries; the rules of the game cease to function beyond the football field, and this is the same with Bourdieu's concept (Anheier et al. 2009), in that fields have limitations and the rules and habitus within that field cease to function at the limits of it. Moreover, just as in league football, the field is not a level one, and those players who have certain types of capital are advantaged because the field depends on, and produces more of, that capital. In footballing terms, some players have an advantage because they have highly qualified coaches, physiotherapists and managers. This advantage means that they do well in championships and leagues and are further rewarded because of this progression. This also means that the field produces more successful individuals and teams, because of the success they already enjoy.

Agents gravitate towards social fields which match their own dispositions and try to avoid those fields which will produce a clash between the field and habitus (Maton 2008). Individuals adjust their expectations regarding the amount of capital they are likely to gain in terms of practical limitations such as education, social class and so on. Thus, there are limitations imposed upon the agents by the field which can lead to people being 'resigned' about their lower position in the field (Webb et al. 2002). This acceptance can lead to a reproduction of symbolic domination as those resigned agents tolerate conditions that would be judged unacceptable by others (Webb et al. 2002), thus reproducing conditions of oppression and illustrating the idea that social games are not fair games. Bourdieu refers to this domination as 'symbolic violence' (Bourdieu and Wacquant 1992) and suggests that people are subjected to different forms of violence such as being denied resources or being treated as inferior but do not challenge the domination, as they perceive their situation as normal. As such, those who are dominated take part in their own domination and subjugation, which is perpetrated unconsciously by those who dominate and those who are dominated through classification systems and participation in society (Bourdieu and Wacquant 1992).

The social world is made up of multiple fields, and those fields have different shapes depending on which 'game' is being played. Bourdieu (1986) suggests that there are various fields, such as intellectual, religious, educational, cultural and so on. These fields represent a distribution structure of types of capital and indicate areas of struggle around the creation, accumulation and possession of goods, knowledge or status

(Navarro 2006); thus the key sites of struggle in a field may well be at the boundaries of the field where it is determined whether the field still has an effect and in terms of the value of the capitals within the field. Fields highlight power relations and individuals experience power differently depending on which field they can access, or what field they are in at a given moment (Gaventa 2003). Fields explain the differential power, for example, that women experience in public or private where they may be the main decision-maker in the home but experience much more limited power outside of the home if they are in lower-skilled or minimum-wage jobs. Each field is hierarchical and has a 'distinction' (Bourdieu 1984) that delineates the powerful from the less powerful; for example, some literature is perceived as high culture, and hence influential, and other literature perceived as 'base' or low cultured. The relationship between habitus and field works in two interrelated ways; the field structures the habitus, and the habitus aids the constitution of the field as a meaningful world (Bourdieu 1984). Bourdieu (1984) insists that practice is always informed by agency, but agency must be contextualised in terms of its relation to the objective structures of culture. As such, the way an individual behaves is the result of the interrelationship between his/her habitus, the field and its structures. Bourdieu's concepts of habitus and field are relational structures, and it is the relation between the structures that provides the key for understanding practice. As Dumais (2002) suggests, an individual's practices or actions are the results of one's habitus and capital within a given field. This means that the concept of the field is powerful as it "facilitates an analysis of the socially differentiated and stratified, without reducing it to a set of discrete and self-contained micro-worlds" (Topper 2001, 410). It uncovers the power relations within society, and without this focus on power, the problem rapidly becomes focused on an individual or group's lack of social capital, rather than the consideration of the historically defined social conditions that have formed and reproduced a structured inequality. Therefore, fields are also fields of struggles that are aimed at preserving or changing the forces of capital (Wacquant 1989).

In underpinning social capital with the concepts of field and habitus, Bourdieu facilitates the analysis of phenomena through a lens that allows sight of the power differentials which are often neglected in broader analyses of society. In particular, Bourdieu's conception of social capital proves useful in analysing the processes by which individuals resettle and rebuild by highlighting the role of social networks and individual 'ways of being'. Bourdieu's ideas are especially useful because they allow us to examine the relationship between structure and agency and, in particular, highlight how individual choices may be constrained by larger structural factors such as laws and policies as well as cultural traditions.

References

Aguilar, J., & Sen, S. (2009). Comparing Conceptualizations of Social Capital. *Journal of Community Practice, 17*(4), 424–443.

Anheier, H. K., Gerhards, J., & Romo, F. P. (2009). Forms of Capital and Social Structure in Cultural Fields: Examining Bourdieu's Social Topography. *American Journal of Sociology, 100*(4), 859–903.

Bourdieu, P. (1977a). Economics of Linguistic Exchanges. *Social Science Information, 16*(6), 645–668.

Bourdieu, P. (1977b). *Outline of a Theory of Practice, Cambridge Studies in Social and Cultural Anthropology*. Cambridge: Cambridge University Press.

Bourdieu, P. (1979). *The Inheritors: French Students and Their Relations to Culture.* Chicago: University of Chicago Press.

Bourdieu, P. (1984). *Distinction: A Social Critique of the Judgement of Taste.* Cambridge, MA: Harvard University Press.

Bourdieu, P. (1986). The Forms of Capital. In J. G. Richardson (Ed.), *Handbook of Theory and Research for the Sociology of Education* (pp. 241–258). London: Greenwood Press.

Bourdieu, P. (1988). Vive la crise! *Theory and Society, 17*, 773–787.

Bourdieu, P. (1989). Social Space and Symbolic Power. *Sociological Theory, 7*(1), 14–25.

Bourdieu, P. (1991). *Language and Symbolic Power* (J. B. Thompson, Ed.). Cambridge: Polity Press.

Bourdieu, P. (1992). *The Rules of Art: Genesis and Structure of the Literary Field.* Stanford, CA: Stanford University Press.

Bourdieu, P. (1993). *The Field of Cultural Production.* Cambridge: Polity Press.

Bourdieu, P., & Passeron, J.-C. (1990). *Reproduction in Education, Society and Culture* (2nd ed.). London: Sage Publications.

Bourdieu, P., & Wacquant, L. (1992). *An Invitation to Reflexive Sociology*. Cambridge: Polity Press.

Coleman, J. (1990). *Foundations of Social Theory*. London: Harvard University Press.

Coleman, J. (1994). *Foundations of Social Theory*. New York: Harvard University Press.

Dumais, S. (2002). Cultural Capital, Gender, and School Success: The Role of Habitus. *Sociology of Education, 75*(1), 44–68.

Edwards, R. (2004). Present and Absent in Troubling Ways: Families and Social Capital Debates. *The Sociological Review, 52*(1), 1–21.

Field, J. (2008). *Social Capital*. Abingdon: Routledge.

Foley, M., & Edwards, B. (1996). The Paradox of Civil Society. *Journal of Democracy, 7*(3), 38–52.

Gaventa, J. (2003). *Power after Lukes: A Review of the Literature*. Brighton: Institute of Development Studies.

Goldthorpe, J. H., & Jackson, M. (2007). Intergenerational Class Mobility in Contemporary Britain: Political Concerns and Empirical Findings. *British Journal of Sociology, 58*(4), 525–546.

Granovetter, M. S. (1973). The Strength of Weak Ties. *American Journal of Sociology, 78*(6), 1360–1380.

Hall, P. A. (1999). Social Capital in Britain. *British Journal of Political Science, 29*(3), 417–461.

Halsey, A. H., Heath, A. F., & Ridge, J. M. (1980). *Origins and Destinations: Family, Class and Education in Modern Britain*. Oxford: OUP.

Haynes, P. (2009). *Before Going Any Further with Social Capital: Eight Key Criticisms to Address*. Ingenio Working Paper Series. Retrieved February 15, 2018, from http://digital.csic.es/bitstream/10261/14203/1/Before_Going_Any_Further_With_Social_Capital__Eight_Key_Criticisms_to_Address%5B1%5D.pdf.

Jones, A. (2016). *Genocide: A Comprehensive Introduction* (3rd ed.). London: Routledge.

Kauzlarich, D., Matthews, R. A., & Miller, W. J. (2001). Toward a Victimology of State Crime. *Critical Criminology, 10*(3), 173–194.

Maton, K. (2008). Habitus. In M. Grenfell (Ed.), *Pierre Bourdieu: Key Concepts* (pp. 49–65). London: Acumen.

Misztal, B. A. (2000). *Informality: Social Theory and Contemporary Practice*. London: Routledge.

Murdock, G. (2000). Class Stratification and Cultural Consumption: Some Motifs in the Work of Pierre Bourdieu. In D. Robbins (Ed.), *Pierre Bourdieu* (pp. 133–159). London: Sage Publications.

Navarro, Z. (2006). In Search of a Cultural Interpretation of Power: The Contribution of Pierre Bourdieu. *Institute of Development Studies, 37*(6), 11–22.

Oliver, C., & O'Reilly, K. (2010). A Bourdieusian Analysis of Class and Migration: Habitus and the Individualizing Process. *Sociology, 44*(1), 49–66.

Portes, A. (1998). Social Capital: Its Origins and Applications in Modern Sociology. *Annual Review of Sociology, 24, 24*(1).

Putnam, R. D. (1995). Bowling Alone: America's Declining Social Capital. *Journal of Democracy, 6*(1), 65–78.

Putnam, R. D. (1996). The Strange Disappearance of Civic America. *American Prospect, 7*(24), 34–48.

Putnam, R. D. (2000). *Bowling Alone: The Collapse and Revival of American Community*. London: Simon & Schuster.

Thomson, P. (2008). Field. In M. Grenfell (Ed.), *Pierre Bourdieu: Key Concepts* (pp. 67–81). London: Acumen.

Topper, K. (2001). Not So Trifling Nuances: Pierre Bourdieu, Symbolic Violence and the Perversions of Democracy. *Constellations, 8*(1), 30–56.

Wacquant, L. J. D. (1989). Towards a Reflexive Society: A Workshop with Pierre Bourdieu. *Sociological Theory, 7*(1), 26–63.

Wacquant, L. J. D. (1996). Reading Bourdieu's "Capital". *International Journal of Contemporary Sociology, 33*(2), 150–170.

Webb, J., Schirato, T., & Danaher, G. (2002). *Understanding Bourdieu*. London: Sage Publications.

3

Migration and Acculturation

Migration is a collective action (Castles and Miller 2009), and migration research is often separated into two groups: the determinants and patterns of migration and the ways that migrants are incorporated into the societies that receive them. Castles and Miller (2009) argue that this is something of a false dichotomy as migration is a process that affects every dimension of human existence, and research should draw on both areas as they inform each other. This book does precisely this, considering the genocidal forces that propel people out of their own country and the responses they received from host societies, exploring the relationship between their survivor status and the re-establishment of life in a new country following forced migration.

Castles and Miller (2009) make the point that only a limited number of refugees manage to migrate to a country beyond their country of first asylum. These are usually people who have financial resources, and cultural capital such as educational qualifications and social networks in their destination country. It can be argued that most genocide survivors lack these indicators, so this research will be exploring what alternatives genocide survivors use to re-establish their lives and how they came to arrive in the UK.

L. Asquith, *Rebuilding Lives After Genocide*, Palgrave Studies in Compromise after Conflict, https://doi.org/10.1007/978-3-030-14074-8_3

The concept of citizenship is particularly important in terms of migration, and Twine (1994) argues that it has three aspects: civil (legal) rights such as being able to own property and the right to a fair trial; political rights such as the right to vote; and social rights, which include entitlement to welfare. Dwyer (2003, 151) notes that "citizenship has a formal legal status but also has a substantive dimension to it", suggesting this substantive dimension is "the extent to which those who enjoy the formal legal status of citizens may, or may not enjoy the rights (including rights to welfare) that ensure effective membership of a national community" (Dwyer 2003, 151).

The word 'refugee' was first used in France in the 1500s (Karatani 2005), and most states have not differentiated between refugees and other forms of migrants until relatively recently. In the UK, the 1905 Aliens Act introduced the first set of immigration control measures, designed to prevent criminals and undesirables from entering the country. Even at this point, attitudes towards Jews were not particularly welcoming, and the key focus of the 1905 legislation was to prevent large numbers of Jews from Russia settling in the UK following their expulsion to the Pale of Settlement on the Austria-Hungary border with Russia. Prime Minister Arthur Balfour suggested in debates about the act that the incoming migration was "an alien immigration which was largely Jewish … [who remain] a people apart" (Klug 2013, n.p.).

Prior to the Second World War, the UK's response to refugees and refugee situations had been piecemeal at best, with no clear 'rescue operation' planned or operationalised. In 1915, 250,000 Belgian refugees arrived in the UK following Germany's invasion of Belgium. They arrived at all major ports and were dispersed throughout the UK. The refugees were initially welcomed: "A group of Belgians detraining at Northampton were met by 'kind-hearted ladies [who] were ready at the station with steaming coffee, buns and sweets.' Such refugees arriving in the English Midlands 'brought home to us the tragedy of their martyred country'" (Purseigle 2007, 76). Indeed, at Victoria and Charing Cross rail stations, there were cheers and celebrations as the buses left carrying refugees to reception centres (Purseigle 2007). When the war ended, the refugees were rapidly returned to Belgium, with employment contracts being terminated and the government offering free one-way tickets back to

Belgium (Kushner 1999). In this case, the migrants were given safe harbour for the minimum amount of time and returned to Belgium as soon as the war ended. There was no consideration of the refugees remaining in the UK and settling here permanently.

As Hitler came to power in 1933, the League of Nations established the office of the High Commissioner for Refugees from Germany, recognising the threat that Hitler posed to the Jewish community in Germany. James McDonald, a US diplomat, was assigned to be the high commissioner, but he resigned in 1935 as a result of the frustration he felt regarding the lack of cooperation he experienced from nations with regard to Jewish refugees (Marfleet 2006). In his resignation letter, he wrote very clearly about the ongoing persecution of Jews and non-Aryans in Germany and again called for responses from all League nations (Marfleet 2006). Most governments ignored this plea, and the British government explicitly rejected the request. In 1937, a message was sent from the British government to the embassy in Paris, which reinforced that the official policy was to do nothing that would trigger further immigration (Marfleet 2006). Even following the annexation of Austria by Germany, officials in London were still of the view that an increase in migration would create both social and labour problems. It was at this point that the Home Office introduced a visa system to control the entry of Jews from Germany and to "avoid creation of a Jewish problem in this country" (Marfleet 2006, 135); the disturbing repetition of the Nazi's language of 'Jewish problem' is noted here. This and the Belgian migrants from the First World War show that the UK has not always been the 'haven' for migrants that it sometimes perceived and portrayed to be (Kushner 2006).

It must be pointed out that the UK was not alone in being reluctant to host any refugees from Hitler's regime; the US had a similar policy and stance. Indeed, the invitations to the 1938 Evian conference on Jewish refugees from Nazi Germany stated quite clearly that "no country would be expected to receive a greater number of immigrants than is permitted by existing legislation" (Marfleet 2006, 135). At the conference, the vast majority of countries rejected any changes to refugee legislation, maintaining that they had already taken in large numbers of refugees—a statement that was untrue. In Britain between 1933 and 1939, only 10,000 refugees were permitted to reside in the UK, with most of these being intellectuals, artists and upper classes such as bankers and financiers, all with assurances that they would not be a drain on the public purse (Kushner 2006). At the conference, only the Dominican Republic made a substantial offer to take in 10,000 refugees to work the land and become rural settlers (Marfleet 2006). Following the November pogrom (called Kristallnacht) in November 1938, the UK reluctantly agreed following public pressure to participate in a programme to help the remaining Jews of Germany to escape, but the government were still insistent that they should be directed out of Europe (Kushner 2006).

The government agreed at this point (November 1938) to participate in the Kindertransport programme. The Kindertransport was the informal name given to a relatively large-scale rescue mission which placed almost 10,000 Jewish children from Germany and the German-annexed areas on trains and boats to the UK. However, this decision was not without its detractors. Comments from the public, recorded in the mass observation archive, point to a reluctance from some people to accept the child refugees into Britain, with one female observing,

> I think people feel sorry for the children now, but they won't like it when their children start to find work, and they find so many Jews in the market at the same time. I think thousands of people feel, too, that these refugees are having a far better time than the children of the unemployed—I do. (Kushner 2006, 155)

This perception of refugees having a better life than the members of the host society is an enduring one. Over 70 years later, in January 2015, the *Daily Mail* ran a story highlighting how asylum seekers were being housed in a 'luxury hotel', with reviews on the review website 'TripAdvisor' highlighting the asylum seekers' potential criminality and how paying guests were being downgraded as a result (Baker 2015).

What is rarely questioned or considered about the Kindertransport is why the UK government rejected calls to allow the parents of the children to come with their children; instead, the Kindertransport project is commonly held as a model of British generosity to the Jewish people. The implications of not considering the selectivity of British immigration procedures at this time mean that connections are not made with current illogical asylum procedures, where some claimants are privileged over others, depending on the nature of their claim: for example, recent cases of individuals who have made a claim for asylum because they have been targeted for their sexuality having to prove that they are gay to the Border Agency in order to be granted refugee status, or being told they cannot be lesbian because they have had children (Cohen 2015; Townsend and Taylor 2014). Moreover, whilst the saving of 10,000 children's lives is in no doubt a good thing, the celebration of the Kindertransport neglects the reality of the situation in that the vast majority of children had their parents murdered and were left in an unfamiliar country, not fully understanding what had happened to them (Kushner 2006). Even in cases where the children were reunited with their parents, the relationship often broke down because of the long separation and trauma caused by the Holocaust. Therefore we should not look back at the UK's refugee regime with rose-tinted glasses, but remember that whilst 10,000 children were saved, those children frequently became orphans and were often treated poorly by their adoptive parents (Benz 2004).

The UK's later refugee regime has been shaped by two key events. Firstly, the refugee crisis following the Second World War, which resulted in thousands of refugees (known as displaced persons) scattered throughout Europe. This led to the 1951 United Nations Convention relating to the status of refugees. This convention defined who was a refugee, what their rights were, and the legal obligations of signatory states, and initially only dealt with those who were displaced as a result of the events of the Second World War. The convention rights were later extended in 1971 by the Bellagio protocol, which broadened the convention's scope to all people and at all times for the signatory countries. Most governments of the time presumed that the refugee problem would disappear given time, once the displaced peoples of the Second World War had been dispersed and resettled, as they had after the First World War. Indeed, there was a period of relative stability that lasted until the 1970s (Marfleet 2006). Refugees (with a few exceptions) mainly came from the territories of the Eastern bloc, and they were rare due to the 'non-departure regime' of the

USSR (Castles and Miller 2009). Consequently, it was easy for the UK to welcome such refugees, particularly as they served as politically expedient propaganda to highlight the corruption and oppression of the Eastern bloc countries (Castles and Miller 2009).

The second key event was the collapse of the USSR and the end of the Cold War that led to an extended period of political instability sending shockwaves throughout Europe. As conflicts arose out of the collapse of communist states throughout Eastern and central Europe (most notably the former Yugoslavia), asylum processes in Western Europe and the US became more politicised, resulting in changes to national legislation. This also produced temporary rather than permanent protection regimes and diversion to safe 'third' countries through a restrictive interpretation of the 1951 Refugee Convention (Castles and Miller 2009). The new nation-states that arose from the ashes of the Cold War tended to be exclusionary and based on principles of nationality that resulted in more forced migrants (Sales 2007). Migration at the turn of the nineteenth to the twentieth century tended to be homogenous groups of migrants, resulting in specific ethnic communities developing such as the Jewish communities of Leeds, Manchester and London and, later, in the 1970s, the Ugandan Asian community in Leicester. However, modern migration has produced an unprecedented number of migrants from a wide range of different countries, which has resulted in not only an expansion of the number of ethnic groups but also differential statuses, patterns and spatial distribution and responses by local communities and service providers. The interplay between these factors has been called 'superdiversity' (Vertovec 2007).

Early integration policy emphasised the importance of migrants maintaining links with co-nationals or co-ethnics. However, later policy moved towards a more assimilationist stance as a result of a backlash against multiculturalism (Cheung and Phillimore 2014). The nationality and immigration legislation that followed the Second World War, especially from the 1990s onwards, defined and redefined British citizenship in a number of ways. The state began to have a central role in constructing an ideology within which minority ethnic communities were seen as a threat to British identity (Dwyer 2003). Indeed, Dwyer (2003, 157) argues that

> the British state has implemented a series of Acts that have negatively impacted upon the citizenship rights and status of legally resident minority ethnic citizens, and simultaneously sought (literally) to exclude non-white people from beyond the geographical boundaries of Britain, attaining formal legally defined citizenship.

Since the 1990s, the regulation of asylum seekers and refugees has become increasingly restrictive with the number of forced migrants growing as a result of proliferation in the number of conflicts and the closing-off of other migration routes (Castles and Miller 2009). The process of determining who a refugee is, is based on the assumption that it is possible to distinguish between refugees and what are termed 'economic' migrants and therefore between forced and voluntary migration, which in reality is very difficult to do (Sales 2007). Indeed, the violence and conflict which force people to flee to new countries are often the results of poverty and economic instability which also propel individuals to move in search of security and a better life (O'Reilly 2012). Moreover, the process of determining refugee policy, whilst based on humanitarian principles, is in reality often based more on foreign policy and concerns over upsetting or offending 'friendly' countries. For example, the UK government refused to accept refugees from Chile in 1973 due to an alliance with General Pinochet (Sales 2007).

The immigration system has over the past few decades increasingly developed a bifurcated approach, wherein the social and economic benefits of migration are welcomed at the same time as the proposal and implementation of increasingly harsher measures to deter asylum seekers (Home Office 2002). Alongside this, the New Labour rhetoric, particularly under Gordon Brown was one of citizenship needing to be 'earned' (Brown 2008). Indeed, the 2009 Borders, Citizenship and Immigration Act placed emphasis on 'temporary residence' and 'probationary citizenship' as being steps on the way to earn citizenship. Even the terminology of the forced migrant has a significance, with 'refugee' having an everyday meaning of someone who has left their home country because of fear of violence and persecution, and a very precise meaning in law, which is interpreted in an increasingly narrow way in the UK. In addition, there is a gendered nature of the refugee definition that reflects male dominance and experience and makes specific assumptions about gender roles (Sales 2007). The asylum claims of women rest on "gender stereotypes of accepted and 'believed' roles" (Edwards 2003, 57). Most importantly, gendered forms of persecution are not included in the convention categories within the definition, and whilst gender persecution is increasingly being recognised, the responses to women at border control are unpredictable at best (Ali et al. 2012). For example, women are often expected to describe and explain their stories of persecution (which often contain violent sexual abuse) to an unknown person, often a male who identifies the slightest inconsistency as evidence of falsehoods (Sales 2007). Moreover, women's residential status is often conditional on their husband's status, and this dependence can lead to vulnerability such as domestic abuse where a woman may have to remain in a violent relationship in order to remain in the UK (Sales 2007). More generally, refugee policy requires refugees to prove their vulnerability in some way, and the refugee identity is not necessarily sought because of a sense of solidarity with others, but because that status and identity facilitate access to services that are denied others (O'Neill 2015).

There was no specific asylum (as opposed to refugee) legislation until the 1990 Asylum and Immigration Act, which introduced the concept of the deserving/undeserving asylum seeker and triggered the start of the dispersal of asylum seekers to areas outside the south-east of the UK (Fletcher 2008). Later on, the 1999 Immigration and Asylum Act removed rights to social assistance benefits from those who were subject to immigration control and replaced them with a voucher scheme. The effect of this act was to widen the gulf "between the social rights enjoyed by UK citizens and those available to asylum seekers" (Dwyer 2003, 161). Hence, forced migrants are effectively excluded from the mainstream social welfare system whilst at the same time their entitlements to support within the asylum system have been reduced (Dwyer 2003). The other key aspect of the 1990 Asylum and Immigration Act was to introduce the concept of no-choice dispersal, whereby asylum seekers would be dispersed and housed throughout the UK to prevent overloading of services in London and the south-east of the UK. The act also removed the responsibility for meeting asylum seekers' basic social security and housing needs from local authorities and moved them to the newly created

National Asylum Support Service (NASS). NASS became responsible for dispersing asylum seekers to reception areas across the country, but typically in urban areas with available housing stock (Phillimore and Goodson 2006). This process has been widely criticised as it removes migrants from cultural groups and support and the relevant dispersal areas are chosen on broadly economic grounds (Phillimore and Goodson 2006) with little, if any, consideration of the impact of dispersal upon the local, often-deprived community. Indeed, seven of the areas that serve as dispersal areas are in the top 20 deprived areas of the UK (Phillimore and Goodson 2006). Alongside this, policies towards asylum seekers have become increasingly draconian, with asylum payments being 50% of basic welfare benefits (Lyons 2017), the refusal of permission to work in some cases, restriction of freedom of movement and compulsory detention whilst asylum claims are appealed (Chantler 2010). The legislation of the 1990s and 2000s also consolidated the link between immigration/residency status and welfare entitlement, a situation which was further complicated by a "stratified system of entitlements that exists within the generic population of asylum seekers/refugees, who enjoy differential entitlements to housing and social benefits depending on formal immigration status" (Dwyer 2003, 162). The combined effect of this is that different categories of displaced people in the UK have different rights, another factor which contributes to Vertovec's (2007) idea of superdiversity.

Furthermore, whilst asylum seekers are in many ways victims in their home countries, they are often labelled as a predator upon the host country's resources and culture, rather than a victim or survivor of an offence (Fekete and Webber 2010). Asylum seekers have been the focus of parliamentary disagreements, are vilified in the media (e.g. see Baker 2015), and face active opposition from right-wing groups such as UKIP which has led to a perception of those who seek asylum as being workshy or having criminal intent, and this focus has not facilitated absorption into the host country. This is in sharp contrast to the official British narrative as a compassionate democracy which provides a safe haven to the persecuted of the world (Friedman and Klein 2008). The tabloid press portrays asylum seekers as uneducated criminals (see *The Sun*, 'Asylum seekers steal the Queen's birds for barbecues', 4 July 2003, or *The Daily*

Star, 'Asylum seekers eat our donkeys', 31 August 2003). In addition, migrants, particularly asylum seekers and refugees, are seen by the media as threatening and different. Indeed, Phillimore (2011, 582) notes that respondents in her research "spoke of feeling criminalised as their identity as an asylum seeker was questioned, they had to tell, retell and defend their story, were detained, dispersed and then made to report to police stations". Often 'liquid' metaphors such as 'flood' or 'wave' are used to describe the arrival of asylum seekers in the UK creating a potent image of a country overcome by waves of people, leading to the belief that the country and its resources are under threat from asylum seekers (Bleasdale 2008). These negative labels are, in Bourdieuian terms, an attempt to keep people in their place by those in a higher class (Erel 2010). This is important to consider for the survivors in this research, as it is fair to assume that they would not have always been welcomed to the UK and seen in a positive light. This may well have had an effect on their resettlement experiences and made re-establishing their lives harder.

Theories of Migration and Acculturation

It is evident that language, country of origin and religion are important in relation to migrant identities. However, Vertovec (2007) argues that methods and channels of migration as well as the range of legal statuses arising from migration are just as, if not more, important in terms of the length of stay, and to what extent migrants access public services and gain employment. Hence, Vertovec (2019) argues that the concept of 'superdiversity' more accurately represents the widely differing statuses within the same ethnic or migratory group. Some members of the group may hold British citizenship, others may be undocumented migrants, and there is a range of other legal statuses in between these two poles. It is important to consider the statuses of forced migrants as "formal and substantive aspects of citizenship are both important if an individual is to achieve effective membership of a national community and enjoy the equality of status that full citizenship promises" (Dwyer 2003, 166). If these statuses are not fully investigated, it can be difficult, if not impossible, to consider the various statuses that migrants have.

"Superdiversity is proposed as a 'summary term' to encapsulate a range of such changing variables surrounding migration patterns—and significantly, their interlinkages—which amount to a recognition of the complexities that supersede previous patterns and perceptions of migration-driven diversity" (Meissner and Vertovec 2014, 542). Hence, superdiversity is, as Phillimore (2014, 568) notes, "associated with intra-group heterogeneity as individuals differ according to immigration status and associated rights and entitlements, gender, age, faith, the reason for migration, class, education levels and more, leading to unprecedented demographic complexity".

It is this demographic complexity that highlights the weaknesses within several theories of migration, particularly economic theories centred on a push/pull model. For example, Ravenstein's laws of migration (cited in O'Reilly 2012) argues that migration has a basis of rational choice and is rooted in the global supply and demand of workers. Castles (2010) argues that such theories do not reflect the reality for most migrants, ignoring wider structural and historical factors such as family dynamics as well as policies relating to refugees and asylum seekers. Hence, migrants are seen as a homogenous group who make rational decisions based on the best-perceived outcome for themselves. Whilst migrants may make some choices about their migration; these choices may well be constrained by wider structural and cultural factors which impact upon some migrants more than others (Castles 2010). Other ideas, such as world systems theories see the entire world as a single, capitalist system, emphasising the unequal distribution of economic and political power. Because theories of this sort focus almost exclusively on the structures of society and how they impact upon individuals, they often fail to recognise individual agency (O'Reilly 2012) and often ignore the complexity of migration (Castles and Miller 2009). They do, however, draw attention to the relationship between colonialism and modern migratory flows and the role of the state in migration (O'Reilly 2012). Therefore, whilst world systems theories do consider the impact of the structure of society upon individuals, they still do not fully engage with the full range of identities and diversities that are present in modern migrant groups.

However, migration systems theory as put forward by Castles and Miller (2009) does appear to reflect this diversity, seeing migration as a complex process, examining the roles of both structure and agency. This approach draws together the interactions of "macro, meso and micro level elements within a wider migration system" (O'Reilly 2012, 46) and allows us to see a clearer picture of the complex nature of immigration and allows a consideration of migration in its historical and cultural context. However, such approaches do not necessarily "fully theorise the interrelationship of structures and agency and spend little or no time thinking through how structures become embodied practice" (O'Reilly 2012, 48). Hence, whilst these approaches begin to consider the relationship of structure and agency, they do not go far enough in thinking about how softer structures such as social norms and rules become embedded within an agent so that they become part of their habitus.

However, by taking a Bourdieuian stance, the migration systems approach can be developed and push forward thinking on the nature of softer structures and their embodiment in the habitus. In particular, O'Reilly's (2012) theory of practice in relation to migrants illustrates the internal and external structures that both facilitate and constrain migrant decision-making. External structures, such as health care institutions, employment and housing markets as well as war and environmental disasters can be seen as 'hard' external structures, in that they are less malleable and exist independently of the desires and wishes of the migrant in question. Social norms, pressures and vague rules are a more flexible form of external structure. The malleability of such structures depends on how much power the migrant feels they have which can be utilised to 'bend' or 'change' such structures (O'Reilly 2012). Structures can also be internalised and can be acquired through socialisation or past practices and, as such, appear in the form of a habitus. "Communities of practice (social and institutional life, if you like) thus provide the context within which an agent is constrained and enabled by the external structures. These are embodied and enacted through the roles and positions of those within an agent's communities of practice" (O'Reilly 2012, 31).

In terms of the processes of migration, traditional thought has again centred on a rational choice approach, seeing migration as a one-off event where an individual moves permanently from one place to another. Because of this, migratory outcomes were seen in terms of how well the migrant became assimilated or incorporated into the host society, with migrants giving up their own culture and adopting the traditions of the host culture (O'Reilly 2012). This, as Castles and Miller (2009) argue, is one-sided assimilation, with the migrant being the one doing the adapting and the assimilating. More recently, we have seen a shift towards multiculturalism and integration. Within these approaches, migrants are seen as distinct but equal, with integration being seen as a process whereby both migrant groups and host societies change and develop new identities (Berry 1997). As such, integration is the result of an individual maintaining their original culture and regularly interacting with other groups. Within this approach, an important focus of Berry's (1997) work is the role of social networks. If migrants do not integrate, they may be marginalised if they have no social networks, separated if they do not mix with the host population or assimilated if they do not retain links with co-nationals or co-ethnics. Integration then needs a connection between the host and the migrant that allows the development of new identities. However, Berry's (1997) approach has been criticised for "assuming integration is unidirectional, monolithic and linear" (Cheung and Phillimore 2014, 520). Equally, there has been little consideration of the society that migrants are integrating into, or examination of how integration is experienced by individuals (Castles 2003). Moving away from this, integration can be understood as "a multidimensional process in which individuals, migrant and refugee community organisations (MRCOs), institutions and society all have a role" (Cheung and Phillimore 2014, 520). In considering macro-, meso- and micro-level 'stakeholders' in the integration process, this concept then becomes allied to the migration systems theory approach and can be seen in Ager and Strang's (2004) Indicators of Integration framework, which draws both on Berry's (1997) work and also on the concept of social capital as put forward by Putnam (1995). Importantly, Ager and Strang (2004) note that there is no clear consensus on what integration actually is. They reviewed over 40 definitions of the term, finding that whilst there was no single definition, there were some clear themes in terms of the public outcomes of integration, the importance of participation and relationships, and the importance of notions of citizenship which shape local and national expectations around integration.

In investigating different understandings of the term 'integration', Ager and Strang (2004) established a framework for a common understanding of integration, devising a model to aid those working in the field of refugee integration. Ager and Strang's (2004) model presents ten key domains of integration in four areas. There are complex interlinkages between all of the domains, and actions in one have the potential to impact upon all the others. This model is not hierarchical, nor do Ager and Strang (2004) wish that integration is seen to occur in a particular, linear way. The first area, 'Means and Markers', is argued by Ager and Strang (2004) to be the 'public face' of integration. This area is underpinned by four domains: housing, employment, education and health. They are called 'means and markers' because success in these areas is an indicator of integration, and are likely to assist in the integration process. Employment serves as a mechanism for income generation as well as aiding language development and the development of social connections. Much of refugee and migrant integration is structured by their experiences of housing, which as well as providing stability also facilitates the development of social connections. Education is a significant marker of integration but also serves as a means towards the goal of integration, creating opportunities for employment and wider social connections. Finally, "good health enables greater social participation and engagement in employment and educational activities" (Ager and Strang 2004, 17).

The three domains within the second area, 'Social Connections', emphasise the importance of relationships and networks to understanding the integration process. Drawing on Putnam's (1995) concept of social capital, Ager and Strang (2004) argue that the domains consist of social bonds, social bridges and social links. Social bonds are seen as connections with a community defined by ethnic, national or religious identities. Without these bonds, "integration risks being 'assimilation'" (Ager and Strang 2004, 19) and migrants do not maintain their sense of identification with a particular ethnic, religious or geographical community. Social bridges span from migrant to other communities, and in doing this, "support social cohesion and opens up opportunities for broadening cultural understanding, widening economic opportunities" (Ager and Strang 2004, 18). Social links include links with local and central government services, and these activities "provide a 3rd dimension of social connection alongside links to one's own community and bridges to others" (Ager and Strang 2004, 20). Migrant engagement with local services, both governmental and non-governmental, as well as civic duties and involvement in political processes, develop social connections that support integration. How broad these networks are depends on a range of factors, not least the migrants' language competency and the length of time they have lived in the UK. Unsurprisingly, those who have been resident in the host country longer and have more competent language skills have wider networks (Cheung and Phillimore 2014). In the third area, 'Facilitators', there are two domains: language and cultural knowledge, and safety and stability. These are central areas of cultural competence, going beyond language acquisition to broader cultural knowledge such as understanding local customs and traditions. Importantly, this area is also focused on the reciprocal understanding by the local community of the circumstances and culture of refugees. In addition, "community safety is a common concern amongst refugees and within the broader communities in which they live. Racial harassment and crime erodes confidence, constrains enjoyment in social connections and disturbs cultural knowledge" (Ager and Strang 2004, 22). The final area, 'Foundation', has one domain: rights and citizenship. Ager and Strang (2004, 4) argue that these are the "basis upon which expectations and obligations for the process of integrations are established", and understandings of nationhood and citizenship fundamentally impact on what is seen and recognised as integration, with both the host and migrant population being influenced by perceptions of rights and citizenship. Hence, this domain assesses the extent to which refugees are able to participate fully and equally in UK society, and "focuses upon the enablement of rights for those ultimately granted full refugee status or leave to remain" (Ager and Strang 2004, 23).

Integration, Bourdieu and Social Capital

Ager and Strang's (2004) model, along with the migration systems approach, can facilitate a new understanding of genocide survivors' migratory and post-migratory experiences, particularly when combined with a Bourdieuian analysis. Migrants have different capacities for resettlement in a new country, with some merely having a vague awareness of the local customs to others having existing family and/or friends in the new country. Forced migrants, however, will suffer from a lack of knowledge about the host country's culture and resources as well as their own personal traumas that they will need to manage. As such, forced migrants such as genocide survivors are already at a disadvantage when it comes to re-establishing their lives and utilising or developing social capital (Castles and Miller 2009). Moreover, they may well be experiencing latent or outright hostility from the host population because of their migrant status. More specifically, survivors' ability to utilise social capital will depend, to some extent, on their cultural capital such as language skills and educational qualifications, which interact with broader societal structures such as immigration policy and the relative rights that are associated with a particular migratory status (Ryan et al. 2008). As genocide survivors often have their education interrupted, their citizenship removed or other human rights derogated, this can mean that survivors hold very little, if any, social capital when they arrive in the host country. Moreover, because of their genocide experiences, many survivors lack trust in others, even in those who are of a similar background.

Trust is a key aspect of many studies of migration and social capital, frequently because of a focus on Robert Putnam's conception of social capital. Quite often, the view of social capital as a panacea to all migratory ills is rooted in Putnam's (1995) conception of social capital, which is one wherein individuals have the highest levels of social capital when they engage in voluntary groups and develop social trust through socialising with members of their community. Putnam's ideas are arguably more dominant than Bourdieu's in the literature about migration, integration and social capital due to media coverage and the general accessibility of his ideas. Indeed, some studies do not even acknowledge Bourdieu's ideas in their overview of social capital theories (Evergeti and Zontini 2006). However, Putnam's conception of social capital does not wholly engage with the wider structure of society and how this may aid or inhibit social capital development (Fine 2010).

Berry (1997) suggests that acculturation is a two-way strategy, wherein the host country has to adapt its institutions to meet the needs of all groups while migrants have to accept the basic values and rules of their host society. For asylum seekers, this is often difficult as they are prevented from engaging in certain 'everyday' behaviours such as employment. Asylum seekers are not permitted to engage in paid or voluntary work, and under the 2006 Immigration, Asylum and Nationality Act, it is an offence to employ someone who has not been granted permission to work. For refugees, this means that the task of finding employment is made significantly harder as employers are wary of employing someone who may not have the correct permission to work. In addition, the 2002 Nationality, Immigration and Asylum Act removed the right of asylum seekers to access work-based learning and request permission to work whilst their claim was being decided. This results in long-term unemployment for many (Phillimore and Goodson 2006), and as Colic-Piesker and Walker (2003) recognised, the way out of the 'refugee' identity, especially for middle-class refugees, is linked to their use of their cultural capital: their skills and qualifications which, if recognised in the host country, can be utilised to develop social capital. Moreover, employment also provides economic capital, which, for many migrants, is first needed in order to develop or access social capital (Hellerman 2006). Asylum seekers are only allowed to work if their claim for asylum has been in process for more than 12 months and they can fill a role on the shortage occupation list, which includes managing directors of the mining industry, geophysicists, cybersecurity professionals with five years' relevant experience and team-leading experience.

However, as previously acknowledged, Berry's (1997) acculturation model has been criticised for assuming that migrants follow the same linear pathway in order to acculturate (Phillimore 2012) and for believing that there is a set of homogenous norms to adopt. Bhatia and Ram (2001), on the other hand, argue that integration is a multidimensional and iterative process, with individuals taking part in an ongoing negotiation between the past and the present, and their host country and their country of origin, recreating their identity in light of their new surroundings. Phillimore (2012), in her assessment of integration policy in the UK, suggests that the most effective integration projects were fixed on developing links and networks between refugees and the wider society and between refugees themselves. These links aided refugees in accessing support and moving their lives forward. Furthermore, contact between the host population and refugees changed community relations for the better. This is an issue that Colic-Piesker and Walker (2003) also recognise, suggesting that in relation to the refugees from Bosnia in the 1990s, the receptivity of the host society had a significant impact on how Bosnian refugees reformed their identities. Thus, networks that build social capital can aid both the refugee and the community. More recently Cheung and Phillimore (2013) have found that the development of social connections aids integration, but crucially the formation of networks was supported by employment opportunities as well as language acquisition, and importantly, Cheung and Phillimore (2014, 520) argue that social networks only "support integration if they provide access to resources that impact on the integration process". However, the most problematic situations were the ones wherein there was a total lack of social networks, and as such, whilst family and friends can reduce a migrant's reliance on formal support organisations, families do aid the formation of networks and facilitate some forms of integration. Indeed, Cheung and Phillimore (2014) suggest that asylum seekers who had been placed in 'support only' housing, and hence living with family and/or friends and only receiving financial support, managed better in terms of integration than those who were dispersed by the UK Border Agency.

Bourdieu argues that capital is 'hereditary' in that it follows a linear progression whereby individuals who are born into some families (and therefore classes) are endowed with the relevant habitus and field in order to utilise their social capital (Bourdieu and Passeron 1990). However, migration disrupts this, as the conditions for producing the habitus are not consistent with the conditions of its functioning. Therefore, migration results in new and different ways of re/producing capital that builds on power relations of either the country of origin or the host country. Erel (2010) suggests that some resources and assets such as language or knowledge can be converted into 'national capital' in order to legitimise belonging. Whilst there is still value placed on certain types of past capital that is transferable and following migration, the migrant often seeks to endow themselves with the host nation's capital by acquiring citizenship of that country and engaging in social activities that befit a member of the host country.

The idea of a choice of identity for new migrants may be something of a fallacy as their choice is controlled and is not made within a vacuum, and is informed by existing power structures (Hanauer 2008). Instead, forced migrants may seek the citizenship of a country for the protection it brings rather than having a desire to 'become' that particular identity. Whilst they have legal citizenship of a country, if they do not or cannot 'become' that nationality through language, family and physicality, they will still be seen as an alien, and not considered to be an integral part of the nation (Hanauer 2008). Therefore, their social capital is limited to that of the legal identity of the host nation, which, whilst useful, does not allow a citizen to participate fully in the social life of the new country.

Moreover, the process of being forced migrants removes most, if not all, of an individual's agency. Forced migrants are forced into victimised roles prior to escaping, and in the case of genocide, survivors may have their legal rights restricted or removed completely. They have to surrender to control by authorities once they arrive in the UK and are expected to conform to the usual model of an asylum seeker. As such, refugees may feel that there is little point trying to regain control of their lives (Nicassio 1985); they become infantilised and, with the resulting stress of living in an unfamiliar country, may feel that the easiest (and best) option is to surrender control to the relevant agencies.

An uncritical reading of social capital could suggest that it is a panacea for migrants and enables social cohesion. This approach when specifically considering migration is the 'rucksack approach' to cultural and social capital, wherein refugees bring with them a package of cultural assets that they are hopefully able to use in the host country. However, this tends to ignore how those cultural and social assets are made convertible in the new country (Erel 2010). This is where Cheong et al. (2007) and Erel (2010) argue that Bourdieu's ideas can aid understanding of migration, especially in recent years where migration has increasingly been negatively framed in relation to terrorism, crime, unemployment and religious fundamentalism. In particular, using Bourdieu's theory breaks the link between social capital and social cohesion and focuses on access to resources. In taking account of the class structure and distinctions in contemporary society, Cheong et al. (2007) highlight the realities of the immigration experience, suggesting that certain types of capital that migrants bring with them become a basis for inequality rather than a cure. Bourdieu's ideas foreground the connections between immigration, social capital and social cohesion and draw attention to issues of power, class and racism. Moreover, as Erel (2010) observes, Bourdieu's theory on social capital enables a 'thicker' description of what is happening, as it considers how the varying forms of capital interact and differentiate between the different states (institutionalised, embodied, symbolic) of capital. Thus, the capital that refugees bring with them from their home countries may not fit perfectly into the host country's ideals, and therefore this may result in negotiations and bargaining over the value of this capital. This is where some individuals may suffer 'occupational downgrading' wherein their qualifications are only recognised to a certain degree; for example, a teacher becomes a teaching assistant because, whilst their experience is recognised, their qualification to teach is not, and therefore, the result is employment in the same field but at a significantly lower status and pay than previously.

Whilst acknowledging the weaknesses of Bourdieu's approach, it is argued here that there is still value in utilising his theory. Bourdieu's ideas on social capital are focused on how hierarchies, conflicts, elites and class structures are reproduced, areas which Fine (2010) suggests are often ignored from contemporary uses of Bourdieu's ideas. Whilst some of Bourdieu's ideas may be a little outdated, such as his ideas on the cultural activities of the elites, this can be accounted for by extending and developing his ideas to take account of developments in culture and class. In using these ideas, practices can be analysed "so that the underlying structuring principles of the habitus are revealed" (Maton 2008, 62). Bourdieu's idea of social capital illuminates the processes that survivors go through when rebuilding their lives. In arguing that social capital helps people get on in life, Bourdieu brings to the fore the role of cultural and economic capital in structuring the amount of success an individual has.

Bourdieu's work, in particular, can be seen as a tool that facilitates the exploration of survivors' experiences in more detail and an exploration of the phenomena discovered through this research, as he has underpinned his idea of social capital with the concepts of field and habitus. It is this further development of social capital that makes this conception the most appropriate one, as these foundational ideas generate a more in-depth analysis of the processes of genocide recovery and the re-establishment of life. These concepts aid the analysis of processes that inhibit or facilitate integration, by shining a light on the structural factors such as asylum and migratory regulations. Factors such as these may allow survivors to resettle effectively, or prevent them from doing so by restricting access to education or employment, which can prevent individuals from developing their cultural capital that the genocide has previously disrupted or destroyed.

Migrants, particularly those who have sought refuge or asylum, initially tend to have limited social capital because of their restricted networks in the host country. Some, such as athletes or business people, may have a surplus of capital, but the majority of migrants have their social capital devalued because of arriving in a new cultural and social context where their familiar networks no longer exist. For forced migrants, those networks that they do have are limited and are usually made up of similar individuals with similarly low levels of capital. Furthermore, alongside these migratory problems, genocide and its resulting diasporas destroy the 'building blocks' of life, such as families, social structures and cultural life, which allow individuals to build up social capital and get access to work, education and a better life. Finally, genocide survivors are often excluded from networks, which reduces their ability to gain employment. Without employment or a means to develop economic capital, survivors have limited opportunities to use economic capital in order to develop social capital and rebuild their lives.

In enabling a rich understanding of how survivors utilise social capital and engaging with the varied forms of capital, Bourdieu's ideas facilitate a deeper analysis by differentiating between different states of institutionalised, embodied and symbolic capital (Erel 2010). Rather than using social capital as a 'catch-all' for a whole range of behaviours and attributes, Bourdieu tried to understand social inequality and why some people acquiesce to power and domination without resisting, arguing that social classes are reproduced through symbolic domination and the education system. In arguing that there was a dominant value in favour of high culture, which is used to express social distinction, he suggested that access to capital is structured by society (Bourdieu 1986) and therefore that the elite in society are the ones who hold and retain such capital.

References

Ager, A., & Strang, A. (2004). *Indicators of Integration*. London: Home Office.

Ager, A., & Strang, A. (2008). Understanding Integration: A Conceptual Framework. *Journal of Refugee Studies, 21*(2), 166–191.

Ali, C. H., Querton, C., & Soulard, E. (2012). *Gender Related Asylum Claims in Europe*. Directorate General for Internal Policies; European Parliament.

Baker, K. (2015). Our Four-Star Hotel Was Turned into a "Soup Kitchen". *Daily Mail*, January 17.

Benz, W. (2004). Emigration as Rescue and Trauma: The Historical Context of the Kindertransport. *Shofar, 23*(1), 1–7.

Berry, J. W. (1997). Immigration, Acculturation and Adaptation. *Applied Psychology: An International Review, 46*(1), 5–68.

Bhatia, S., & Ram, A. (2001). Rethinking Acculturation in Relation to Diasporic Cultures and Postcolonial Identities. *International Journal of Cultural Relations, 44*(1), 17.

Bleasdale, L. (2008). Under Attack: The Metaphoric Threat of Asylum Seekers in Public-Political Discourses. *Web Journal of Current Legal Issues, 1*(1), 1–17.

Bourdieu, P. (1986). The Forms of Capital. In J. G. Richardson (Ed.), *Handbook of Theory and Research for the Sociology of Education* (pp. 241–258). London: Greenwood Press.

Bourdieu, P. (1988). Vive la crise! *Theory and Society, 17*, 773–787.

Bourdieu, P. (1989). Social Space and Symbolic Power. *Sociological Theory, 7*(1), 14–25.

Bourdieu, P. (1991). *Language and Symbolic Power* (J. B. Thompson, Ed.). Cambridge: Polity Press.

Bourdieu, P., & Passeron, J.-C. (1990). *Reproduction in Education, Society and Culture* (2nd ed.). London: Sage Publications.

Brown, G. (2008). *Managed Migration and Earned Citizenship*. Speech to Members of the Third Sector and Local Government Representatives in North London.

Castles, S. (2003). Toward a Sociology of Forced Migration and Social Transformation. *Sociology, 37*(1), 13–34.

Castles, S. (2010). Understanding Global Migration: A Social Transformation Perspective. *Journal of Ethnic and Migration Studies, 36*(10), 1565–1586.

Castles, S., & Miller, M. (2009). *The Age of Migration* (4th ed.). Hampshire: Palgrave Macmillan.

Chantler, K. (2010). Women Seeking Asylum in the UK: Contesting Conventions. In I. Palmary, E. Burman, & K. Chantler (Eds.), *Gender and Migration* (pp. 104–138). London: Zed Books.

Cheong, P. H., Edwards, R., Goldbourne, H., & Solomos, J. (2007). Immigration, Social Cohesion and Social Capital: A Critical Review. *Critical Social Policy, 27*(1), 24–49.

Cheung, S. Y., & Phillimore, J. (2013). *Social Networks, Social Capital and Refugee Integration*. Birmingham/Cardiff. Retrieved December 15, 2018, from http://www.birmingham.ac.uk/Documents/college-social-sciences/social-policy/iris/2013/nuffield-refugees-integration-research-report.pdf.

Cheung, S. Y., & Phillimore, J. (2014). Refugees, Social Capital, and Labour Market Integration in the UK. *Sociology, 48*(3), 518–536.

Cohen, C. (2015). Home Office Tells Nigerian Asylum Seeker: "You Can't Be a Lesbian, You've Got Children". *The Telegraph*, March 4.

Colic-Piesker, V., & Walker, I. (2003). Human Capital, Acculturation and Social Identity: Bosnian Refugees in Australia. *Journal of Community and Applied Social Psychology, 13*(5), 337–360.

Dwyer, P. (2003). *Understanding Social Citizenship* (2nd ed.). Bristol: Policy Press.

Edwards, A. (2003). Age and Gender Dimensions in International Refugee Law. In E. Feller, V. Turk, & F. Nicholson (Eds.), *Refugee Protection in International Law: UNHCR's Global Consultations on International Protection*. Cambridge: Cambridge University Press.

Erel, U. (2010). Migrating Cultural Capital: Bourdieu in Migration Studies. *Sociology, 44*(4), 642–660.

Evergeti, V., & Zontini, E. (2006). Introduction: Some Critical Reflections on Social Capital, Migration and Transnational Families. *Ethnic and Racial Studies, 29*(6), 1025–1039.

Fekete, L., & Webber, F. (2010). Foreign Nationals, Enemy Penology and the Criminal Justice System. *Race and Class, 51*(4), 1–25.

Fine, B. (2010). *Theories of Social Capital*. London: Pluto Press.

Fletcher, E. (2008). *Changing Support for Asylum Seekers: An Analysis of Legislation and Parliamentary Debates*. Sussex Migration Working Paper No. 49. Retrieved January 2, 2019, from http://repository.forcedmigration.org/show_metadata.jsp?pid=fmo:5695.

Friedman, E., & Klein, R. (2008). *Reluctant Refuge: The Story of Asylum in Britain*. London: British Library.

Hanauer, D. I. (2008). Non-Place Identity: Britain's Response to Migration in the Age of Supermodernity. In G. Delanty, R. Wodak, & P. Jones (Eds.),

Identity, Belonging and Migration (pp. 198–217). Liverpool: Liverpool University Press.

Hellerman, C. (2006). Migrating Alone: Tackling Social Capital? Women from Eastern Europe in Portugal. *Ethnic and Racial Studies, 29*(6), 1135–1152.

Home Office. (2002). *Secure Borders, Safe Haven*. London: HMSO.

Karatani, R. (2005). How History Separated Refugee and Migrant Regimes: In Search of Their Institutional Origins. *International Journal of Refugee Law, 17*(3), 517–541.

Klug, B. (2013). *The Balfour Project*. Retrieved August 13, 2018, from http://www.balfourproject.org/the-other-arthur-balfour-protector-of-the-jews/.

Kushner, T. (1999). Local Heroes: Belgian Refugees in Britain During the First World War. *Immigrants and Minorities, 18*(1), 1–28.

Kushner, T. (2006). *Remembering Refugees*. Manchester: Manchester University Press.

Lyons, K. (2017). 'How Do You Live on £36.95 a Week?' Asylum Seekers on Surviving on Their Allowance. *The Guardian*, August 21. Retrieved December 22, 2018, from https://www.theguardian.com/world/2017/aug/21/asylum-seekers-allowance-surviving-charities-counting-pennies.

Marfleet, P. (2006). *Refugees in a Global Era*. Hampshire: Palgrave Macmillan.

Maton, K. (2008). Habitus. In M. Grenfell (Ed.), *Pierre Bourdieu: Key Concepts* (pp. 49–65). London: Acumen.

Meissner, F., & Vertovec, S. (2014). Comparing Super-Diversity. *Ethnic and Racial Studies, 38*(4), 541–555.

Nicassio, P. M. (1985). The Psychosocial Adjustment of the Southeast Asian Refugee: An Overview of Empirical Findings and Theoretical Models. *Journal of Cross-Cultural Psychology, 16*(2), 153–173.

O'Neill, M. (2015). *Asylum, Migration and Community*. Bristol: Policy Press.

O'Reilly, K. (2012). *International Migration and Social Theory*. Hampshire: Palgrave Macmillan.

Phillimore, J. (2011). Refugees, Acculturation Strategies, Stress and Integration. *Journal of Social Policy, 40*(3), 575–593.

Phillimore, J. (2012). Implementing Integration in the UK: Lessons for Integration Theory, Policy and Practice. *Policy and Politics, 40*(4), 525–545.

Phillimore, J. (2014). Delivering Maternity Services in an Era of Superdiversity: The Challenges of Novelty and Newness. *Ethnic and Racial Studies, 38*(4), 568–582.

Phillimore, J. (2015). *Migration and Social Policy*. Cheltenham: Edward Elgar Press.

Phillimore, J., & Goodson, L. (2006). Problem or Opportunity? Asylum Seekers, Refugees, Employment and Social Exclusion in Deprived Urban Areas. *Urban Studies, 43*(10), 1715–1736.

Phillimore, J., & Goodson, L. (2008). Making a Place in the Global City: The Relevance of Indicators of Integration. *Journal of Refugee Studies, 21*(3), 305–325.

Purseigle, P. (2007). The Reception of Belgian Refugees in Europe: A Litmus Test of Wartime Social Mobilisation. In J. Crawford & I. McGibbon (Eds.), *New Zealand's Great War: New Zealand, the Allies and the First World War.* Auckland: Exisle Publishing.

Putnam, R. D. (1995). Bowling Alone: America's Declining Social Capital. *Journal of Democracy, 6*(1), 65–78.

Ryan, L., Sales, R., Tilki, M., & Siara, B. (2008). Social Networks, Social Support and Social Capital: The Experiences of Recent Polish Migrants in London. *Sociology, 42*(4), 672–690.

Sales, R. (2007). *Understanding Immigration and Refugee Policy.* Bristol: Policy Press.

The Daily Star. (2003). *Asylum Seekers Eat Our Donkeys.* August 31. Page 1 Headline.

The Sun. (2003). *Asylum Seekers Steal the Queen's Birds for Barbecues.* July 4. Page 1 Headline.

Townsend, M., & Taylor, D. (2014). Home Office Wouldn't Believe I Was Gay: How Do You Prove It? *The Guardian*, February 8.

Twine, F. (1994). *Citizenship and Social Rights: The Interdependence of Self and Society*. London: Sage Publications.

UK Lesbian and Gay Immigration Group. (2018). *Still Falling Short.* Retrieved December 29, 2018, from https://uklgig.org.uk/wp-content/uploads/2018/07/Still-Falling-Short.pdf.

Vertovec, S. (2007). Superdiversity and Its Implications. *Ethnic and Racial Studies, 29*(6), 1024–1054.

Vertovec, S. (2019). Talking around Super-Diversity. *Ethnic and Racial Studies, 42*(1), 125–139.

4

New Lives: Initial Adaptation

In its most general sense adaptation is defined by Berry as referring to "changes that take place in individuals or groups in response to environmental demands" (1997, 13). However, whilst all migrants have to adapt to a new way of life when they migrate, genocide survivors have to make a further adaptation that is unique to that particular group. As well as adapting to a new language and a new country, genocide survivors have to adapt to the fact that many of their family were intentionally killed and that they have been targeted for death because of their identity. This means that genocide survivors have to adapt to a new understanding of themselves as well as their new surroundings. Bourdieu's ideas on social and cultural capital (Bourdieu 1993) aid understanding of this form of adaptation by facilitating the identification of features that apply particularly to genocide survivors. For example, the majority of survivors lack financial capital when they arrive in the UK; hence, they are dependent upon any cultural capital they have that will be recognised by the host population. In addition, Bourdieu's concept of the linguistic habitus (Bourdieu 1991) aids analysis of the nature of survivor talk and how survivors are perceived by the host population when they arrive in the UK.

L. Asquith, *Rebuilding Lives After Genocide*, Palgrave Studies in Compromise after Conflict, https://doi.org/10.1007/978-3-030-14074-8_4

This central category of adaptation encompasses the early efforts of survivors to adapt to their new way of life and their struggles for independence as well as their practical, longer-term responses to their experiences such as recreating a family. It also draws in the strategies survivors use when seeking to develop their social capital and how they adapt to struggles for employment and training. Finally, this category of adaptation aids a consideration of the way in which survivors change over time, particularly in respect of the way that they speak of their experiences, adapting the way they talk in order that their story is heard.

This chapter explores survivors' migration and early acculturation experiences in order to examine how genocide survivors and their families utilised and/or developed their social capital in the time soon after the genocide. It examines how individuals and families utilise the relationships they have within their field, that is, how they make use of the contacts they have that will recognise their status or qualifications and, as such, help the survivor or their family in some way. In focusing on the initial adaptation experiences of genocide survivors, this chapter considers how they left their home countries and what influenced their choice of destination country and how the genocide experiences of survivors have affected their initial resettlement and re-establishment of their lives.

Utilising Existing Social Capital

Survivors use a variety of strategies in order to escape genocide and make their way to a place of safety. However, most survivors of genocide lack financial capital because it has been removed from them (e.g. in the case of Holocaust survivors and the Nuremberg Laws) or because they did not have any to begin with, or because they had to leave it behind with wider family or friends when they escaped. This means that many survivors had to rely on other resources, such as their social capital and networks, in order to escape and migrate to another country.

The survivors in this research left their home countries in two main ways. Some escaped prior to the start of the genocide, others left some time after the genocide had ended, and still others spent time in refugee or displaced persons camps prior to their eventual migration. Whilst the individuals in this research all had very different genocide experiences, there are some commonalities in their migratory experiences.

The Kindertransport

Escaping prior to the genocide usually required economic capital, either to pay someone to aid escape or to pay for the required travel documents. Occasionally, schemes were set up in order to facilitate escape, the Kindertransport being one such scheme; and in this research, two survivors had been part of the Kindertransport scheme. This was a scheme aimed at the rescue of 10,000 children from Nazi Germany, organised in response to the UK government's easing of restrictions relating to certain categories of Jewish refugees. As such, it was the parents of these children who made use of their financial and social capital in order to send their children to safety. The survivors described their parents' plans to escape Nazi-occupied areas by using their existing social, cultural and financial capital. One survivor also explained how those plans changed regularly and how that affected their resettlement. Henry's father's initial plan to escape to China fell through, and so Henry's parents decided to prioritise the children in their attempts to escape.

> He [Henry's father] found out about the Kindertransport system, talked to us about it, and said, "We need visas to come to England or America, or wherever we are going, and it's very hard to get a visa for four people, a family, so if you're there it only leaves two, and so it will be easier, and we'll see you in a couple of months."

Henry's father had to utilise his contacts within his 'field' in order to get a place on the Kindertransport for his children. In this case, this was the Landsman family who had become an acquaintance of Henry's father through their dealings with Henry's grandmother. Without the aid of this family, it is more likely that Henry and his sister would have died during the Holocaust. Each Kindertransportee required an individual or family in England to act as a guarantor, to ensure that these children would not become a burden on the British state. By utilising his financial and social capital, Henry's father was able to protect the lives of his children by finding a guarantor, in this case, the Landsmans, who would agree to look after them. It is important to note here that social capital was a powerful tool in this situation and Henry's father had this capital because he was middle class. It is unlikely that a lower-class or poorer family would have had such contacts outside Austria, especially given the limited communication opportunities in the 1930s. Henry's background was also evident in the fact that his father was exploring migrating to China, again a step not open to many people due to the prohibitive cost of such a move. Henry's case demonstrates the value of social capital and related financial capital. Even when the trip to China was no longer viable because of Henry's father being robbed of his money, he was still able to utilise his non-tangible assets—his reputation and contacts—in order to secure an escape for his children.

Rebecca was also a Kindertransportee, but at four years of age was significantly younger than Henry when she arrived in the UK alongside her seven-year-old brother. Like Henry, her parents planned to escape the Nazi occupation by going to Shanghai, and her father successfully managed this. Her mother was not Jewish and elected to remain in Germany, where she took part in the Rosenstraße protest, wherein a group of non-Jewish women protested the arrest of their Jewish husbands. Following this protest, Rebecca's mother went into hiding until the end of the war. Rebecca's father succeeded where Henry's had failed in getting to China, and again unsurprisingly economic capital played a part, with his passage to China paid for from the sale of jewellery that was smuggled out of Germany. Similarly, economic capital facilitated the escape of Rebecca and her brother, as her parents were able to pay for a place on the Kindertransport. Rebecca has no recollection of whether her parents knew her initial foster carers, or whether they were placed there by the Refugee Children's Movement (which organised the Kindertransport), but it was not long before the relationship with their foster carers broke down, and they were moved.

> My mother actually brought us over because she was not Jewish, she was able to get a holiday visa and come on the Kindertransport with us. But of course, she had to go home. I don't have any memory of saying goodbye,

> nor has my brother who was 7. So we don't know to this day, how long she stayed and whether she actually said goodbye or whether she put us to bed and crept out… The first foster family was an elderly rector in Kent, who … became very ill and died and his very much younger wife who had no children of her own didn't want to look after children and was very cruel to us. She didn't want us anymore, so they had to find somewhere else.

Thus, Rebecca and her brother were refugees who were at the bottom of the 'pile', with all the family economic capital used up in order to escape from Germany and no ability to pay anyone to care for the children once they arrived in the UK.

When Henry and his sister arrived in the UK, the expectation was that they would be with the family for only a couple of months until Henry's parents managed to escape and collect them.

> The idea was that this would be a very interim thing, 2 or 3 weeks maybe, a couple of months at the maximum. I was 13 at the time; my sister was 15, she was with me.

Subsequent letters from Henry's parents indicated that their plans regularly changed because of increasing restrictions put in place by the Nazis. In 1940, Henry's father died of a heart attack when he was being arrested. The letters to Henry and his sister eventually stopped in 1942, when his mother was taken to Izbica, a ghetto in Poland, and then transported to Sobibor, where she was murdered.

Bourdieu's ideas also aid understanding of why Henry's mother and father were not able to escape Hungary. Bourdieu (1986) argues that structure both constrains our choices and limits the recognition of capital. An individual's social capital is not recognised by everyone in every situation, and there are limits to the field in which the social capital operates. Essentially, social capital fails to be recognised when the field no longer has an influence on the capital. Like foreign currency, social capital can only be used in the relevant fields; outside of this field, the capital loses some or all of its worth. This was the case when Henry's father could access support from his field to enable Henry's escape, but his field did not extend to anyone who could aid his own escape. Those within his field, most of whom were Jews, would likely have been in the same position as him because of the anti-Jewish regulations (Nuremberg Laws) that were in place, which limited the amount of money and property that Jews could own. What is apparent then is that the new structure of Austrian society limited Henry's father's field; the laws and general attitudes towards Jews were such that individual adults seeking to escape found their field, and therefore their social capital, very restricted. Their capital (i.e. their reputation, skills and qualifications) was no longer recognised or had, at the very least, been significantly devalued. The wider structure of anti-Semitic laws and regulations combined with the view that Jews were dangerous and problematic had a significant impact on the recognition of their capital. This also explains why Rebecca's father was able to escape, as he left Germany prior to the enactment of restrictions on the movement of Jewish people, and as such, the broader societal structure facilitated, rather than inhibited, his escape.

Leaving After the Genocide

Those in the study who left their country after the genocide attempted to identify ways of using or developing their capital, with some survivors being strategic in their decision-making in order to make the most of their social capital. Julien decided to come to the UK after escaping the genocide in Rwanda by swimming across Lake Kivu to the Democratic Republic of Congo. He returned to Rwanda once the genocide was over but found that he could not resettle there due to his lack of trust in others. Julien did not initially plan to leave Rwanda, but a friend who saw his unhappiness encouraged him to do so. This individual could get him an illegal passport at a time when it was becoming very difficult to leave Rwanda.

> Actually, I didn't plan it myself; I went to … I was selling medicines, and I went to buy medicines there. One day I went there, and a friend of mine told me, "I can do you a passport." I think you got a passport via someone who had a visa, so the whole thing was very easy, and they just changed my … moved his picture to my one somehow, I don't know what they did. And then you have to pay some cash; I spent about three … 3000 dollars, to pay people involved.

Illuminée, another Rwandan survivor, made plans to leave Rwanda with her cousin who had gained a job working for Oxfam in the UK. In order to leave, Illuminée first needed to get a passport, but by then the Rwandan government were wary of issuing passports as they were concerned that the perpetrators of the genocide would try to escape justice by leaving the country. However, the first civil servant that Illuminée met was a former high school colleague. "He was so pleased to see that I was still alive, and he said he would do anything to help me." Illuminée's friend processed her application, and it is the fact that she knew someone in the passport office that allowed her application to be processed with no hitches, and her passport and visa arrived within a week. If Illuminée had not known the passport official, it is feasible to suggest that she may not have been able to get a passport at all, or at the very least, the process would have taken significantly longer.

Like Illuminée, Julien was able to make use of a contact in his field who could aid him in leaving Rwanda. Importantly, this contact recognised Julien as a victim and, in recognising his 'victim' status, opened the door for Julien to use his social capital that could aid his escape. However, this status is not universally recognised because there were limits to the 'field' of being a genocide survivor where the status of being a survivor actually becomes problematic. For example, Halima, a Darfuri survivor, found that despite escaping genocidal violence in Darfur and claiming asylum as soon as she arrived in the UK, she was still viewed with suspicion by Border Agency staff and subject to strict residential and reporting controls. When initially reporting to claim asylum, Halima was told, "Tell the truth. If you tell us any lies, we'll punish you by putting you in prison." During the meeting with the UK Border Agency (UKBA), she indicated that she did not know the name of the airline she flew to London with, and the UKBA officer responded, "I don't believe you. I don't believe you for one moment." Later in the interview, Halima was asked for proof of marriage, which she could not provide, and was also asked about the whereabouts of her husband. When she indicated that she did not know where he was, the officer said,

> You claim to be married, but there's no certificate. You claim to have a husband, but you don't know where he is… How can you not know which country your husband is in? It's impossible.

Social capital is especially important for those individuals escaping genocide. Very few survivors had the financial capital to move independently, and the genocide itself would have disrupted and restricted their pre-existing social capital, rendering any social capital that remained vital in order to facilitate their escape.

Use of Symbolic Capital

For Julien, his symbolic capital of being a genocide survivor was recognised by a friend, and this recognition triggered the process which would see that cultural capital begin to be transformed into social capital, eventually resulting in Julien being given a passport which would get him out of the country. Julien did pay some money for this passport, but as with all things illicit, they are not offered to everybody. In this case, it was Julien's status with his friend that facilitated the transaction, with his financial capital coming later. Without his contact, it is unlikely Julien would have been able to obtain a passport.

Passports act as symbolic capital, affording the holder specific rights and freedoms. Tabitha, a Holocaust survivor, spent a number of years stateless following the war and eventually managed to gain a South African passport. Four days after gaining the passport, Tabitha and her husband boarded a boat to the UK, with Tabitha's South African citizenship aiding her resettlement in the UK.

> When I came here, I was already allowed to work and everything because I came as a South African citizen and South Africa was then still in the Commonwealth, so that made it easier.

Thus, the migration regulations worked in Tabitha's favour and aided her resettlement as she was allowed to work, easing financial worries and aiding her acculturation in a new country. In this case, Tabitha's social capital was not with the individual who aided her in getting a passport. Instead, the passport became the social capital itself. The South African passport (and by implication, the South African nationality) was part of the group of countries known as the Commonwealth. Thus, Tabitha's field was all those countries that had signed up to be a part of the Commonwealth; her passport had currency in a number of countries in terms of resettlement and work permissions. Beyond the Commonwealth, her passport would not have held the same value, particularly in terms of working permission. For Tabitha, the ability to begin work immediately was a luxury rarely afforded to most other forced migrants. The ability to work not only provides a steady income but also allows an individual to adjust personally to their new life, and for the host country's citizens to adjust to the presence of migrants (Suedfeld et al. 2005). In this case, the passport was more than just a travel document. For individuals such as Tabitha, it represents a status of belonging, something that is especially important for genocide survivors who have often had all their citizenship rights removed. The impact of this removal of citizenship is evident in Tabitha's testimony:

> I needed a passport, and I went to the Hungarian embassy for a passport. They said, "You didn't go back to Hungary, so you lost … you didn't get back your nationality." I was born and grew up in Hungary, but I had no nationality now because I didn't go back after the war. I made … I usually don't shout… I don't fight shouting, I fight otherwise, but I don't fight shouting. But here I really started to scream. I said, "What people are you? I was born there, grew up there, was there until my 20th year. How can you say that I'm not Hungarian?" They said, "Anyway, no, we can't give you a passport."

Hence, Tabitha's evident upset at being denied her citizenship illustrates how important it is; it goes beyond nationality and draws in an individual's sense of identity, from where they were born to how long they lived there. It embodies the holder with a sense of belonging and a status of being a legitimate citizen. Therefore, individuals have made strategic use of their social capital either through gaining passports or through the use of economic capital in order to effect escape to a safe country. Thus, whilst choices may have been constrained by structural problems such as where passports are accepted, survivors and their families still attempted to make choices within those structural constraints.

A key method of acculturation for all migrants is employment. Modern genocide survivors are initially unable to work in the UK due to the restrictions placed upon them by asylum legislation. However, Holocaust survivors who arrived in the years following the war had significantly greater freedom in this regard. Jack's father was able to use his field through his employment in a bank to make possible the family's migration just after the war.

> Well, my father worked for a bank in Hungary… Allied to that, a friend of my father's offered him … 3 of them decided to emigrate before the war. One had some money, one had the technical expertise, and my father was going to be the sort of administrator, but my father was the youngest of the three. So he was still military age, so he wasn't allowed to leave. So the other two came to England and built up a small factory and said to my father, "Well, if and when the war is over, we'll keep a job for you." So the bank helped my father to get permission to live here.

The bank had British shareholders and, as such, was able to facilitate Jack's family's migration to the UK at a time when migration from Hungary was becoming restricted due to the rise of Soviet control which imposed strict migration controls on the non-German parts of the population. Because the bank (and, therefore, Jack's father's field) extended to the UK, it meant that Jack's father was able to access help. If Jack's father had been employed in a more 'working class' or lower-status role within the bank, such as a cashier or cleaner, it is unlikely that he would have been able to capitalise on the social capital which being a managerial employee of the bank endowed upon him.

Why the UK?

Many survivors came to the UK simply because it was the most convenient place to escape to, or because relatives were already in the UK. Others planned their migration in some detail. Sarah is one such Holocaust survivor who, after being released from Bergen-Belsen concentration camp, was taken to Sweden to recover from her experiences.

Following this, the Swedish government sent her to Canada for resettlement, where she remained until 1962, by which time she had met her husband. Migrating to England was, therefore, her first chosen and planned migration.

> We were kind of looking forward to it, you know, you scrimp and save, and you save a bit of money, and you pay for the fare, for the passage, and we came here to London, in 1962.

Unlike most other respondents, Sarah's migration to the UK was not a hasty decision made in the light of the threat from a genocidal aggressor. Rather, it was a considered, planned move which involved saving up and finding a place to live. Sarah's choice was partially influenced by the persecution she had previously experienced in Hungary, which caused her to reject her Hungarian nationality. She made a choice about her nationality, opted to become Canadian, and then gained dual citizenship after moving to England.

> I became a Canadian citizen, and that's the most important document because I lost my … I didn't want anything to do with Hungary. So having been given that, I valued it. We came to live here, Canada would not allow us, I wanted to retain it… I have nothing to do with Hungary, a place I was born, a place which persecuted us, a country that let us be deported, that let my family suffer so much. [Sarah, from Hungary]

At the time that Sarah and her husband moved to the UK, Canadians were not entitled to retain their citizenship and hold British citizenship. Sarah and her husband waited until the Canadian Citizenship Act of 1976 was passed which permitted dual citizenship and then gained British citizenship. She chose to retain her Canadian citizenship as a safety net, doing so because of the loss and denial of Sarah's identity during the Holocaust. The idea of giving up citizenship (and therefore, arguably, an identity) is an alarming one for those who have previously had citizenship forcibly removed from them. For Sarah, it was better to have two identities than none, retaining a Canadian safeguard, should life in the UK not work out. Thus, survivors do make strategic decisions, even when faced with significantly constrained choices.

However, for some, the move to England was an opportunity seized, rather than a specific or strategic plan. For example, the migration of Lili, a Holocaust survivor, was triggered by a chance meeting with some English customers dining in her mother and father's restaurant in 1952.

> One of the customers said, "Well, we're moving to England, you can come and stay with us. We will pay you; we have a 15-year-old, we both work and it would be really nice to have somebody at home."

Lili's parents were restaurateurs, had quite a large field, and could draw on a range of contacts. It was because of this large field—and related social capital—that Lili was able to first experience living in the UK. She returned to France three months later but did eventually return to the UK as a permanent settler.

Thus, social capital has a complex nature, especially its relationship with cultural and economic capital. Furthermore, the way in which 'field' works is also complex, and it is reliant on factors such as the habitus and how it was formed, as well as the macro-social structure in place. The impact of the wider social structures cannot be underestimated when considering the initial resettlement experiences of genocide survivors. These structures constrain the choices of the survivors and limit the ways in which their capital can be recognised and utilised. As a result, survivors escape their home countries in any way they can, either legally or illegally. For example, the Kindertransportees were able to escape because of the financial and social capital of their parents—financial because each family had to guarantee that their child would not be a 'drain' on UK resources, and social because families had to find someone willing to foster their child once they arrived in the UK. Others used illicit means to access a passport, while survivors such as Tabitha planned their migration and were able to make use of their symbolic capital in the form of a passport, which enabled and facilitated her migration and resettlement. Equally, Jack's father planned his migration and was able to migrate to the UK with his employer. When survivors are able to plan their migration, they are able to resettle more effectively initially, and a key aspect of this is the provision of and ability to access employment.

Early Adaptation Experiences

It is unsurprising that in recovering and moving on from genocide survivors face a number of challenges and difficulties that continue to affect them for a significant period afterwards. Rosenfeld (2011) suggests that it is possible to speak fully about life after Auschwitz only by being aware of the legacy of the camp, arguing that for the majority of survivors the suffering continues and there is no closure. Furthermore, alongside psychological problems such as post-traumatic stress disorder, survivors also face a number of other more 'existential' problems, that is, problems which go beyond the practical issues of finding housing or employment, such as their adaptation to new cultures and ways of life. Barbara Schwartz Lee, a Holocaust survivor and psychoanalyst, points out that it is important that these broader issues are considered, arguing that the consideration of Holocaust survivors must be broadened out from a narrow focus on post-traumatic stress disorder. This is because the wider context which affects how people react to trauma is ignored by much of the literature (Schwartz Lee 1988), and as such, we know very little about the social impacts of survival. Indeed, she argues that recovery happens in people's *lives*, rather than in their psychologies. Therefore, the practical and social aspects of re-establishing life should be considered. This chapter now considers these problems and discusses how survivors understand the issues of independence and dependence, considering the strategies they use to reduce isolation and examines what may inhibit or facilitate their adaptation and integration into the host society.

Public perceptions of genocide survivors tend to be based on media images of concentration or refugee camps that housed weak, vulnerable individuals. This image of vulnerability is also evident when considering the children who were part of the Kindertransport programme prior to the Second World War, with the transportees being presented in the media as "bundles of forlorn and helpless childhood" (Angell and Buxton 1939, 11). Both of these representations emphasised the dependence of the survivors, either on the liberating troops or on families willing to take the children in. At this point, it was inconceivable for most to consider that survivors will exercise agency in their lives, especially in the years immediately after the genocide. However, this research examines the extent to which survivors do exercise agency, from leaving their country and arriving in a new one, to finding employment and rebuilding their family.

Cultural Attachments

Migration can be a very traumatic experience and, perhaps unsurprisingly, having some familiar cultural attachments around can significantly aid resettlement. DeVries (1996) suggests that the re-establishment of life is aided by cultural processes such as being involved in families and support groups, especially if there is cultural acceptance of the trauma within the group that has occurred. Prior to the war, Zakiah's parents had divorced, and Zakiah was brought up by his paternal grandparents.

> I was brought up by my grandmother and … not unfortunately … but they were very orthodox Jews and in Poland, in the early '30s, you know, they … through ignorance or whatever, you know, to them, and especially because of their religion, divorce was worse than death, and I never wanted to come … so … I was brought up in a very Orthodox home, and after the war, I thought my mother was dead. That's what they told me, and I never heard from her. My father, of course, he got killed somewhere, I don't know where.

His mother had escaped to the UK via Belgium, and had met and married an Englishman. She managed to contact Zakiah whilst he was in the hospital after the war, and he moved to the UK to be with her in 1947. Whilst he barely knew his mother, living with someone who came from his own country but was also familiar with the English language and culture must have provided a 'cultural cushioning' of some form, especially in terms of language development. His mother's ability to speak both English and Polish would have meant that Zakiah was able to communicate in his native language that provided some familiarity in a strange new country at the same time as learning English. In addition to this, Zakiah spent a large amount of time with 'The Boys', a group of individuals who were a similar age, had all experienced comparable things during the Holocaust, and met regularly as a group following their migration to the UK.

> But it was like you said; it was very tough for the first 6 months. Until I found those boys that came here in 1945. Then, then … I always say that … whenever I am in a school to do a talk, I always also … it's written in Martin Gilbert's book 'The Boys' what I said when I first saw them. They had a dance in a church hall, and I knocked on the door, and they opened the door, and I looked and the first words I uttered I said: "At last I've found my family again."

Bourdieu's argument is that the habitus can change, but only slowly, and this is seen in this case. Whilst Zakiah came to the UK on his own, his life with his mother, whilst difficult, allowed his habitus to change slowly, as he would have been able to engage in familiar habits such as speaking his own language and eating familiar food. In addition, his regular meetings at the youth club, again with individuals similar to him, resulted in a slow-changing habitus, which is significantly less traumatic for an individual to experience. For Zakiah the change in habitus was not as obvious as it was for other survivors, who may have been older or had limited literacy skills in their own country. Other survivors' migratory experiences following genocide could have been exceptionally traumatic, as their habitus will have been fixed for a significantly longer period. Therefore, survivors who are younger and have some form of 'cultural cushioning' are more able to begin recovering more quickly.

Whilst wider society at the time had not accepted the impact of the Holocaust, Zakiah's immediate group were all survivors and therefore knew and understood the impact the genocide had, and it is possible that this understanding facilitated Zakiah's relatively rapid re-establishment of his life. In addition, those who have a sense of belonging and feel socially included benefit from the 'shielding cushion' that a supportive community provides (Shklarov 2012). For Zakiah, 'The Boys' were this shielding cushion between him and wider society; he could talk about his experiences (or not) as needed. In addition, he was amongst a group of people who were similar to him economically and socially. Zakiah's experiences correspond with research by Kalayjian et al. (1996), which also found that culture served as a coping mechanism following genocide. In addition, Sheftel and Zembrzycki (2010) suggest that for many Holocaust survivors, it was easier to begin their lives anew when they did not have to forget their past or where they came from. Therefore, this 'bubble' of familiarity facilitated a smoother change in Zakiah's habitus, rather than the jolting change that many survivors experience, which in turn led to his increasing independence.

Role of Family

Some survivors managed to live with their family when they arrived in the UK, making a presumption that this would aid their resettlement. However, Kitty found that her family were unable or unwilling to assist her in the way she wished when her uncle told her that he would not pay for her to return to school. Nonetheless, Kitty managed to gain employment because of a family contact as her Aunt Olga managed to circumvent immigration rules about permanent employment. She arranged for Kitty to begin a nursing training course; however, this was not Kitty's choice, and in many respects, Kitty felt that she and her mother, having been taken in by a relative, were in a poorer position than many other refugees were. When talking of financial assistance for survivors in the UK, she said:

> We two, being supposedly under the wing of a relative who had vouched for us, could get no assistance at all.

The initial jubilation that Kitty felt when she first arrived in the UK decreased significantly with the realisation that not all family networks are helpful and supportive and her family, in particular, would not be able to aid her in her wish to complete her education. In Kitty's case, her family controlled how and what opportunities Kitty accessed, by directing her into a particular form of work rather than the education that she wanted. This means that Kitty's family limited her choices, rather than facilitating them.

Illuminée lived with her cousin when she first arrived in the UK after leaving Rwanda and managed to access some English-language lessons through her local church as she felt she needed to learn the language in order to participate in English life fully. However, her cousin, whose children Illuminée was looking after in the UK, was angry with Illuminée, saying that she "was not in Norwich to be a student". Similar to Kitty, it is evident that instead of facilitating access to education, the family did in fact attempt to prevent access to it.

It is apparent that arrival in the UK with some family or with those from a similar cultural background aids resettlement. The problem with this is that very few survivors actually arrive in the UK with their whole family; the majority of the survivors in this research lost a large part of their family to the genocide prior to arriving in the UK. It has been well recognised that many Holocaust survivors sought to rebuild their family as soon as possible after the war ended; in 1946, Germany had the highest Jewish birth rate in the world (Grossman 2003). Rebuilding and being part of a family was a way of reidentifying themselves and reconstructing life, and provided a re-entry into 'normal' humanity. Furthermore, the presence and recreation of the family was seen as a biological 'revenge' against the Nazis, with the baby boom being seen by many as an act of symbolic revenge (Grossman 2003). This is common to all genocides, but occasionally, a few fortunate families do survive as a small unit. Sefik, a survivor from Bosnia, was one such person who did come to the UK with his parents and immediate family. Like Zakiah, this aided the re-establishment of his life because he was able to speak his own familiar language at home, but additionally, unlike Zakiah, Sefik was able to go to school, which further aided his language development and his resettlement.

> Err, to be honest, the first few months, maybe five, six months, life in high school was extremely hard even though we had all the support that we needed, but … we had additional English lessons outside the normal, regular timetable. So I would say after maybe six, seven months I would say I had a fairly good standard of English after that period and obviously just developed as the time progressed and so on.

Sefik was also given extra language classes along with a small number of other Bosnians who had also arrived as part of the Bosnia refugee project. Despite this support, Sefik still found his initial migration difficult.

> It was hard, you know, you couldn't speak, and there were all these people, you know, your fellow students wanting to know so much about you and the staff and all the teachers and like … you don't know what's going on.

As noted earlier, between the Second World War and the early 1990s migration to the UK was relatively limited, but the Bosnian war led to a significant number of refugees arriving in the UK. Rather than being a lone individual who could have migrated for any number of reasons, there were now several hundred Bosnian refugees arriving in communities, whose plight had been the focus of news reports for several months. As a result, it is unsurprising that there was curiosity about these new people and their experiences, but this curiosity served to isolate the refugees as they were evidently marked out as 'different'. However, due to having regular access to people from the same cultural background that had experienced similar things in Bosnia, this isolation was relatively short-lived. What is interesting about Sefik's experience is that rather than just meeting up and talking, his peer group from Bosnia formed a football team which trained regularly and played matches against other local teams. This gave Sefik and the other young Bosnians a focus and a way of re-establishing their identities.

> There's a very very small community of Bosnians here in West Yorkshire, but that was one way we could all sort of meet, or get together, twice a week for training sessions and then Saturday we could meet together, play football.

This small community helped Sefik resettle, and is evidence that the dispersal policy in current asylum legislation is fundamentally flawed. By separating communities, recovery is inhibited. The ability to meet and talk with co-nationals or co-ethnics appears to be especially important when those individuals have experienced significant trauma.

Like Sefik, Jack, a Hungarian Holocaust survivor, came to the UK with his parents. Despite having the cultural 'bubble' of having his family with him and this aiding his entry to the UK, life was still challenging because Jack felt isolated.

> It was difficult because we didn't … apart from one Hungarian family who … people who owned the factory who … he was my father's boss, so it was difficult to be friends … so we didn't know anybody.

Whilst Jack had his immediate family, he had lost most of his wider family (grandparents, aunties and uncles) in the Holocaust, and unlike Sefik, he did not have a wider Hungarian community around him, which meant that his loss of family was made more acute by his early experiences in the UK.

> You could see that the other … do you know Tyneside? The family plays a much stronger part in people's lives than in other parts of Britain. People go back to Tyneside, and they say "God's own country" type of expression. And so we were lonely in that sense.

Jack did not yet fit in with the host population, and the intense focus on family reinforced what had been lost during the genocide. In this context, the family focus of the Newcastle people served to emphasise Jack's change in habitus, so he became acutely aware of this change. However, one event that did combat Jack's isolation and aided his adaptation was joining the local Scout troop. Despite being born into a Jewish family, Jack was baptised in an attempt to protect him from the anti-Semitic policies of the Nazis and was taught from an early age that he was a Christian, not a Jew. When his school headmaster in the UK found out that Jack was a baptised Christian, he suggested that Jack join the Scouts as a way of meeting new friends and settling in. This gave Jack a whole group of friends very quickly, which both aided his language development and confirmed his status as 'not Jewish' and therefore the same as everyone else.

Joining in with cultural activities aids recovery and the re-establishment of life (Phillimore and Goodson 2008), and in this research, it was found that the groups engaging in these cultural activities did not have to be made up of a majority of dominant host society members. For example, for Zakiah and Vincent, 'The Boys' were all Holocaust survivors, but meeting with them still aided resettlement and integration into the host society as they were able to meet together and, if needed, talk about their experiences, which gave them a valuable outlet that was not available to them from the host country. They also aided each other in understanding unfamiliar practices and gave guidance on where to go for work or training.

Reconnecting with Families

Other survivors had a more challenging time, and this seems to be a result of arriving in the UK on their own and needing to adapt very quickly to the English way of life. The children of the Kindertransport, in particular, were uprooted and sent to a new life in a country they had usually never heard of, often sent to relatives or parents' acquaintances they had never met. Those who appear to have had the most difficulty are those who have two families: a foster family and a biological family. In this research, there were two such people. One participant, Rebecca, had been part of the Kindertransport scheme. The other, Judith, was part of a similar scheme that sent unaccompanied children to the US at the end of the Second World War. While most children never saw their biological parents again, a few did manage to survive and sought out their offspring after the war. It is worth noting at this point that this experience seems to be a phenomenon tied to the Second World War. Genocides after this time did not involve such a large humanitarian effort in terms of refugees, nor did they have the vast numbers of unaccompanied children that the Holocaust created. For these children, the reconnection with their biological parents was actually deeply upsetting, especially when they were returned to their home country.

> My foster-mother, who said, "You're one of the family, we love you," had to take me to Germany and leave me there, which in my experiences was the Kindertransport in reverse, only I wasn't four, I was 14.

Judith also struggled with being reunited with her parents:

> I didn't remember my natural parents, they were terribly traumatised, completely impoverished and it was very tough. I'd had a strong relationship with my foster family, but that broke down as well as I got into my teens.

Bourdieu's theory can aid understanding of these experiences because, for those two individuals, the change in situation occurs suddenly and more than once, which leads to isolation from both families. Bourdieu's view that the habitus can change only slowly means that if there is a sudden change, as was the case with Rebecca and Judith, a 'void' results where individuals do not know how to act or behave. Their previous habitus no longer 'works' but there is nothing to replace that habitus with. Consequently, individuals struggle to make sense of their experiences to settle in either location. For Rebecca, returning to Germany after the war was problematic not only because of not knowing her biological parents and being separated from her brother but also because she had grown up around the British propaganda of how dangerous Germans were.

> Suddenly everything familiar had disappeared: home, parents, language. Every familiar signpost had vanished, and Germany really was a frightening place in 1949, and of course, I believed all the propaganda about nasty Nazis in jackboots jumping out to shoot you in the comics I read and was petrified and very very angry, it just wasn't going to work.

Rebecca's 'English' habitus served to alienate her further from German society as her habitus had been constructed with the idea that Germans were the enemy and were dangerous. As a result, when she was taken back to Germany, Rebecca's habitus prevented her from resettling.

Rapid changes disrupt or even destroy the habitus, which in these cases prevented Rebecca and Judith from bonding with both their biological and adoptive families, and reinforced their isolation from wider society. Rebecca did not feel at home in her birth country, nor did she feel fully accepted in the UK once she returned. Similarly, Judith moved backwards and forwards between her biological and adoptive parents, not feeling at home in either. Both Judith's and Rebecca's field was limited as a result of this split between biological and foster families, as Judith was unable to build links in either country as a result of moving between the two, and Rebecca had her trust in others destroyed by being removed just at the point she had settled in. This meant that Rebecca was unwilling to develop her field because she was wary that as soon as she began to trust them, she would have to move again. Thus, for Rebecca, the habitus that developed after she returned to the UK was centralised on notions of the inability to trust, both in people and in situations. Because the habitus is formed slowly, it takes on those experiences that are repetitive; in this case, Rebecca's experiences of being moved around led to the habitus incorporating this lack of trust in others. Thus, the dominant theme in Rebecca's life for this time was a lack of trust. This lack of trust tended to manifest itself as a drive for independence, or a need for others to be dependent upon them.

Adaptation Through Independence and Dependence

Independence and agency are generally encouraged in society; a lack of reliance on others is seen as positive and is applauded, especially in migrants where there is a fear they may become dependent on the state. Several survivors indicated a need for independence, and Zakiah was one such case. He recalled the reasons for setting up his own business and emphasised his fears about depending on others.

> I felt, I'm working for him and what happens if he dies, I'll be working for my wife, her sister, her mother and I said, "if something happens, they'll tell me to go, to hop it", and I said "no, I've got to…" and my wife agreed, she was more for it than I was.

Zakiah's fear was that he would have to depend on others for employment and, therefore, money and resources, which is quite probably linked to his genocide experiences. This is because he was unable to trust anyone for fear they would turn him into the Nazis, or that they would steal his property or food. Survival during genocide is a very individual experience; survivors are concerned only with their own and immediate family's survival. Trust is rare during such a 'total' conflict, and consequently, independence and a lack of trust in anyone is a way of ensuring survival. Therefore, Zakiah's post-genocide desire for independence is an understandable reaction to his earlier fears about survival. Zakiah's 'genocide' habitus informed his experiences after the genocide had ended, albeit in a non-destructive way. As a result, Zakiah's need for independence in terms of survival is perfectly understandable when viewed in relation to his previous genocide experiences as these experiences resulted in a habitus that prioritised independence.

Leaving the Genocide Behind

In becoming independent, survivors often have to ignore their emotional and psychological suffering. This issue was recognised by Rosenfeld, who says, "Out of necessity, one learns to live with such pain, to disguise it or suppress it or otherwise evade a direct confrontation with it, but these manoeuvres work at best to tame the suffering, not eliminate it" (Rosenfeld 2011, 190). This suppression is often psychologically unhealthy; Hunt and Gakenyi (2005) argue, for example, that those who experience genocide and migration have greater psychological problems than internally displaced persons. Despite this, survivors in this research did not talk about the genocide having a continuing effect on them. Instead, they spoke of moving on and being self-sufficient, leaving the genocide behind them. Two survivors cited their independence and recovery being an active choice, and something they actively pursued, rather than something that occurred naturally. Zakiah did this by suggesting that he did not allow the Holocaust to have a continuing effect on him:

> How can you forget when your whole family was killed? It doesn't mean that you've got to live it. I moved on. I built a family, I built a business, I built a family, and I don't ... the Holocaust does not come into it.

In rejecting the continuing effects of the Holocaust, Zakiah affirmed his own agency and stated what *he* did, casting aside the idea that the Holocaust impacted on his ability to rebuild his life and on the surface Zakiah's experiences have the appearance of decision-making and independence but, in reality, it was the slow adaptation of the habitus which aided his resettlement. Zakiah's experiences show how having the time to develop language and having a 'softer' entrance into life in a new country results in a less traumatic transition. This is due to Zakiah's habitus being re-formed when he still had links to his culture and support from his friends and mother. Furthermore, he did not have to undergo any protracted asylum procedure, and as Zakiah is also white, he looked no different to the dominant host population, meaning that he did not stand out. As a result, his recovery and resettlement were facilitated by this relatively quick acceptance into, and of, UK life. In short, Zakiah was young and the 'right' colour, and had family and friends to aid his resettlement and recovery.

Need for Other People

After initially striving for independence, Zakiah began to recognise that he did need other people around. As he became more established as a person and had rebuilt his life to the point of getting married and having children, he was able to recognise that he did need faith as well as other people around, something that he acknowledged in his interview when discussing why he went into business for himself.

> I think … the reason for it was also that I like people, I need people … I'm in a supermarket, I talk to people … I love people, and there I was almost alone. It wasn't the thing for me… Then you get older, you get married, and you have a family, and you start thinking. Then I thought… Well, I can't say to anyone, "Don't be silly, there's no such thing as God." I don't know. Nobody can say there is; nobody can say there isn't. You cannot deny something you don't know … I go twice a year I'm in a synagogue. I might be more if I go to a wedding, but I only go Yom Kippur, and the Jewish New Year, for the simple reason that I want to remember my family, after

> all, they were religious, and I want to say a prayer for the dead which one says … that I haven't got the luxury of saying it when it happened when my father died or was killed I don't know, I haven't got a grave for him.

This is the point at which we can see the habitus, having had more time to develop, becoming more nuanced. Independence was still clearly important to Zakiah as he set up his own business, but he recognised that alongside that independence there was a need to be around people, to have contact with others, and relaxation in terms of his ideas on faith and religion. Thus, the habitus develops from his immediate post-genocide habitus to one that combines independence with the confidence of a migrant who has found their place in the dominant host society. This 're-established' habitus illustrates how Zakiah's way of life is now a mix of pre- and post-*genocide* experiences that are also tied in with post-*migratory* experiences.

However, the concept of independence goes beyond personal independence. For Julien, a Rwandan survivor, his concern was state independence and how the perceived independence of the UK was a factor in his choosing to come to the UK.

> Because of the relations there, Rwanda's relations with Belgium for example, a French colony, Belgium, France, I was not happy with the behaviour, so I decided to come to this country.

Many Rwandan survivors felt that the French and Belgian governments facilitated the genocide, either through their previous role as colonial powers or through the arming and training of the militia which went on to commit the genocide. Consequently, Julien saw his migration both as an adventure and as an expression of his independence; he rejected moving to Belgium or France as a result of their perceived involvement in the genocide despite having a sister living in both countries, as well as being able to speak French. Thus, Julien's independence is in his physical migration and choice of the host country, rather than personal independence. Despite Julien's field being limited, and his family being elsewhere in Europe, he still made a choice to come to the UK, where arguably his field was most limited. However, Julien may have felt that whilst his field would initially be more limited, it may be a better 'quality' field that is more trustworthy. As he felt that both Belgium and France were complicit in the genocide, it may have been difficult for him to be governed by those countries. That is, the lack of trust would have prevented him from settling in those countries.

Pride in Independence

Once survivors established themselves in the UK, many of them took pride in their independence, seeing their lack of dependence on others as a positive step in their acculturation. Several Holocaust survivors in this study spoke of their pride in their own independence. As mentioned above, Zakiah took great pride in his achievements that allowed him to be independent such as running a successful business. Lili's independence was expressed as a reaction to the identity of refugee, being very clear that she rejected the label of refugee and the connotations of dependence that the word invoked.

> It was a very good marriage, my stepfather and my mother, but even in the Jewish community in Nice, they were somehow, I just can't tell you why, they kept on having this status, when I look at it, of refugees. By leaving them, I was stopping the refugee. I did not consider myself a refugee in England at all. Well, to this day I've never considered myself a refugee.

In rejecting the status of refugee, Lili asserted her separation and independence from both her parents and her experiences, and her pride that she could remove this label. Lili attributed most of her independence to her relationship with her husband.

> When I married, he didn't want a woman at home, so he encouraged me to go to Pitman's [typing] college.

This must have been quite unusual at a time when wider British society still expected the majority of married women to remain home and be a homemaker. This unusual status is something she recognises:

> He needed someone to stand up to him, to be independent. I really don't know a single woman of my own age who would have travelled in Colorado, rented a car… I was invited to a wedding in New York and decided to stay in the States for a month… I really was a traveller. 1982 I travelled to India for one month on my own … and I don't know a single girlfriend who's done that.

Lili felt that her freedom was something unusual and she linked this independence and freedom to her Holocaust experiences:

> Within the marriage when the children were old enough, I became a risk taker; I just can't tell you what I did not do. And I also think that had something to do with the Holocaust, because having survived, having married so young, I was going to experience, and I was going to live.

This desire to experience life fully led to her meeting another man with whom she had an affair.

> It ended up me telling my husband, "Look, I've got this other man in my life", and my husband used to look up reasonably priced hotels for us … he said to me, "I have to get used to the fact you have two men in your life."

Lili's husband's reaction is unusual, and his acceptance of the situation reinforced her independence by allowing her the freedom to see other people. In reflecting on his acceptance, Lili said simply, "He allowed me to live."

Lili's experiences here point to a habitus that again had slowly developed over time, with a key aspect of that habitus being independence. Unlike Rebecca, Lili's migration was planned and took place over a longer period. She was happy to migrate and saw the migration as being a positive choice, rather than having it imposed upon her. In recognising her agency, Lili felt more in control of her life and, as such, was able to assert her independence more freely. The idea of independence was very important in Lili's habitus as it was one thing she felt she must pass on to her children.

> Basically I don't feel that they need me. I think if anything happened to me I think they would cry at my funeral, but on the whole, they don't, which probably I did a good job as a mother or a grandmother.

For Lili, not being needed was positive; it demonstrated independence, which was to be encouraged as it enabled survival. Dependence on others was not good because it inhibited survival and could have led to emotional pain, which she references when discussing her genocide experiences.

> I think probably the worst bit was my mother during the war would say "I only live and fight to live because I have got you as a child". And the moment that the danger was over, I sort of became slightly redundant, and that really was absolutely horrible.

Thus, Lili's response to become independent and to foster independence in others was to ensure that she did not experience that rejection again. Lili was not alone in responding to her experiences by desiring to be independent. Judith also identified a very clear reason *why* she needed to be independent.

> Because my parents were so hysterical and overprotective and I was so resistant to any … really … contact with them, I went the other way. Because loss was just assumed, I made my children very independent… I didn't get close enough to my children. There was just … nothing lasts forever, and they must be independent.

Here Judith's habitus had developed in response to a specific set of events that had a significant impact upon her. When they arrived in the UK after the Holocaust, Judith's parents became very fearful of other people, especially anyone who was not overtly Jewish, and consequently sent Judith to a very orthodox Jewish girls' school. It was this overprotectiveness that Judith found claustrophobic, especially as she had not experienced this with her foster-parents. When her parents, whom she did not remember, took Judith back to the UK, this served to highlight the 'break' in her habitus, and as her new habitus developed, it was in direct opposition to these experiences.

Reliance on Others

Whilst these survivors' habitus had developed to prioritise independence, other survivors responded in almost the opposite way and relied on a specific individual. Rebecca was a Kindertransportee and was sent to the UK with her older brother. She relied on him a great deal, to the point that when she refused to eat because she was unhappy at being placed with her foster-parents, her brother would steal food from the larder and encourage her to eat during the night, which prevented her from becoming ill. In return, when her brother developed hepatitis, Rebecca sold a doll to enable her to buy apples so he could eat 'an apple a day'.

> Psychologically that kept him going. Medically, I don't know how he managed to eat the apples. So we were very close, and still are.

Like Joan and Lili, Rebecca's experiences during the genocide influenced her parenting style, but unlike them, she did not seek to encourage independence. Rather, she sought to keep children and parents together. When her son was five or six years old, he required a tonsillectomy and Rebecca spent a significant amount of time searching for a hospital that would allow her to remain with her son during his stay in the hospital.

> I just knew that he was a very anxious child and I couldn't let him go into hospital without me … after that, I worked for years to promote the idea that small children need their parents more than ever in the hospital.

Rebecca responded very differently to her separation from her parents. Whilst Judith's habitus led her to focus on independence, Rebecca's led her to ensure that she would not be separated from her children if she felt they needed her. This shows how the same traumatic conditions can produce different habitus' in different people. Whilst Judith and Rebecca both experienced foster care and being reunited with their biological parents, their response to these events was very different.

Bourdieu argues that the habitus is informed by one's position in the world. Both Rebecca and Judith had similar positions in society and were culturally similar to each other; therefore, according to a simple reading of Bourdieu, their habitus should have developed in a similar way. This did not happen in this case, as their habitus led them to very different responses, with Judith seeking independence and Rebecca ensuring she was available to be depended upon. This difference is partly explained by considering Judith's parents' behaviour, which was very overprotective and risk-averse. However, this difference in habitus may also be due to structural factors that influenced the development of the habitus. Whilst Rebecca and Judith were culturally similar at the point of migration, Rebecca was sent to the UK even as Judith arrived in the US as an 'unaccompanied minor'. It could be that the national narratives of the countries they found themselves in also influenced their habitus. For Judith in the US, the habitus may have been influenced and modified by the national narrative of the 'American Dream', a concept that promotes independence as a way to success.

Conversely, Rebecca was sent to the UK through the Kindertransport scheme, and rather than the 'American Dream', she lived through the war narrative of working together for freedom and, after the war, saw the inception of the welfare state. Thus, it is suggested here that because of this more 'paternalistic' national narrative, Rebecca's habitus developed in a different direction and focused on the dependence of others on her. This, in fact, illustrates the flexibility of Bourdieu's ideas. The habitus operates in relation to a social field, "and therefore the same habitus can produce very different practices" (Jenkins 1992, 82). He recognises that external structures such as states can influence the development of the habitus as well as key individuals within the fields, and this has been illustrated here. Both Rebecca and Judith, whilst having similar post-genocide experiences, had very different fields, with Judith having a limited, and possibly significantly more homogeneous, field as a result of her parents' choices. Rebecca's field, on the other hand, whilst being similarly limited, was a little more heterogeneous, with Rebecca having gone to a local, non-faith-based school. Rebecca's and Judith's experiences resulted in differing habitus because of the differential impact of individuals within the fields, and larger societal structures influencing the development of the habitus.

Adaptation Through Risk-Taking and Trust

Surviving genocide and migrating afterwards is risky by its very nature. The Kindertransport programme was risky in that parents and children did not know if they would ever be reunited, and parents were sending their children hundreds, often thousands, of miles away on their own, frequently to individuals they barely knew. Research has already discussed that survivors often find trusting in others difficult following genocide (Ajdukovic and Corkalo 2004), and three Holocaust survivors in this research made a direct reference to their mistrust of others in the aftermath of the genocide. Furthermore, as mentioned above, Julien referred to his lack of trust in other countries when he moved to the UK. When discussing trust, Sarah referred to an incident fairly soon after the genocide that was common amongst Holocaust survivors who had been kept a prisoner in the camps.

> They used to give us a bit of pocket money and I used to go out and spend the pocket money on raw … what was that … raw bacon and that was fantastic. I put weight on, and you know, at first, I used to hide my food, under the pillow, under the bed, under the sheet because I never knew, is it going to come the following day.

The fear of lack of food was considerable for those who had been kept in camps on near-starvation diets; as such, the lack of trust in the availability of food is understandable and unsurprising. Equally, many survivors have talked of being unable to remain in their country of origin because they could not trust their neighbours (Corkalo et al. 2004). Jack recognised this when talking about the process of migration:

> So it would have caused immense difficulty, had we stayed, partly because there was such an atmosphere of mistrust. You never knew whether your neighbour took part in your persecution and took your furniture and clothes and so on. So there was never the civic trust that society would need.

It is interesting that Jack refers to civic trust, that trust is not just personal, but acts on a wider level in a society, where individuals have trust (or not) in the community in which they live. In Rwanda, there is a focus on rebuilding civic and community trust following the genocide. One of the key responses to the genocide has been the Gacaca trials, which are a community resolution traditionally used with financial disputes. The aim of Gacaca is to promote community resolution by allowing the community to come together and find out the truth regarding a particular genocide event and to rebuild trust in those communities. Julien was sceptical about the ability of Gacaca to rebuild trust, saying,

> They told us Gacaca would help, but the government … interfering and the way … and the survivors, I don't think it helped survivors at all… It's very complex, very complex, with the government interfering as well … some people know the top people in the government so we cannot touch them, so what's the point?

The idea of trust in communities is one very much related to both Coleman's and Putnam's conception of social capital; however, Bourdieu's ideas, whilst not being focused on trust in the same way that Putnam's and Coleman's are, do consider the issue of trust in the community by drawing on the ideas of field and habitus. In doing so, Bourdieu's ideas suggest that if individuals feel that they can no longer trust the agents in their field, then it becomes exceptionally difficult to begin rebuilding or utilising a field because of the concern that this breach of trust may occur again. As Julien notes, processes such as Gacaca, which attempt to engender trust in communities, are fraught with difficulties, and trust cannot be rebuilt in such a top-down manner where the government expect voters to forgive, irrespective of their experiences. In addition, following an event such as genocide an individual's habitus may have changed to the point that their way of living no longer 'fits' with the habitus of others who live in their community, especially when others in that community were perpetrators during the genocide. Julien's experiences of Gacaca show this, in that he felt that the government was enforcing a change upon the population for which it was not ready and which it did not accept. The Holocaust survivors in this study made little mention of the role of justice and did not link it to their trust or distrust of society, whereas it was a particular issue for Julien. This contrast may well be due to the more recent nature of the Rwandan genocide and the involvement of both the International Criminal Court and the Rwandan government in justice processes, rather than the more abstract Nuremberg trials which focused only on those at the very top of the Nazi hierarchy.

The final discussion of trust came from Rebecca, who talks of how her experiences as a Kindertransportee led to a significant breakdown in trust between her and her parents:

> My parents, who were nice people, they wanted a sweet little four-year-old and hadn't a clue how to handle an adolescent off the rails. They let me go back to England … but I completely lost my trust in human beings; I'd been so messed about. But I had the animals.

Rebecca lived on a farm with her foster-parents, and whilst she rejected both her biological and foster-parents, she found solace in looking after the animals on the farm. This lack of trust in humans took a significant time to recover from, and Rebecca credits her husband with her being able to regain trust in others:

> Without my husband's endless patience I would have never regained my trust in human beings. He complained endlessly, "You don't trust me, you don't trust me", and I suppose I didn't really know what trust was because I couldn't understand why he complained. I had developed a way of functioning where I trusted nobody but myself. You know, little things, he would say that he was going to do something, and I would act as though he hadn't said he was going to do it.

Because of her experiences during the Holocaust, Rebecca's habitus quickly developed into one which assumed that people could not be trusted as a result of the severe trauma she experienced. Her husband's 'endless patience' points to her habitus changing very slowly over a number of years following the Holocaust. Thus, the rapid change in habitus took a number of years to 'rectify' because of the trauma she experienced.

Allied to the concept of trust, several participants raised the issue of risk, either in terms of their own risky behaviour during and following the genocide, or risk aversion because of their genocide experiences.

Zakiah took risks in setting up a business, fearing that the alternative would result in dependence on others. Julien also took risks when he was escaping the genocide: firstly, in swimming across a lake to escape the genocidaires, and secondly, through migration to the UK rather than joining his sisters in France and Belgium. Moreover, as above, both Lili and Judith discussed their risk-taking in the context of their genocide and post-genocide experiences. As already mentioned, Judith's parents sent her to an ultra-orthodox Jewish school.

> My family were sort of, they weren't religious, they were very traumatised and they didn't particularly want anything to do with religion at that stage, but because they were so terrified of the outsider they sent me to an ultra-orthodox school.

Thus, Judith's parents' risk-averse nature was a result of a lack of trust in others who were not evidently Jewish. Two other survivors also acknowledged the influence of their parents' risk-averse natures on their later lives. These participants recalled their parents' attempts to protect them from being targeted by having them baptised. For Jack, the rise of Hitler convinced his parents to get him baptised:

> Hitler came to power in 1933, so many parents, shall we say, middle-class parents who had Jewish backgrounds decided that the children they were going to have, they were going to have them baptised into the Christian church because it would be a way of … they could see what Hitler's influence was going to be a malign one.

These early experiences influenced Jack to the point that even now he does not identify or see himself as Jewish, stating during his interview that he had no connection with that faith. Jack's parents' lack of trust in the future thus fundamentally changed Jack's identity. This also happened to Rebecca, who was baptised and brought up as a Christian, again in an attempt to protect her from the Nazis, but unlike Jack, later converted to Judaism alongside her husband.

> My [Jewish] father converted to Christianity; my mother was Protestant Christian. My father converted I think because he thought that that might

> save the family … they thought it would protect us against antisemitism, which of course was rife in this country, right across Europe.

As Jack mentioned, baptising the young in an attempt to protect them was a relatively common practice among the middle-class, (usually) assimilated Jews. Often known as 'hidden children', those baptised into the Christian church learned the prayers and public rituals of Christianity in an attempt to keep their Jewish identity hidden, even from their closest friends (Heberer 2011).

Risky Individuals

However, risk was not only something that genocide survivors perceived; the survivors themselves could be seen as risky, and one survivor was perceived as a risk by the British government.

> Did you know about the "enemy aliens" that we were labelled as in England? Some guy sitting in an office, some mandarin in Whitehall, soon as the war broke out came to a conclusion that "how do we know that these 10,000 children aren't spies"? So we were labelled as enemy aliens, then we had to go to the police to register ourselves… We were on a curfew throughout the war. We had to be indoors by 11 o'clock, and whenever we moved house, changed jobs we had to go to the police and present this book until, eventually, they said, "No, I don't think they are spies after all". Every move we had to do we had to report.

This classification of individuals as 'enemy aliens' was only applied to those of German or Austrian descent; other countries were deemed victims of Nazi aggression and therefore not enemies of the allied forces. As Henry mentions, they were regulated and subjected to stricter control. In some cases refugees were interned in camps; some 27,000 were interned in total, despite the vast majority posing no risk whatsoever (Cesarani and Kushner 2013). More recently, as acknowledged earlier in the literature discussion, migrants have been perceived as a risk by the media, with forced migrants being portrayed as a threat to resources within the UK and often detained in immigration removal centres. For many survivors then, they go from being in a risky situation to being seen as a risky individual. This perception of survivors as risky inhibits the re-establishment of life, as they are less able to form relationships in the community that would aid their resettlement.

Despite the perception of genocide survivors as being helpless and forlorn, they do utilise whatever agency and social capital they have to effect escape and migration. As such, regardless of survivors frequently having very little economic capital, their social capital is brought into play in order to escape and migrate. Once arrived, survivors' early adaptation experiences are often improved by being able to live/work/socialise alongside others who have had similar experiences. However, alongside this 'cultural cushioning', the resettlement of survivors is also aided by engaging in cultural activities alongside the host population.

It is evident that culture has a significant impact on the individual and can both aid and inhibit acculturation and resettlement. Several survivors found that having access to aspects of their home culture whilst in a new country aided their resettlement significantly. This is relatively unsurprising; most migrants keep something of their home life with them when they migrate, through either speaking their home language with their family or eating familiar foods. Bourdieu's ideas on habitus are useful here as for those survivors who were able to retain some form of cultural 'bond' and therefore maintain their cultural habitus and way of being appeared to (at least initially) fare better than those who were simply transplanted here with no cultural links or markers which resulted in an adapted habitus. Hence these 'cultural buffers' are very important to survivors in terms of their resettlement. Having familiar people or cultural attachments around aids resettlement because it provides a familiar link to the survivor's previous habitus. This means that survivors have something familiar to 'cling' to in their new surroundings, whether that is being able to speak their first language or talk to others who have had similar genocide experiences or grown up in a similar area or with a similar background.

However, what seems to cause distinct problems for genocide survivors is the situation that both Rebecca and Judith found themselves in, wherein they were initially fostered by one family, but then several years later were reunited with their biological family. This resulted in their newly developed habitus becoming disrupted again, which led to relationship breakdowns for both survivors. What appears to have happened in these two cases is that if the habitus is viewed as 'recently repaired' from the first traumatic experience of genocide and forced migration, then like something which has been broken in half and repaired, the habitus appears to develop a weak point which is related to those experiences of loss of family. This means that this disruption is felt more keenly because the survivors remember the experience from the first time around, and the habitus is disrupted once more. This disruption is reinforced by the impact of the survivors' field changing again which compounds the unstable habitus as the survivors have to begin again in terms of friendships and relationships. This results in survivors being aware that they are different from the host population and having to manage the resettlement process again.

A habitus which involves a sense of independence can aid the re-establishment of life for genocide survivors as they feel that they are moving away from being a survivor and are starting to be perceived as a 'normal' member of society. The vast majority of survivors saw dependence on others as a weakness or vulnerability that they wished to avoid at all costs. This illustrates the slowly changing nature of the habitus; even years after the genocide, dependence is viewed as a weakness because reliance on others could lead to death. However, for those separated from their parents, their habitus could change to one of requiring that others become dependent upon them, as it is at that point that an individual is useful and needed.

Those who survive genocide have often done so through being wary of others, hiding or pretending to be someone they are not. As such, the genocide infuses the habitus with a lack of trust and a lack of faith in others. This is often aggravated by survivors' post-genocide experiences wherein they may have had a hostile reception in their host country, or not had their experiences acknowledged as valid. This results in a reluctance to rely on anyone, which in turn reduces the survivor's 'field': the network of individuals who could provide access to opportunities and support. Likewise, for survivors like Judith's parents and Jack, the concern over being at risk was linked to a lack of trust in others, which resulted in fear of 'the other' and a cultural cocooning in order to protect themselves. However, some survivors such as Lili actively took risks in an attempt to stop being the 'survivor' with all the baggage that that particular status entailed. This risk-taking led to a broader field being developed as survivors were more open to meeting new people and experiencing new activities and, consequently, a habitus which accepted risk and trust in others.

It is important to note that survivors' backgrounds have had a significant impact on their departure from their home country and their arrival in the host country. Those who were quite young managed (initially at least) to resettle quite quickly. For Judith and Rebecca, it was the reappearance of their biological parents that caused significant problems. Sefik's experiences highlight the impact of different asylum regimes; as he was part of a wider United Nations project which brought Bosnian refugees to the UK, his resettlement was supported significantly more than those who had experienced the Holocaust, or the Rwandan genocide. This was particularly because the Bosnia project housed co-nationals and co-ethnics together in communities, rather than the random dispersal pattern that the current asylum policy dictates. Being based in an area with others from the same cultural background facilitated integration and enabled Sefik to set up a football club that developed links with local and regional football teams that were made up of the host society.

The roles of the macro structures within society are exceptionally important when considering the resettlement and re-establishment of life for genocide survivors. Along with experiencing all the challenges that forced migrants face, genocide survivors also manage the results of being targeted for their identity, for who they were. Thus, genocide survivors migrate not only to escape imminent death but also because of their inability to trust in the future in their home countries. Consequently, whilst the larger societal structures may constrain choices, survivors will utilise their capital in any way possible (legally or illegally) in order to escape that environment. Thus, they still exercise agency wherever possible, according to their capital and field. This means that those 'receiving' the survivors must not base their expectation of what a survivor is on one particular escape experience or migration method. The utilisation of agency is a key part of a survivor beginning to rebuild their lives; prior to migration, survivors have had their agency and identity targeted and removed where possible through the dehumanising of individuals and groups and laws created to limit movement. As a result, survivors escape and migrate through a variety of means in order to get to safety.

Survivors used their social capital in many ways in order to leave their home country and enter the UK. A particular aspect of this capital was class based, especially in terms of those who arrived as part of the Kindertransport scheme. Both Rebecca and Henry came from middle-class families who had a range of contacts who could facilitate the foster care of their children in the UK. In addition, both families had the required finance that paid for the children to access the Kindertransport in the first place. Bourdieu's argument that economic capital is the key-stone of all other capital is worth exploring here, as the charity organising the Kindertransport (the Refugee Children's Movement/RCM) or the child's parent had to pay a guarantee of £50 (equivalent to £3300 in 2019) to cover the cost of their child's eventual return to their country of origin. This resulted in many children not being rescued because their parents were unable to pay the cost of the transport. However, those who were rescued by the Refugee Children's Movement were subject to an assessment of need, with the charity only rescuing those who were at risk of death because of being in a concentration camp or having been orphaned. Thus, in some cases, it was the children who were least able to pay who were chosen to be taken on the Kindertransport.

Consequently, economic capital, whilst underpinning the Kindertransport as a whole, did not mean that all families had to be able to afford to pay for their child. Instead, it was the *recognition* of that lack of economic capital that resulted in children being selected. Consequently, a more nuanced understanding of Bourdieu's views of economic and, subsequently, social capital is required. The concept of economic capital as the foundation of all other capital still holds ground here, but it is not the holding of economic capital that facilitates social capital; a lack of economic capital can see an individual being offered opportunities because they were recognised as lacking money. Thus, it is not as simple as arguing that an individual who lacks money will not be able to access opportunities, but rather out of those who lack economic capital, there are some whose lack of economic capital is *recognised* as a barrier and are therefore supported by organisations such as the RCM. It is not the 'holding' of economic capital that is key, but access to it through whatever means, and in particular the recognition of that lack of capital can result in either opportunities being denied or additional support being given.

The role of economic capital is more nuanced than it first seemed. Whilst the simple fact of having money does, unsurprisingly, aid escape, a complete lack of money can also aid an individual if that lack of money is recognised as a barrier to safety by an organisation or individual who has the economic and cultural capital to do something about it.

Familiar culture can aid survivors because it provides them with a cultural link to their pre-genocide habitus. In providing this link, a familiar culture can aid initial resettlement, and as such, initial resettlement is aided by familiar cultural markers in the form of the habitus, aided by opportunities for survivors to become independent and establish new ways of life which aid acculturation into the new country.

References

Ajdukovic, D., & Corkalo, D. (2004). Trust and Betrayal in War. In E. Stover & H. M. Weinstein (Eds.), *My Neighbour, My Enemy*. Cambridge: Cambridge University Press.

Angell, N., & Buxton, D. (1939). *You and the Refugee*. Harmondsworth: Penguin.

Berry, J. W. (1997). Immigration, Acculturation and Adaptation. *Applied Psychology: An International Review, 46*(1), 5–68.

Bourdieu, P. (1986). The Forms of Capital. In J. G. Richardson (Ed.), *Handbook of Theory and Research for the Sociology of Education* (pp. 241–258). London: Greenwood Press.

Bourdieu, P. (1991). *Language and Symbolic Power* (J. B. Thompson, Ed.). Cambridge: Polity Press.

Bourdieu, P. (1993). *The Field of Cultural Production*. Cambridge: Polity Press.

Cesarani, D., & Kushner, T. (2013). *The Internment of Aliens in Twentieth Century Britain*. London: Routledge.

Corkalo, D., Ajdukovic, D., Weinstein, H. M., Stover, E., Djipa, D., & Biro, M. (2004). Neighbours Again? Intercommunity Relations after Ethnic Cleansing. In E. Stover & H. M. Weinstein (Eds.), *My Neighbour, My Enemy*. New York, NY: Cambridge University Press.

DeVries, M. W. (1996). Trauma in Cultural Perspective. In B. A. van der Kolk, A. C. McFarlane, & L. Weisaeth (Eds.), *Traumatic Stress: The Effects of Overwhelming Experience on Mind, Body, and Society* (pp. 398–413). London: The Guilford Press.

Grossman, A. (2003). Gendered Perceptions and Self Perceptions of Memory and Revenge: Jewish Displaced Persons in Occupied Postwar Germany as Victims, Villains and Survivors. In J. T. Baumel & T. Cohen (Eds.), *Gender, Place and Memory in the Modern Jewish Experience.* London: Vallentine Mitchell.

Heberer, P. (2011). *Children during the Holocaust.* Plymouth: AltaMira.

Hunt, N., & Gakenyi, M. (2005). Comparing Refugees and Nonrefugees: The Bosnian Experience. *Anxiety Disorders, 19*(6), 717–723.

Jenkins, R. (1992). *Pierre Bourdieu.* New York: Routledge.

Kalayjian, A., Shahinian, S., Gergerian, E., & Saraydarian, L. (1996). Coping with Ottoman Turkish Genocide: An Exploration of the Experience of Armenian Survivors. *Journal of Traumatic Stress, 9*(1), 87–97.

Phillimore, J., & Goodson, L. (2008). Making a Place in the Global City: The Relevance of Indicators of Integration. *Journal of Refugee Studies, 21*(3), 305–325.

Rosenfeld, A. H. (2011). *The End of the Holocaust.* Indiana: Indiana University Press.

Schwartz Lee, B. (1988). Holocaust Survivors and Internal Strengths. *Journal of Humanistic Psychology, 28*(1), 67–96.

Sheftel, A., & Zembrzycki, S. (2010). "We Started over Again, We Were Young": Postwar Social Worlds of Child Holocaust Survivors in Montréal. *Urban History Review, 39*(1), 20–30.

Shklarov, S. (2012). Theory through the Eyes of Child Survivors of the Holocaust. *Kavod: Honoring Aging Survivors: A Professional Journal for Care Providers and Families, 2*(Winter), 1–10.

Suedfeld, P., Paterson, H., & Krell, R. (2005). Holocaust Survivors and the World of Work. *Journal of Genocide Research, 7*(2), 243–254.

5

Resettlement and Reintegration: Adapting to Life in the UK

In explaining how genocide survivors use and develop social capital, it is important to remember that the majority of survivors arrive in the UK with very little in terms of material goods. Therefore, they have to make use of any *cultural* capital they have, as it is often the only resource available to them. However, as this chapter shows, this can be beset with problems. Cultural capital depends on its recognition in order to begin the conversion into social capital, and survivors in this research often found that the cultural capital they held was not recognised to the same degree as at home, if at all. This meant that survivors sometimes had to start afresh, rebuilding their economic, cultural and social capital from the beginning. The discussions in this chapter illustrate the different ways survivors re-established or recreated their capital, from gaining employment and accessing support that aided acculturation and facilitated resettlement through to engaging in sport and cultural activities as a way of illustrating their social capital and being accepted by the broader community.

L. Asquith, *Rebuilding Lives After Genocide*, Palgrave Studies in Compromise after Conflict, https://doi.org/10.1007/978-3-030-14074-8_5

Resettlement and Reintegration: The Role of Education and Employment

Phillimore and others have recognised that education and employment are vital ways of aiding acculturation (Cheung and Phillimore 2013; Phillimore and Goodson 2008; Phillimore 2012). A key issue which must be borne in mind here is that of the participants in this research: many were Holocaust survivors who arrived in the UK at a time when there was almost zero unemployment and the government was beginning to consider 'importing' a workforce from Commonwealth countries in order to meet the growing need for industrial workers. This was also a time when mothers were not expected to work, and women's employment outside the home was still restricted to part-time, menial roles. Hence, different economies and legislations affect survivors' ability to access work and education in different time periods. It is noted that the lack of an (specifically English) education often caused a problem for survivors.

> But how could one be fitted for any job without at least a basic English education? We approached a Jewish community to see if they could help, only to be told that there were no funds for people like me … Looking back, I think what makes me most bitter against the Nazis, even after all this time, is the education of which they robbed me.

Illuminée echoed this story when she discussed settling in the UK.

> How does the only Rwandan in Norwich get a job? I had no recognised qualifications. My education had been put on hold when I fell pregnant and was effectively terminated by the genocide.

All of the survivors in this research who accessed education in the UK found that it benefited them either directly through the gaining of qualifications or indirectly, such as through developing a wider social network. Those who attended school in the UK were able to learn English quickly and were provided with a 'ready-made' social network. Those who accessed education later in life found that education had benefits beyond that of gaining a qualification. Five participants in this study were of compulsory school age when they arrived in the UK, and they were required to attend school and acknowledged that attending school helped them resettle and, in particular, learn English.

> It was realised that I was breaking the law, in the sense that I wasn't going to school. The school leaving age was 14 at the time … but then I went to school with this boy [the son of Henry's foster-parents], who was my age and that was my start of English education, at 13 and a quarter … of course now my English would grow, lots of mistakes but lots of laughs.

As well as attending school, extracurricular activities can also aid acculturation. Henry's experiences illustrate this, where he developed his field at school by performing well during a swimming lesson.

> I just dived in and as I said I was a pretty good swimmer for my age and I did three or four lengths, just went up and down, but I was the only one in the water, I couldn't understand it so when I finished and had enough I walked out, there was a big roar of applause, and it appeared on that day they were actually handing out 50 metre, 50 yard certificates, and I'd just done about 75 yards and consequently I've now got a certificate.

The 'big roar of applause' cemented Henry's acceptance into school life. Jack also had a similar experience, again through his sporting activities.

> I started swimming, and there was a school swim … they pronounced it 'gala' … swimming gala. I won so many races and immediately established my credibility.

In contrast, school had a different significance for Rebecca, who did not seek to prove her prowess in anything, and instead found school a refuge from all the upheaval she had experienced.

> It was like coming out of a nightmare into paradise. The teachers summed me up, and I remember them saying, "Do you like stories?" and I loved stories. "What kind of stories?" "Animal stories," so they provided me with

> lots of books, Felix Salten particularly, and I sat quietly at the back of the class, reading and making no problems at all. They knew how to deal with potentially problematic children, which many schools didn't.

Rebecca and her brother were the only refugees at her school, and therefore, there were no other students from familiar cultural backgrounds or with similar experiences who could aid her resettlement. Others, such as Sefik, found that being part of a group of refugees was helpful, despite starting at a school halfway through the year, and he found being with others who were at the same stage as him in terms of language development, and who had experienced similar things, especially useful.

> What we did at lunchtimes and break times, we would have our little group, and we would meet, and then we would have an additional English lesson just for us as a group because that was one of the things that helped us improve our language and develop more quickly.

This helped Sefik, which is evidenced by the fact that he went on from school to undertake a sport and leisure GNVQ before undertaking a degree in sport and nutrition and a PGCE in post-compulsory education, subsequently gaining a job at a local college. Having British qualifications helped Sefik as they were recognised easily by all colleges and employers, and evidenced a particular standard that was widely understood, thus acting as Sefik's social capital.

The Impact of Family and Class Background on Education

The influence of family and class background in accessing education was especially evident in some narratives. Whilst all of the survivors interviewed showed indicators of middle-class status such as their occupation or their place of residence, class statuses can and do change. Vincent originally came from a poor family who lived in a shtetl (a small town with a large religious Jewish population who spoke Yiddish) in Hungary. Zakiah's background was equally poor, having been brought up by his grandparents following his parents' divorce. For these two individuals, their class background was effectively wiped out by the genocide, and Victor, in particular, had to begin again, having no family at all. Those who had adoptive families were unsurprisingly influenced by their background. Both Rebecca and Jack went straight to university after they had completed their A levels. The fact that they had completed their A levels is of itself impressive, given that they both arrived in the UK unable to speak English and traumatised from their experiences in the genocide. They were encouraged to go on to university by their parents (foster-parents in the case of Rebecca). Both families could be considered middle class, and, therefore a university education was expected of them. What this shows is that culture and class do have an influence on individual trajectories that can override even extreme external influences such as genocide. For these two individuals, there was a family expectation that overrode their genocide experiences. That is, despite their experiences leaving them with little, if any, social capital, their families were of the appropriate class that could prepare them and support them in going to university. This shows how cultural capital can operate independently of economic capital. For Rebecca, her foster family provided the cultural capital that facilitated her studies and encouraged her to go to university, despite her initial reluctance.

> I finished my education … I went to university, which my father insisted. At that time I just wanted the animals, but he was right. He insisted I went to university and there I discovered a whole world beyond the farm.

Rebecca's genocide experiences in terms of her lack of trust in others made her reluctant to go to university, but she must have gained enough faith in her foster-parents to trust their judgement in encouraging her to attend university. Going to university widened Rebecca's field and the qualification, acting as social capital, enabled her to go on and develop a career in psychotherapy, focusing on the experiences of the Kindertransport and the effect it had on survivors psychologically. For Rebecca, then, like several of the survivors in this research, her education provided social capital that significantly aided her progression through life.

Even if survivors were adults when they arrived in the UK, education was still important to them. Julien made a choice to come here in part in order to access education. Once Julien had had his status as a refugee confirmed, he began to establish himself in the UK, getting help and support from the Medical Foundation for Victims of Torture charity as well as meeting his wife, also a genocide survivor from Rwanda. Once married, Julien went to college and undertook undergraduate and postgraduate degrees in business, commerce and finance. These degrees gave him the knowledge to be able to set up the support organisation 'Hope Survivors Foundation' that supports Rwandan survivors living in the UK.

Purpose of Education

People develop social capital through gaining qualifications that can be utilised to develop a career further or through employment, however circuitous the route. As already discussed, several interviewees were of school age when they arrived in the UK so were placed in schools as per the legal requirements and then followed parental (or foster-parental) expectations regarding higher education or employment. Whilst education is a valuable tool in developing social capital, sometimes the motivations for engaging in it are less instrumental and more focused on personal, rather than professional, development.

Jack, Judith and Henry all attended school in the UK; however, Judith, during her school years, moved between her biological parents in the UK and her foster-parents in the US. This led to a disruption in her schooling to the point that she was unable to fulfil her foster-parents' expectations of becoming a doctor. In this case, her foster-parents' social capital could not overcome the disruption that this regular moving caused. Even though Judith's foster family were of a class which would have facilitated the progression to becoming a doctor, Judith's experiences of moving between two sets of parents as a result of the disruption of the Holocaust meant that she was unable to achieve her expected career. This was because her education had been significantly disrupted, and therefore, she could not achieve the grades required for medical school. Judith eventually returned to education as a mature student in the early 1970s, undertaking A levels followed by a degree in history at the London School of Economics (LSE).

Sarah, a Holocaust survivor, also undertook a history degree later on in life, graduating from Middlesex University when she was 60 years old. Neither woman indicated that they engaged in education to benefit professionally; rather, they emphasised their desire to learn: education for education's sake. Sarah referred to the gratefulness she felt at being allowed to study and how that motivated her.

> When somebody gives you something—that's the survivor's legacy—somebody gives you something a little good, you magnify it a million times over … It's the joy of learning … and the generosity of teaching.

By linking her status as a survivor with her learning experiences, Sarah explained her attitude towards learning. The gift of education needed to be grasped with both hands, not because of the career advancement it could have brought but because it was an opportunity which was denied during the genocide. As well as achievement, education can also have benefits for the wider family. Sarah was able to develop her social network through her children's schooling, by meeting other parents.

> [the] children went to local schools, through them I made a few friends, and that was very helpful the schooling, and I met people. Nice, good people in my road in Hendon, and that's what it was. You know you hear; you listen, you learn from others what they do, what they're planning. And so when they got educated, I went to school myself.

Sarah developed links and connections with a wide range of people who provided her with a network of individuals whom Sarah could emulate in terms of language and culture. This aided her resettlement in the local area and eventually gave her the confidence to go back to school herself, and in seeing her children's education Sarah realised that it was possible for her to make up for her own disrupted education.

Like Sarah, Judith also undertook a degree for the pleasure of learning rather than career advancement. However, she was able to use her degree in order to gain information about her family. Because of her many moves during the Holocaust and afterwards, Judith was not aware of her family history and what had happened to her family during the Holocaust. Judith used her degree and her university contacts to facilitate her access to archives that contained information about her family and the events of the Holocaust.

> I originally wrote [to the National Archives] saying I was a child [survivor] and they more or less wrote back saying for your own good you're not allowed to look in, terribly patronising. Having graduated from LSE and I mentioned it to my tutor, and he wrote saying I was a research student, so of course, I got into all the archives.

Thus, Judith utilised her cultural capital in an attempt to understand what happened to her family, rather than for any professional gain. The use of cultural capital aided her emotionally and helped her to understand where she had come from. In the context of genocide, it is not the case that a survivor's cultural capital will always be recognised; in order for their 'survivor' cultural capital to be recognised, the individuals need to be perceived as valid by those who have the power to recognise them as such. In addition, the recognition of those experiences (and thus recognising their cultural capital) also needs to be seen to be in the best interests of the survivor themselves. In Judith's case, her experiences were seen as valid, but it was perceived to not be in her best interests to recognise those experiences and thus recognise her cultural capital.

Starting Small and Working Hard

In general terms, several of the Holocaust survivors, having had time to reflect on their early years in the UK, spoke of 'starting small' and 'working hard' as a way of getting on and re-establishing life. For some, this referred to going to school then university. For others, it was about starting their own business or starting off in menial jobs before moving through the ranks. In terms of employment, Zakiah and Henry were both told that they would be joining the family business, starting at the bottom. Whilst this work was initially helpful, neither of them particularly wanted to do this, and both sought new jobs as soon as possible, with Henry finding an engineering apprenticeship and Zakiah setting up his own stationery business. It must be borne in mind here that whilst Zakiah's and Henry's first jobs were basic and menial, this was no different to any other young boy starting work in the years after the war. Julien also set up his own business, but his business was related to his experiences as a genocide survivor. Julien's social capital derived from his experiences as a survivor with this work role being directly related to that of being a survivor. As a consequence, his social capital of *being* a survivor facilitates his working life; it gives authority to what he does in the support organisation. Without this capital of being a survivor, he may well be viewed as less 'appropriate' for the role, and it is argued that it is the cultural (and ultimately social) capital that he holds which allows Julien to command respect in his role. His experiences qualify him and endow him with social capital that a non-survivor would not be accorded.

Likewise, Sarah's work was low skilled and low paid. She was found a job in Canada by the organisation that initially looked after her whilst she was there. Her role was to write sizes on shoes, one of the few jobs she could do as Sarah could not yet speak English. It is not uncommon for new migrants to access low-skilled jobs as such jobs often have a high turnover of staff and consequently regularly advertise vacancies.

Exploitative Employment and Denial of Work

Sometimes employment is exploitative, particularly if the migrant does not have the correct working permissions, something that Tabitha discussed:

> I was stateless 12 years, I was an asylum seeker, and I travelled with a false passport, and I worked without any working permission and was very badly paid as a result and 'course I had to change places because, for instance, I was working at a weavers doing bobbins for 10 hours, just doing bobbin for one weaver and then he wanted to sleep with me as well. He paid me very badly, but on top of it, he wanted to sleep with me, so I left him … Yes, you were certainly exploited if you had no working permission.

Only Tabitha explicitly discussed feeling exploited by her employer and was also the only participant to make reference to experiencing sexual harassment. As such, this is an atypical case, in this research at least. One explanation for this could be that Tabitha was older than most of the other Holocaust survivors in this study and was of working age when she arrived in the UK. As such, she was thrust immediately into the world of work, unlike other survivors who had a chance to acculturate at school. However, whilst Tabitha's case is unique within this study, it is a very common occurrence for survivors and forced migrants to find themselves in low-paid, exploitative work, especially if that work is illegal (Anderson and Rogaly 2005). In her attempts to develop her economic capital, Tabitha recognised the vulnerable position she was in and how her lack of status opened her up to exploitation by unscrupulous individuals. Survivors who are in this position have no choice as they have no employment protection or rights whilst they are working illegally (Black et al. 2005). Even in 'legal' work, migrants may find themselves experiencing exploitative practices such as the withholding of wages, or excessive deductions being made from wages for housing costs (Anderson and Rogaly 2005). Whilst Tabitha is the only respondent in this research to raise the issue of exploitation and illegal working, it is of some concern for asylum seekers from more recent genocides such as Darfur and Syria. Given the time that is taken for asylum claims to be processed, and the extreme poverty asylum seekers experience, it is unsurprising that they may seek illegal employment of one form or another (Black et al. 2005). Importantly, asylum seekers are not allowed to work, as Halima noted.

> I had inquired about working as a doctor or even a nurse, but I'd been told that asylum seekers weren't allowed to work.

The denial of the opportunity to work, for Halima, meant that she could not begin to be part of society, nor could society become used to her presence.

This potentially exploitative employment may continue the trauma that migrants may have experienced prior to migration, because it reinforces their fragility and vulnerability, especially in relation to situations where migrants have been and continue to be sexually exploited (Wright and McKay 2011; Anderson and Rogaly 2005). In addition, these exploitative roles only further their social capital in the field of illegal employment. References cannot be given, and those jobs will not appear on any CV. As such, they provide very little for the survivor, except purely economic capital.

Taking Risks

The development of social capital sometimes depends on individuals who are prepared to take risks in some way. Two of the Jewish interviewees in this study evidence what is termed in Yiddish as 'chutzpah', which is sometimes a negative term implying rudeness and insolence, but in business terms often means 'nerve' or 'courage'. Henry showed this when he decided he needed to be more independent, like his older sister. Until this point, he had been working in his foster-father's menswear business delivering suits, a job which he felt had no future as he was not learning a trade.

> About the middle of 1940, I decided to take a day off, and I went to an area of London with lots of engineering companies, and I knocked on doors and asked them if they wanted an apprentice. I was lucky on about the fifth call, and that was that.

Zakiah showed a similar attitude in setting up his own business.

> I started on my own, and my wife said to me, "We have got no money in the bank. What will we eat?" and I said, "So not worry," and straight away on Monday morning went out to see people.

Many people may find the idea of 'cold calling' companies and asking for a job uncomfortable and would avoid it. However, in terms of the development of social capital, having chutzpah helps, as it means individuals are more likely to seek out opportunities in order to succeed and are less likely to be defeated when faced with negative responses. The more opportunities an individual seeks out, the more likely it is that one of them will succeed and aid that individual's development of social capital. For Zakiah in particular, his confidence and chutzpah seemed to be borne out of his Holocaust experiences, in that his attitude to life was set in his experience of surviving when thousands of others did not, and therefore he must make the most of the opportunities presented to him.

> In life, you've got to have luck. Be in the right place at the right time, dodge the bullet or whatever … you get up and start all over again … If you work, you'll get there. I can tell you most of our boys that came here, you know, the Holocaust survivors, 90% did work for themselves. I mean, maybe they're not multi … there are some millionaires as well, but most of them had a good life.

Their potential employers recognised Harry's and Zakiah's confidence or nerve as a positive characteristic. Once recognised, it acted as social capital by enabling them to gain employment. It appears that Zakiah's motivations stem from his survival experiences in that he explained his success by hard work and luck. Luck aided his survival during the genocide and led to opportunities in work, and hard work he believes enabled him to make the most of the opportunities that came his way.

Resettlement and Reintegration: The Role of Support Groups

Organisations such as support groups play a key role in recognising and validating a survivor's cultural capital. Bourdieu (1986) suggests that individuals derive 'profit' from belonging to a group by enjoying certain privileges that they have not necessarily earned individually but by virtue of being a member of the group. This section of the chapter covers three aspects of support. Firstly, the role of ordinary community groups in supporting genocide survivors is discussed. These groups are not set up with the intention of specifically supporting genocide survivors, but instead have a different focus, for example, sports teams and uniformed organisations. Secondly, formal support organisations, those set up with the specific intent of supporting either forced migrants or genocide survivors, are examined. Finally, the role of sibling support is considered, focusing on two survivors who came to the UK as youngsters alongside their older siblings. The problem of inappropriate support will also be explored, that is, where survivors have been offered support that is wholly inappropriate for their particular circumstances, as well as times where survivors have rejected the help offered.

Community Groups

These are groups that are not created with the specific intent of supporting survivors to come to terms with their experiences; rather, they are often pre-existing groups which often have a specific focus such as Scout troops, the Boys' Brigade, music groups or football teams. These groups usually consist of the dominant (host) population with often only two or three migrants in them. However, migrants themselves sometimes set up such organisations if there are no such groups already in existence, or if those that do exist do not meet the needs of the migrants. Robert Putnam's (2000) conception of social capital draws heavily on the role of community groups in developing social capital, arguing that such groups are the 'glue' which hold a community together and prevent the collapse of the community into chaos. Equally, James Coleman (1994) identified that the weak 'bridging' capital between group members aids the development and progression of society. However, both these approaches see social capital as something that communities, rather than individuals, hold. Thus, whilst recognising Coleman's and Putnam's ideas, there is still a focus on Bourdieu here.

Several of the survivors in this study were involved in local community groups of one form or another; two joined the Scouts/Boys brigade, another joined a choir, whilst three interviewees (all male) took part in sporting activities. Three survivors were part of 'grassroots' groups set up by survivors themselves.

Some groups provided an opportunity for survivors to mix with people who were of the same ethnicity. Henry, a Holocaust survivor, joined the Jewish Boy's Brigade because his foster family's son already attended the group. Developing friends allowed Henry to acculturate and settle in. The leader of the group was aware of Henry's background, as when it came to the time of their annual camp, and Henry was asked to go with the group,

> Captain Lang came up to me and said, "Are you coming to camp?" So I said, "No, I don't have the money," and he said, "I didn't ask you about the money, I said are you coming to camp?" I said, "How can I go?" He said, "We'll take care of that," and they took me to camp for nothing, which was nice.

Whilst Henry's primary purpose of attending the Boy's Brigade may have been to enjoy himself and make friends, the Brigade, by supporting Henry financially in this way, facilitated the development of his social capital. According to Bourdieu (1986), economic capital is one of the building blocks of social capital, and without it, it is difficult, if not impossible, to develop social capital. By assisting Henry's inclusion on the camping trip and compensating for his lack of economic capital, the captain also provided an (albeit unintentional) opportunity for Henry to further develop his social capital by taking part in activities that were normally restricted to those who could afford them.

Like Henry, Jack found joining a group provided friendship.

> I was very lucky that the headmaster said "What were your interests in Hungary?" I said, "I used to play sport, and I was a member of the scouts," and he called over a boy and said to him, "This boy lives near you and might be interested in joining the scouts," and I did and it gave me lots of friends at once.

Thus, the boys' group appeared to be very useful for both Jack and Henry in broadening their field, which facilitated contact and relationships with a wide range of individuals who had the potential to provide opportunities in the future. In addition, membership of these groups provided access to a wide range and a large number of people who could aid their adaptation to life in the UK. In particular, because Jack was a member of the Scouts in Hungary, there was some continuity for him as whilst the language and broader culture may have been different, the Scouts are a global movement that has the same values and activities worldwide. For Jack, this meant that as well as accessing a large group of friends all at once, he was able to have a link with his past whilst acculturating to life in the UK; there was a familiar thread that eased his transition into his new life.

Receiving Charity

Some survivors did not join a specific group but found support from local charities. Tabitha, a Holocaust survivor, was given support by a Jewish charity. However, unlike other respondents in this research, Tabitha did not find the support provided appropriate and the help it offered actually served to alienate her further.

> The Jewish charity organisation had not many people for charity, needing charity, and I was one, and they indulged in it. I said that I must get a dress or something, and they sent me a big case with clothes and not one thing fitted me. Everything was torn. They went out of their way to send me things. Or somebody said "She's hungry, she needs to eat," and there was a ball or some occasion at a Jewish club that had lots of boiled potatoes left and sandwiches that had been left a day, two days before and they were sent over to me which was pretty frustrating and degrading.

Tabitha did join a choir once she arrived in the UK, and this did provide her with friends to a certain extent. However, the support she received from some people was again inappropriate for her.

> I went to town, and I met [the music director's wife], and she said, "Oh, how lovely to see you, come we shall have something to eat"... she ... took me to into a tearoom and went to the counter and ordered something. And she ordered me a double portion of cheese sandwiches, and she ordered tea and when it came then she got up and she said, "Well, I have to leave, I ordered a double portion because you must be hungry," and I must say, I started to cry and walked out and didn't eat anything because it was so degrading, the whole thing. That she couldn't wait even to eat with me.

Tabitha came from an upper-middle-class family in Hungary; her father was a doctor, and she was a teacher. As such, her migration may have been especially traumatic for her as not only did she move to an unfamiliar country, this migration also resulted in her being in a lower-class status, that of migrant, and as a result, her habitus was significantly disrupted. This explains her response to the charity support she received. As well as not feeling she was a good recipient for charity, she felt that the charity she received was not appropriate for someone of her class. This shows that her habitus had not adjusted to her new status as migrant and her way of thinking was still rooted in that of an upper-middle-class young woman from Hungary with all the cultural trappings that this entailed. This is also apparent in Tabitha's response to the clothes donated to her. In the 1950s in Britain, there was still an attitude of 'make do and mend' when it came to clothing, and it must be questioned as to why Tabitha did not merely accept the clothes and repair them. Whilst Tabitha may have been responding to the treatment she felt was below her status, her experiences show how damaging inappropriate support can be for a genocide survivor. Irrespective of whether her treatment from the group was particularly poor or Tabitha's response to the support provided was inappropriate, as a result, Tabitha felt degraded and deeply ashamed of her new status.

Other survivors were not able to access support due to their previous nationality. Judith, a Hungarian Jew, was initially not able to access compensation for her genocide experiences because compensation was only paid to German nationals. All other nationalities were seen as victims of war, rather than identified as victims of Nazis. Judith eventually received a small amount of compensation in 2009, when she was paid £2500. Again, the lack of recognition of Judith's status as a survivor reinforced a survivor hierarchy whereby her experiences were seen as less valid than other survivors by mere virtue of the fact of her nationality. This is further explored in Chap. 7.

Participation in Sport

One activity that proved useful in aiding survivors' resettlement in the UK was participation in sport, particularly team sports such as football. Whilst individual sports such as swimming can serve to establish status, team sports enable survivors to begin to fit in with the host population slowly, providing a managed situation in which everyone has a role and understands what he or she should do. Like the Scouts, the ability to play a sport such as football acts as cultural capital, facilitating acceptance and absorption into the host community but in manageable 'chunks'. Games such as football do not necessarily require the ability to confidently speak the host language, provided that the rules of football are understood by all the players. Football and similar team games can then act as a form of cultural capital, similar to educational qualifications but that have an effect in the social sphere rather than facilitating employment or something similar. Importantly, whilst joining a team sport where the majority of members are representative of the host community aids integration, joining a team where the members are made up of the refugee community also aids resettlement, but in a different way. When migrants join groups such as sports teams that are made up of other migrants, they are able to meet with others who have had similar experiences. Specifically, sports teams allow survivors to come together without needing to talk about or explain their circumstances to anyone. Sefik helped set up a team specifically for Bosnians living in the Yorkshire area.

> Some people used to live just opposite the football pitch, some people used to come from different parts of Yorkshire, and we would meet there and train. But yeah, that was one thing that helped us all settle down.

A football team made up purely of survivors could have been very inward-looking, resembling Berry's (1997) idea of 'separation' in terms of strategies of integration. That is, the survivors in the team could have remained separate from the community, only dealing with other groups. However, Sefik's team engaged with the wider host community who provided support in a number of ways.

> We had help from people, English people in terms of setting up the club, joining the league, attending meetings, you know, committee meetings and things like that, and also getting stuff like sponsorship deals … so yeah, that definitely helped us settle down, yeah.

Whilst the football team could have been seen as quite insular in that it was made up purely of migrants, it also facilitated engagement with the broader community, but in a structured, managed way that also informed the community's response to the migrants to a certain extent. Again, by proving their abilities on the field, the survivors could then break into other areas of life; like swimming, the ability to play football well acts as currency in social situations and illustrates to the host population that these migrants have skills that can be useful in British society. This can be best illustrated by examining two contemporary sporting stars: Fabrice Muamba and Mo Farah. Fabrice has become well known in the UK because of his collapse from a heart attack midway through a football match. He came to the UK in 1994 as an asylum seeker from the Democratic Republic of Congo. He was able to make friends through playing football at school and was signed to Birmingham City football club in 2003 when he was 15. He later transferred to Bolton Wanderers. Again, the elite athlete Mo Farah was a refugee from Somalia who arrived in the UK in 1991, unable to speak English. He is now a double Olympic gold medal holder after representing Great Britain at the 2012 and 2016 Olympic Games and world champion in the 5000- and 10,000-metre athletic events. Both cases illustrate how their sporting achievements have overridden their status as 'foreigner' or 'asylum seeker'.

However, there is also a negative aspect to involvement in sport, such as if someone does not understand the rules of the game, this could serve to alienate them further. For example, Henry had never played cricket until he came to the UK and spoke of his bewilderment whilst playing it at school:

> I watched people coming out with three sticks and a brick and another one with another three sticks and a brick. I thought, "They look vicious; they can't be throwing those about." I stood there in amazement. Then the guy came out with what I eventually knew was called a bat, and I didn't know how they were going to hit these three sticks … I didn't understand this at all; it seemed so odd … The teacher said to me, "Stand there, and when the ball comes to you, you throw it to him over there." "That's all I have to do, that's cricket?" and he said, "No, that's what you're doing today, there's more to it" … I stood there for 20 minutes, and the ball never came anywhere close, and I thought, the English are mad! Of course, I was used to football, and tennis and stuff like that, I could understand that. But I

> couldn't understand why they were running, none of it made any sense. While I was puzzling this out the ball eventually came to me, and the asphalt playground was on a slope, so the ball bounced next to me, and it started running up this slope, so I thought I won't throw it to him, I'll wait until it comes back, so I stood there waiting for it to roll back, then everybody shouted run, run! I was really mad; I'd been stood there for 20 minutes, why is there a hurry now to get this ball back, it will keep another second.

Whilst sport can aid a survivor's acceptance into a group, as seen with Sefik, Henry and Jack, it can also serve to alienate if an individual does not understand the rules or purpose of the game. Henry's recollections of his first experience of cricket illustrate how confusing sport can be for those who are unfamiliar with the rules. Several of the participants in this research utilised some form of group, whether a particular support group, musical or sporting group or a medical charity. Those who did not access support groups tended to be those who were younger and attended school, which also served the same function as support groups. Informal support groups are invaluable for the resettlement and re-establishment of genocide survivors' lives, provided the survivors understand the rules or values associated with that particular group. If they do not, then joining the group may initially serve to alienate them further.

Sibling Support

It is not surprising that siblings provided support for each other during genocide; it has been recognised in research on migration and trauma that siblings are a positive support to each other (Boyd 1998; David 1969). However, such support may not necessarily be provided by biological siblings, but by anyone who can fulfil that role of close supporter and adviser.

Rebecca and Henry both came to the UK with elder siblings, through the Kindertransport. Henry's sister was two years older than he was, and Rebecca's brother was three years older than she was. Both of them spoke of the support provided by their older siblings, both in helping with language learning and in wider social processes such as gaining employment. Beyond this though, Rebecca felt that her brother saved her life, both literally and figuratively.

> My brother used to raid the larder at night and feed me … which really did save my life … the companion who used to bath us … she pushed me under the water, and if he hadn't shoved her aside and yanked me out of the bath, I would have drowned. I don't know how much truth there is [in that story], but psychologically he saved my life.

Henry's relationship with his sister was quite different in that he did not have the same dependence on his sister that Rebecca had with her brother. This may well be due to the age difference, as Rebecca was much younger than Henry when she arrived in the UK and was dependent upon her brother to a greater degree. Instead, Henry sought guidance from his sister about his career. When he saw his sister moving out and getting a job, he decided to do the same, and he continued to consult her about his options.

> I grew up ever so quickly, you know, quite a different person, and I decided—with my sister, my sister was good guidance—that I needed to get a technical education.

As mentioned previously, Zakiah saw 'The Boys' as his family and relied on them as much as Henry and Rebecca relied on their siblings. Even now, Zakiah sees that particular group of people like family.

> We are still a family, very much so. I once asked my daughter—one of my daughters is a counsellor—and I said, "Tell me why is it that none of us needed counselling?" and she said, "Very simple, because you always had a big family, and the big family are the boys and the girls".

In attributing 'The Boys' with the reason why they did not need counselling, Zakiah highlights how, in being a replacement family, 'The Boys' did much of what would have been expected from a normal family relationship, supporting and counselling each other.

Formal Support Organisations

The use of social resources by survivors is not just limited to the physical act of migration, but also setting up life in a new country. For some survivors, charities and support agencies provided additional resettlement assistance. However, not all survivors are provided with formal support when they arrive in the UK and accessing support is to some extent a lottery, with survivors, especially Holocaust survivors having to be in the right place at the right time. Those who experienced genocide in Rwanda or Bosnia had more chance of accessing formalised support as there has been a significant move towards managing and providing asylum seekers and refugees the support they may initially require. When Holocaust survivors arrived in the UK in the late 1940s and early 1950s, there was no real concept of a 'refugee', with the term only being defined in the UN Convention relating to the Status of Refugees in 1951. While there was legislation relating to the admission of 'aliens', there were few regulations relating to the limitation of individual movement once individuals had been permitted to enter the UK. Controls relating to the movement of asylum seekers were introduced more recently, and thus survivors of the more recent genocides have been subject to control measures that are more stringent but also are given more formal support than were the survivors of the Holocaust. This can be seen in Sefik's experiences, where the UK government facilitated his migration and resettlement, and consequently he was never identified as an asylum seeker. This, along with the media coverage of the events in Yugoslavia, meant that many Bosnians felt welcomed, a sentiment Sefik shared:

> Welcomed, I think it is the right word, I think. We were provided with everything we could expect. We were basically treated like everyone else, I would say.

Thus, Sefik felt like just another person, not marked out for having a 'problematic' identity such as an asylum seeker, and the support put in place facilitated his resettlement. The Bosnia project could be seen in this case as an almost perfect example of integration as defined by Berry

(1997). For Berry, integration is where new migrants develop relationships with the host community whilst still maintaining their own culture. In Sefik's case, this was aided by being able to attend school and gain British qualifications, a form of cultural capital that resulted in Sefik feeling as though he fit into British society very quickly. At the same time, he could associate with other Bosnians by playing football and living in a community alongside others who were also Bosnian.

Another programme which appears to have had a similar success was one run by the Central British Fund (CBF), a Jewish charitable organisation which gained permission from the British government to bring a number of Jewish orphans to the UK after the war. The CBF found 732 youngsters throughout Europe, and they were dispersed across the UK in groups. Some went to Windermere, some to London and some to Northern Ireland. Their stories have been documented by Martin Gilbert in his book *The Boys* (1997), and Vincent, like Sefik, agrees that they were welcomed.

> We were very well looked after; we had good facilities for sleeping and enough food to eat. We had the opportunity to learn a little English, and we were doing sports, football and things like that which was really great because it developed our minds a little, and also we grew up a little bit, you know because we were all very thin at the time, but we gained a lot of strength.

This organised programme aided entry into a range of cultural activities which would aid resettlement and facilitate the development of relationships between Vincent and 'The Boys'. Unlike spontaneous migrants, Vincent and the others were gradually introduced to aspects of British culture rather than having to manage this transition on their own. Furthermore, this convalescent period also seemed to serve as an acculturation period for Vincent. By learning English and playing sports, they were learning how to fit in within society, but they were learning as a group who had had similar experiences and could support each other. Vincent, along with other child survivors, formed the Primrose Jewish Youth Club, which further facilitated the boys support needs and provided a place to go which served kosher food as well as provided sporting activities. Being a member of the youth group allowed the survivors to meet young people in the host country with a similar religious and national background, if not similar genocide experiences. This meant that the boys already had things in common with some of the dominant population, and this further aided their settlement and rehabilitation. The youth club provided a point whereby the migrant Jewish population could integrate and acculturate into the dominant Jewish population which itself is a minority group within the UK. Zakiah explains,

> Look, you can't just … disperse like that; they need somewhere to meet together because it's their family, they've got nobody. I was one of the few people who had somebody like a mother. So, they started a club … I honestly believe that had it not been for that, we would have … quite a few of us would have not have survived, or they would have had problems.

The youth club meant that these survivors could continue to retain some familiarity of their home culture whilst at the same time, through work and education, settle into part of the wider community which did not share their all their cultural norms and behaviour. For Vincent,

> it was like a second home for us, and that was really a great opportunity for us to develop friendship and most of us are still great friends.

Indeed, the day Vincent was interviewed he had been to the wedding of the daughter of one of the original youth club members, and Zakiah, another interviewee, remains good friends with Vincent. For Zakiah, the youth club was a substitute for his family. As mentioned previously, Zakiah only came to know his mother after the war, as until then he had been brought up by his grandparents. Consequently, Zakiah did not really feel he had a 'proper' family, as his mother was a stranger to him when he went to live with her after the war, and both his grandparents had died during the Holocaust. He found much-needed support from 'The Boys', who also had similar experiences to him. It seems, then, that not only does support need to be individualised, but allowing genocide survivors to recover alongside those with similar experiences, and often of the same age, facilitates recovery and resettlement.

This is why genocide survivors differ from 'other' forced migrants. They have been targeted because of who they are, and consequently support from those who understand what it means to be targeted for their identity is vital. The Primrose youth club ran until 1949 when it lost its lease. In 1963, several of the original 'Boys' set up their own charitable foundation called 'The 45 Aid Society'. This charity aims to remember those who died, support those who need help and tell others about what happened during the Holocaust.

There were many examples of formal yet 'ad hoc' support groups happening all over Europe and in the US following the end of the war, and Sarah was initially sent to Sweden following the Holocaust, where she recovered physically from her experiences and found her time in the hospital there also aided her emotionally.

> I made a good recovery, and I put on weight, and I must always say that I remember when one of the Swedish doctors I think he was, he took me out and I was holding his arm, and he said, he turned to me and said, "I've got a daughter like you". I can't remember what language he spoke, at that time I could only speak Hungarian, a bit of German and that made such a huge impression on me. Still, tears come in my eyes because although it seems such a simple statement, at that time, you know, I was so dehumanised and humiliated and forlorn and lost and depressed that that really has jolted me into … into an amazing kind of … life again, you know. So that was probably one of the greatest therapy I received.

These convalescent camps/hospitals, therefore, led to a 'soft' introduction to life after genocide. They enabled survivors to recover from their physical injuries and deprivations before worrying about employment, housing or financial issues. These experiences allowed survivors to create a permeable 'bubble' around themselves that protected them from the wider stresses and strains of everyday life but at the same time allowed them to experience culture in their host country. This again gives prominence to Berry's (1997) concept of integration wherein survivors live a dual life of retaining their own culture whilst developing relationships with the dominant community. Once recovered, Sarah was sent to Canada to resettle.

> I was told, "You're going to Canada". I went to Canada; I was by then 16; no, '48 I was more, I was 17 … and as I said, with all the other refugees, to Toronto. Life became sort of more … what shall we say … I wouldn't say normal, but having to fit in, you know, to an existing community … Nobody said "Did you have an education? Have you got a skill? Perhaps we could help you to learn to speak the language?" There was never, no agencies, nothing that could further our … you know, self-esteem, let alone anything else.

As soon as Sarah and the other refugees had recovered physically from the genocide and were not showing any extremes of mental trauma, it was assumed that they were ready to carry on their lives. There was no consideration of how their experiences might affect them in the future, and therefore no ongoing support was provided for them. However, it must be acknowledged that no government had had to deal with a population which had experienced trauma on this scale before, and many did not know about the ongoing effects of trauma.

The change in awareness between now and the immediate post-war time can be seen most clearly when considering Julien's experiences. Julien, as a survivor of the Rwandan genocide, was initially helped by the Medical Foundation for the Care of Victims of Torture, who supported him financially as well as psychologically. Despite this awareness of the psychological effects of trauma, Julien still feels that Rwandan survivors are,

> kind of … forgotten, a notebook, it's more broken. That's why I'm teaching, talking to people is very important. I don't know if British people are so ignorant, they don't, some people, every time I talk to them they cry, they don't know about the things in Rwanda now, all they know about is the genocide.

In this discussion, Julien is referring to the general awareness of events and what happened after the genocide, suggesting that in the UK people are aware of the genocide, but not what happens afterwards. The life afterwards is virtually unknown and how people recover is not considered beyond a psychological viewpoint. Because of this, Julien proposed developing a support organisation for Rwandans living in the UK.

> I had the idea of a UK-based organisation, so with friends, we thought it would be good to meet up, we had so many survivors' problems, and counselling wasn't, counselling wasn't helping at all. So there were some of them who were seriously ill, and I told myself it was trauma that seemed to affect the mental health or something.

The Hope Survivors Foundation was developed with help from Holocaust survivors in order to meet the needs of genocide survivors from Rwanda, particularly in the areas of education, legal assistance, psychosocial support and HIV/AIDS. In setting up this organisation, Julien focused on practical aspects of re-establishment such as education and legal assistance, and the foundation facilitates the development of social capital for survivors. By accessing this one organisation, survivors can then access a range of support needs and assistance, which aids survivors in building their own social and cultural capital. Part of Julien's work was to set up mutual support groups, where Rwandan survivors talked to Holocaust survivors, as it was felt that this was more help to them than traditional counselling models.

> Counselling is not happening; it's kind of a western thing. Counselling is … for a survivor … it's very difficult to counsel a survivor because it's trust, there's background, so many things.

For him, the traditional model of support did not help.

> It's very difficult because we … erm … in general, survivors we are … opened … we are not there yet. When you talk to Holocaust survivors, they start talking about … they have only a few left, so just start talking about what happened, even the second generation is doing that, the whole thing.

For Julien, Rwandan survivors are different to Holocaust survivors as they are expected to talk about their experiences like Holocaust survivors do, but have not had the time to re-establish and recover, and are not ready to talk about their lives. For him, talking is not just emotionally draining, but "it's like you're living there". Julien's views seem to suggest that the Holocaust survivors' approach of re-establishing first and talking later is an appropriate strategy. However, this could also be related to

Bourdieu's (1991) ideas of the linguistic habitus. It could be argued that genocide survivors do not have the linguistic skills to describe what has happened to them because the events of genocide are often indescribable. Therefore, their linguistic habitus has been disrupted to the point of being unable to speak about their experiences. Again, this illustrates the value of broadening this study beyond Holocaust survivors and including survivors from other genocides. Julien's experiences highlight the significant differences in support between the Holocaust and Rwanda. Whilst Holocaust survivors were left very much to 'get on with it on their own', this had a positive element, as they were not pressured into talking about their experiences. Survivors of more recent genocides appear to have been encouraged to talk about their experiences, but as Julien mentions above, this may not necessarily be a positive thing, particularly when dealing with survivors from non-Western backgrounds who may have different cultural attitudes towards talking about trauma.

Education has a key role to play in the lives of survivors for several reasons. Firstly, it allows survivors to acquire qualifications that can then act as cultural and social capital and facilitates survivors' further acculturation and resettlement. Secondly, it allows them to develop and expand their networks and therefore provides them with a broader field that could further aid their resettlement. However, there is a more general benefit, which is that survivors are provided with an opportunity that may well have been previously denied them because of the genocide. Thus, as well as providing practical help and resources, education also fulfils a more personal need to be seen as 'valuable' or worth investing in.

Likewise, employment also aids acculturation and resettlement but also provides survivors with a sense of worth and value as they are recognised as contributing to the host country. Support groups, whether formal or informal similarly provide survivors with opportunities to acculturate, but this research has found that the make-up of the groups is not as important as the opportunity to socialise and develop networks. If support groups are made up of the host population, this again provides opportunities for acculturation. Those that are made up of migrants also provide opportunities to acculturate and re-establish lives, but in a different way, as survivors are able to come together and talk about the challenges they face in their new country.

Bourdieu and Passeron (1990) stated that education is misrepresented as a meritocratic institution that rewards individual ability over hereditary privileges; instead, they argue that education maintains the current social order with all its hierarchies and reinforces the gap between people who already hold cultural capital and those who seek to gain it (Bourdieu and Passeron 1990). Universities, in particular, are the guardians of the dominant culture within society, and as a result, they separate the cultured from the uncultured. In saying this, Bourdieu indicates that education merely reproduces the status quo, and individuals aspire only to what is possible for their position in society. For example, Webber and Butler (2007) found that social class and social background were the crucial factors in academic performance in UK secondary schools, to the extent that the school's success was dependent not upon its teachers or curriculum, but on the class background of the pupils who attended it. However, individuals or specific groups may gain from education something more than the qualification itself. For example, for the respondents in this study education reduced the gap between survivors and the host society and facilitated the development of their cultural capital in the form of qualifications that were recognised by society as valid. Attending school allowed survivors to expand their field and to develop both cultural and social capital. Going to school enabled individuals to meet a large number of people from a wide range of backgrounds and cultures. This broadened the individual's field, as a result of the friendships and acquaintances made during school.

Furthermore, gaining British qualifications results in the development of cultural capital, which means that young people are more likely to be able to access jobs and further education once they leave school. For example, the degrees that Julien gained in the UK allowed others, particularly possible funders, to recognise him as competent as his degree conferred upon him particular skills and knowledge and, therefore, social capital, as the cultural capital he holds in the form of his degree is recognised. Even in cases where the survivor has come from a working-class background, education still aids resettlement as it provides access to language learning and a set of qualifications, which are perceived as valid by the wider host community. For them, education facilitated a move from a refugee or migrant 'dependent' status to being perceived as a productive member of the host society. One possible explanation for this is that survivors still had aspects of their 'home' habitus, which for many was rooted in the middle classes. This means that survivors aspired to the expectations embedded in their 'home' habitus and did not conform to the expectations of those at the bottom of the society. Like a bumblebee that flies because it does not know it should not be able to, the survivors aspired to the behaviours of their original classes, unaware of the fact that their status and position as one of the lowest in society should preclude them from such aspirations and achievements. Thus, their cultural capital, their 'way of being', ensured their progression in life. However, Bourdieu suggests that success in school is not just a matter of writing and speaking, but *how* an individual writes and speaks. Sefik, for example, who came from a more working-class background, had his resettlement aided by attending a school that already had a large working-class ethnic minority population who were mostly Muslim in background. Education, then, does aid acculturation, as Phillimore (2011) recommends, and it does provide an opportunity to gain qualifications, expand fields and learn English. However, it (usually) maintains the social order by introducing them to the same class that the survivor was in before the migration (Webber and Butler 2007; Reay 2006). Where this does not appear to happen is where survivors do not maintain any links with their past culture, either through choice or through the fact that their family had been killed, and they retained no links with their previous country.

Cultural capital can be gained at school through success in a particular area, whether that is academically or through extracurricular activities such as sport. This was seen in Henry's case where being able to swim competently acted as his cultural capital. By acknowledging this cultural capital in terms of his swimming capability, the pupils at Henry's school allowed the conversion of this cultural capital to social capital. This cultural capital of his swimming skills served as evidence for the rest of Henry's character, and thus he was accepted into the group on the strength of that event. Being accepted into the group gave Henry a wider network or 'field', and whilst these were children, this broader field still allowed Henry to resettle and acculturate more fully.

Bourdieu has tended to see cultural and social capital as being beneficial in terms of class demarcation and 'moving up' in the world. However, this case highlights that these capitals can have less tangible benefits. In Judith's case, using her degree in order to access information about her family history and experiences showed that for her cultural capital had emotional as well as practical benefits. Bourdieu has argued that capital can be transformed from one arena to another. However, Judith's 'cultural capital' of being a survivor with the knowledge of the Holocaust that this entailed was not accepted as valid by the National Archives and she was not able to use her cultural capital as a survivor; indeed, this was seen as a problem. Instead, she had to utilise her social capital of being a student of history at a UK university. These capitals are different; cultural capital, in Judith's case, is the knowledge she had as a survivor, that is, her experiences of life during the Holocaust. Her social capital as a student was her networks of contacts that were available to her through her 'membership' of being a student at a university. Even though Judith's cultural capital as a survivor was acknowledged, it was not seen as the 'right' sort of capital for the National Archives, and thus cultural capital may not work in different fields or may be recognised in different ways.

Bourdieu's thoughts on the transferability of social capital can aid understanding here. For cultural capital to be converted into social capital, it has to be recognised. If it is not recognised, then the individual cannot utilise it to improve their lives. For example, in Zakiah's case, he has met (amongst others) the Queen and the prime minister because of his cultural capital as a survivor. However, the capital he gained as a survivor would not have aided him in his business life, nor did his business life lead him to meet royalty or those in high political office. In Zakiah's case, his cultural, and therefore social, capital was not recognised in terms of his employment status because it had no relevance; his experiences did not provide him with skills that would have been recognised as vital in the stationery business.

Much of the support for survivors was provided either by survivors of a similar background or by organisations which fostered 'middle class' values such as the Scouts or Boys Brigade. Bourdieu's (1986) ideas shine a light on the processes involved in these groups. In terms of the Boy's Brigade, Henry derived the 'profit' of attending camp, despite the fact that he lacked the financial capital to access it. This camp allowed Henry to be a full member of the Boy's Brigade and, importantly, be seen as such by the other boys. This fostered acceptance and allowed Henry to develop his friendship group. Whilst Henry was a young boy, this acceptance into the group aided his language acquisition meaning that he was able to access more cultural activities that would have further aided his acceptance and acculturation into British life. Being part of a group such as this means an individual becomes part of the community; this facilitates members in making contacts that could prove useful later on in life. However, it is important to note that Henry could also fit in with this particular group because his background prior to migration was also middle class, and whilst there were some differences culturally between Austria and England at this point, certain social activities such as boys' groups were common throughout Europe. When support was provided at a subsistence level, as in Tabitha's case, it was felt to be degrading, illustrating a conflict between the class of the survivor and the expectations of the support group. In addition, Bourdieu (1986) recognises that individuals who belong to a group profit from their membership of that group even though they may not have earned it. In this context, survivors 'profit' from being a member of a group which is made up of middle-class individuals as they will also be afforded the same opportunities, irrespective of their economic capital.

In terms of sporting groups, Bourdieu's (1986) concept of habitus brings clarity here as Bourdieu saw habitus as 'the rules of the game'. Henry had no understanding of the rules of cricket, and whilst this on its own may not be problematic, for a migrant seeking to acculturate and appear the same as everyone else, this lack of knowledge shows their difference from the host population, serving to reinforce the sense of isolation that some survivors feel. Bourdieu (1978) claimed that sporting preferences are based on cultural and social reproduction, with different sports having different positions in the social and cultural hierarchy. Participation in cultural activities is rooted in cultural and social reproduction, and engaging in sporting activities that are familiar provides a link to the survivor's previous culture and habitus. This can be seen in Sefik's case, where his football team provided a link to his Bosnian culture and habitus.

Sefik played football, generally perceived to be a sport of the working classes. Thus, some survivors generally manage to re-establish their lives based on their 'home country' status because of their habitus and general expectations about what they will achieve in life. In particular, their general expectations are formed by the survivors' cultural background, but also by survivors who see their success in life as a response to the genocide and its perpetrators. Survivors see their success as retaliation against those who attempted to kill them; not only did they survive, but they survived well.

However, there are exceptions, as illustrated by Vincent's experiences. Vincent came from a relatively poor family who lived in a small shtetl in Eastern Europe. Given Bourdieu and Passeron's (1990) assertions about the reproduction of class, it could be expected that Vincent would have remained in a 'working class' habitus but instead he became very much middle class in terms of his employment (running a small business), his housing (a middle-class area of north London) and his outlook on life. What is important about Vincent's experiences is that he lost his entire family to the Holocaust, and was brought to the UK through a rescue programme after the war. As a result of this, Vincent had to start again; as he was 17 when he arrived in the UK, he did not go to school, which may have put him in the trajectory of a particular class. Instead, he initially spent time at a convalescent camp along with a number of other Holocaust survivors. He then moved to London, living in a predominantly middle-class Jewish area. Whilst it is possible that Vincent's habitus may not have been fully formed prior to leaving his home country, and therefore, it would have been much easier to form a new habitus, it is argued that it is the *post*-Holocaust experiences which particularly aided his progression into the middle class and, significantly, his living alongside other middle-class Jews as he began to rebuild his life.

For genocide survivors, community groups provide opportunities to integrate with the local community through cultural activities that also allow the host community to adjust to the migrants living there. Those local groups, whose members include a number of similar migrants, aid resettlement by providing a safe place for migrants to go without the need for explaining their experiences. Formal support organisations can be useful for survivors, but often only in a specific area such as psychological support or financial aid. Siblings (biological or assumed) often provide a combination of both the above forms of support. They provide counselling and psychological help as well as help each other to adjust to the new life they are encountering. Where individuals have been separated from siblings, it is evident that this has produced an extra trauma in their lives, and this finding adds credence to the argument from many refugee organisations that families should be kept together wherever possible. In addition, there appears to be no difference between the support provided by biological siblings and those individuals who are merely close friends.

Few survivors in this research noted having problems gaining access to employment or education. However, this does not mean that this is still the case now. The majority of survivors in this study were Holocaust survivors, arriving in the UK at a time of plentiful employment and only limited restrictions on employment for migrants. Survivors arriving in the UK now are subject to significant restrictions through the asylum system, often for a long period of time, which does affect future employment prospects as well as arriving at a time of low availability of jobs, living in a time of recession and relatively high levels of unemployment.

Equally, the younger survivors managed to complete their education and found that engaging in education aided their resettlement by broadening their field and providing opportunities to develop social capital. In addition, those who gained qualifications in the UK found that these qualifications aided their progression into work as they do not need 'translating' from a different education system. However, education only aided resettlement so far, and often this was because of previous class statuses.

Survivors re-establish themselves best when they can be with their families or those similar to them in terms of ethnicity and experiences and can access education or work that is appropriate for them. These findings support Greene's (2002) research that argued that supportive families and participation in Jewish organisations allowed Holocaust survivors to renew their lives. However, by utilising Bourdieu's ideas, this research has enabled us to see the mechanisms of this renewal process, centred on rebuilding social capital, and has illuminated the processes by which individuals rebuild their cultural and social capital. Education and employment broaden survivor's fields and aid the development of social capital by providing a network of individuals who may provide opportunities in the future. However, accessing education and employment can be challenging, and as social capital is not transferable, just because an individual has capital in one field does not mean it is recognised in another field. Support that is inappropriate in some way often serves to reinforce the ideology of the perpetrators of genocide by denying identity or experiences and illustrates to the survivors that they are different in some way, even just through their class status. Appropriate support is often that which is a side effect of membership of a particular community or sporting group and aids survivors by helping them acculturate into the new community.

References

Anderson, B., & Rogaly, B. (2005). *Forced Labour and Migration to the UK, London*. Retrieved December 22, 2018, from http://ituc-csi.org/IMG/pdf/Forced_labour_in_UK_12-2009.pdf.

Berry, J. W. (1997). Immigration, Acculturation and Adaptation. *Applied Psychology: An International Review, 46*(1), 5–68.

Black, R., Collyer, M., Skeldon, R., & Waddington, C. (2005). *A Survey of the Illegally Resident Population in Detention in the UK*; Home Office Online Report 20/05 London, Home Office. Retrieved January 2, 2019, from https://www.researchgate.net/profile/Michael_Collyer/publication/265115805_A_survey_of_the_illegally_resident_population_in_detention_in_the_UK/links/5458b9d30cf2cf51648351d2/A-survey-of-the-illegally-resident-population-in-detention-in-the-UK.pdf.

Bourdieu, P. (1978). Sport and Social Class. *Social Science Information, 17*(6), 819–840.

Bourdieu, P. (1986). The Forms of Capital. In J. G. Richardson (Ed.), *Handbook of Theory and Research for the Sociology of Education* (pp. 241–258). London: Greenwood Press.

Bourdieu, P. (1991). *Language and Symbolic Power* (J. B. Thompson, Ed.). Cambridge: Polity Press.

Bourdieu, P., & Passeron, J.-C. (1990). *Reproduction in Education, Society and Culture* (2nd ed.). London: Sage Publications.

Boyd, M. (1998). Gender, Refugee Status and Permanent Settlement. *Gender Issues, 16*(4), 5–21.

Cheung, S. Y., & Phillimore, J. (2013). *Social Networks, Social Capital and Refugee Integration*. Birmingham/Cardiff. Retrieved December 15, 2018, from http://www.birmingham.ac.uk/Documents/college-social-sciences/social-policy/iris/2013/nuffield-refugees-integration-research-report.pdf.

Coleman, J. (1994). *Foundations of Social Theory*. New York: Harvard University Press.

David, H. P. (1969). Involuntary International Migration: Adaptation of Refugees. *International Migration, 7*(3/4), 67–81.

Gilbert, M. (1997). *The Boys: Triumph Over Adversity*. London: Phoenix.

Greene, R. R. (2002). Holocaust Survivors: A Study in Resilience. *Journal of Gerontological Social Work, 37*(1), 3–18.

Phillimore, J. (2011). Refugees, Acculturation Strategies, Stress and Integration. *Journal of Social Policy, 40*(3), 575–593.

Phillimore, J. (2012). Implementing Integration in the UK: Lessons for Integration Theory, Policy and Practice. *Policy and Politics, 40*(4), 525–545.

Phillimore, J., & Goodson, L. (2008). Making a Place in the Global City: The Relevance of Indicators of Integration. *Journal of Refugee Studies, 21*(3), 305–325.

Putnam, R. D. (2000). *Bowling Alone: The Collapse and Revival of American Community*. London: Simon & Schuster.

Reay, D. (2006). The Zombie Stalking English Schools: Social Class and Educational Inequality. *British Journal of Educational Studies, 54*(3), 288–307.

Webber, R., & Butler, T. (2007). Classifying Pupils by Where They Live: How Well Does This Predict Variations in Their GCSE Results? *Urban Studies, 44*(7), 1229–1253.

Wright, T., & McKay, S. (2011). *Undocumented Workers' Transitions: Legal Status, Migration, and Work in Europe*. London: Routledge.

6

Identity and Adaptation

Genocide survivors who migrate to a new country have to manage a changing sense of self. New identities, such as that of a new nationality, become open to them, while others are no longer valid. One particular element of this changing self is whether the individual sees themselves as a survivor, a victim, both or neither. This chapter explores how survivors manage this adaptation of identity over time and whether they come to see themselves as a survivor, alongside exploring the concept of a hierarchy of survivors.

The notion of 'being a survivor' is one which has seen much discussion and debate between those who have experienced genocide and those who study it (see Fackenheim and Huttenbach 1999; Meierhenrich 2007; Skjelsbaek 2006). Given that the UN definition of genocide is any of the proscribed acts, committed with "intent to destroy in whole or in part" (UN 1948), those who survive genocide are both 'victims' of genocide and 'survivors' of the same crime. As a result, those who experience genocide may well identify themselves as a victim, survivor, both or neither. Both terms are value laden; the term 'victim' often conjures ideas of weakness and vulnerability, whereas the term 'survivor' can imply strength and recovery. The individual may not feel strong or recovered, and being

L. Asquith, *Rebuilding Lives After Genocide*, Palgrave Studies in Compromise after Conflict, https://doi.org/10.1007/978-3-030-14074-8_6

a 'survivor' may put undue pressure on him/her to be a certain individual who has conquered a traumatic experience (Skjelsbaek 2006). This concept of the 'survivor' does not allow for people who have physically survived but feel that mentally they are still very much a victim. Spalek (2006) argues that this tension between physical and mental survival is one that presents challenges when considering how to define a survivor and what it means to be a survivor. For some, it is an identity as a result of an individual physically surviving an experience. However, there is a finer-grained debate around the nature of survival and the 'granting' or acceptance of the survivor label. This chapter explores these nuances and discusses how individuals come to see themselves as a survivor and what that status means to them.

The chapter also explores the idea that genocide survivors constitute a 'field' (in the Bourdieuian sense) in themselves and discusses how this field functions and affects survivors. Hence, this chapter considers who becomes dominant and achieves a higher status in a field and how that may occur. Finally, the chapter considers how survivors talk about their experiences and how memory (especially institutional and broader societal memory of genocide) affects the retelling of their stories.

Defining Identities

Halima initially had no choice over how her identity was defined, and when she arrived in the UK, specific identities were imposed upon her. As she was seeking asylum because of her victimisation in Darfur, her first identity was that of an asylum seeker, then victim and, later still, a refugee. The nature of the asylum system means that claims are checked for veracity before allowing the label 'victim', which then allows the label 'refugee' to be applied. For someone to become a refugee, their previous victimisation needs to be recognised by the relevant authorities (in this case, the UK Border Agency).

The refugee/asylum seeker identity can be problematic. When refugees first leave their homeland, the ties they have in the form of social roles, status, groups and networks are severed, resulting in disconnected and shattered identities. While migration profoundly affects people, migration itself is not a threat to identity; it is the change in social context that is problematic (Timotijevic and Breakwell 2000). In particular, migrants who have no home to which they can return, or whose country has disappeared (e.g. in the case of the former Yugoslavia), are those who are most likely to experience threats to their identity. Their experiences in their country of origin often result in a belief that their actions cannot affect or change what happens, which may influence their self-efficacy and self-esteem, and produce a view that the world is unstable and unpredictable (Timotijevic and Breakwell 2000). Thus, this lack of control and consequent instability challenges their identity. Moreover, when individuals arrive in their host country, they may be given an "administrative or bureaucratic identity of 'refugee' which is almost always seen as undesirable and as an 'identity' to be shed as quickly as possible" (Colic-Piesker and Walker 2003: 338). To shed undesirable identities, refugees need to rebuild their identity in the new environment, drawing on previous roles and statuses alongside their new identity (Colic-Piesker and Walker 2003).

However, contrary to this previous research, Halima initially fought to be recognised as a refugee as this status would provide her with the security of knowing she would not face returning to Darfur. Her identity as an asylum seeker was unstable and could be removed at any time should the UK government decide that returning her to her country of origin would not risk her life. For Halima, the refugee identity was desirable, as it would have provided stability and safety; if awarded refugee status, the threat of being returned to Darfur would have ceased and she would have been given leave to remain in the UK. Becoming a refugee would have allowed Halima more agency than that which she had as an asylum seeker. In particular, being a refugee would have allowed Halima to begin work.

> All I wanted was to stay here in peace and safety. I wanted my dignity back, and I wanted to contribute to this society. I was a trained medical doctor, and I knew this country needed doctors. But instead, the Home Office forced us to live on handouts while arguing that my story was a pack of lies.

Working would have enabled Halima to provide for herself and her family. Moreover, it would have shown to the broader society that she was not the drain on resources that she was perceived to be. The way an individual enters and is seen initially in a country has an impact on how the host population defines them and how they see themselves. Those who are labelled as asylum seekers are often seen as or represented as parasites, reliant upon the state and draining the state of valuable resources, or overloading the host country in some way (see Klocker and Dunn 2003; Syal 2014; Foxton 2013). Those who can work as soon as they arrive, such as those from within the European Union (EU), are often perceived slightly more favourably; if nothing else, they are less visible as they engage in the same behaviours (such as commuting and working) as the host population. Asylum seekers, on the other hand, are housed in specific accommodation and are more 'visible' in local communities, which can result in negative perceptions of the individual.

Dan Bar-On suggests that "from a legal-historical point of view, a Holocaust survivor can be defined as anyone who lived under Nazi occupation during World War Two and who was threatened by the policy of the 'Final Solution' but managed to stay alive" (Bar-On 1998: 100). As with the definition of genocide itself, this is a problematic area. Bar-On's definition does not allow for those who escaped to neutral countries or managed to leave Eastern Europe before the war through legitimate means such as the Kindertransport. Furthermore, Bar-On's definition only concerns itself with Holocaust survivors, and it does not inform understanding of who can be a genocide survivor beyond the Holocaust. It is essential to define genocide survivors as a group, not least because being identified as a survivor may lead to an acknowledgement of suffering, both in monetary and in moral terms.

In 1999, an article by Emil Fackenheim in the *Journal of Genocide Research* (Fackenheim and Huttenbach 1999) was given the header 'The Voice of the Survivor' by the editor, Henry Huttenbach. Fackenheim objected strongly to this label in a letter to the editor published in a later issue of the journal. In the letter, Fackenheim stated that he was not a survivor as he experienced only a concentration camp and "only a person who survived a murder camp is a survivor" (Fackenheim and Huttenbach 1999: 463). If Fackenheim's understanding of survivor status were to be applied to other genocides, then no one could be classed as a survivor as death camps were unique to the Holocaust. Instead, a specific definition of a survivor for each genocide would be required, reflecting the circumstances of each genocide. This is impractical, given that it is possible to recognise aspects of acts that are common to all genocides. Moreover, Ben Shephard, when considering the after-effects of the Second World War, suggests that "[m]ost of the Jewish displaced persons in camps in Germany in 1946 were not, strictly speaking, 'Holocaust Survivors', that is, survivors of the concentration and death camps; they were Jewish refugees who had fled to the Soviet Union from Poland in 1939" (Shephard 2010: 5). Thus, there is debate over who is seen as a survivor and what that status means.

In response to Fackenheim, Huttenbach argued that there is no 'official' definition and that Fackenheim's definition was flawed and not useful to genocide studies (Fackenheim and Huttenbach 1999). In disagreeing with Fackenheim's point that only those who survived death camps should be classed as a survivor, Huttenbach suggests that there is, as a result of Fackenheim's assertion, an implication that others who did not experience death camps are 'lesser' survivors or not survivors at all. Huttenbach suggests that if those who experienced concentration camps are not survivors, they must be 'something else' and cannot simply remain unchanged; they have experienced an extreme event that altered their life course, posing the question: if these individuals are not survivors, then what are they? He further questions why someone is so protective over the term 'survivor', concluding that there is nothing to be gained by such hair-splitting. He also argued that this hierarchy is something specific to Holocaust survivors, giving the example of how the survivors of the Armenian genocide did not seem to engage in this 'pecking order' of survivorship.

Thus, the identity of the survivor is bound up in politics beyond the physical survival of genocide. In this respect, some survivors hold what Bourdieu (1984) termed 'symbolic capital', that is, capital which is often seen by others as prestige, honour or respect and is often the result of previous experience or knowledge. Those survivors who have experienced concentration camps (in the case of the Holocaust and Bosnia), and Rwandans whose families were killed with machetes and they themselves survived by hiding under bodies, are often seen as 'stereotypical' survivors. As a result, these survivors would hold large amounts of symbolic capital that would place them at the top of the hierarchy, reinforcing a specific narrative around the survivors' experiences. The creation of such hierarchies is an act of symbolic violence, causing non-survivors to misrecognise reality because of not seeing the underlying power relations. Because of this symbolic violence, a skewed position of this social world is legitimated, and the social order (in this case of the survivors) is stratified and reproduced.

The issue of who is recognised as a survivor has significant implications, not least regarding practical issues such as compensation for suffering experienced, but also for the development of identity and the perception of the self. Frank (1997) suggests that those who suffer illness form what he termed a 'remission society', where despite having recovered from their illness, people are still viewed as different. This idea can be applied to genocide survivors, who are fundamentally changed by their experiences, and instead of returning to 'normal' life, they carve out a new existence in 'survivor society' similar to how cancer survivors inhabit the 'remission society'.

Illuminée wholly rejected the idea of being a survivor, mainly because of her experiences during the genocide, when multiple men raped her. Illuminée was convinced that she had been infected with HIV/AIDS because of these rapes, to the point that she did not undergo testing for HIV/AIDS, saying,

> Deep inside I 'knew' that I had AIDS. My time in Norwich with Esther and the children should have been a period of recovery from the Genocide. But I was constantly troubled by dark thoughts. I had convinced myself that I was not a 'true' survivor. I was under sentence of death thanks to the disease that was taking hold of my skinny frame.

While this was traumatic for Illuminée, what was even more challenging was her discovery that she did not have AIDS and was going to survive.

> The news traumatised me. I had been expecting to die and had been living in a kind of limbo. Now I realised I was going to live I somehow had to come to terms with the genocide and plan a future … I could not cope with this realisation and was literally struck dumb.

Illuminée illustrates the complexity of survivors' identities; coming to terms with life and death is traumatic, and their status as survivor or victim has a significant impact on their recovery. It was the unexpected news that Illuminée would live which caused so much trauma for her because until this point, because of her experiences, she had expected to die. Thus, Illuminée's status as 'survivor' became relevant and therefore particularly problematic to her only when it became evident that she would, indeed, survive. All survivors in this research referred to the idea of being a survivor at some point, and they all talked about their attitudes towards their status. Zakiah was not sure what a survivor should feel like, which illustrates the problems with Fackenheim's conception of a survivor. Zakiah had been in Auschwitz and would easily be recognised as a survivor under Fackenheim's definition. Despite this, he had reservations.

> I don't feel like a survivor; I don't know what a survivor should feel. I feel like anybody else, and my friends, nobody knows me as Zakiah the survivor, they all know me as Zakiah, everybody knows me as Zakiah all over, including Gordon Brown and her majesty the Queen.

Zakiah suggested that he was known for being 'just him' rather than a survivor, but the reason he has met so many people, including Gordon Brown, MP, and the Queen, is that he is a survivor, and has met these people as a result of talking about his experiences during the Holocaust. It is Zakiah's survivor identity that allowed these events to happen, rather than his achievements in work or sport. It is his habitus as a survivor and the fact that his field is made up of survivors that have facilitated those meetings with Gordon Brown (the prime minister at the time) and the Queen. It was Zakiah's experiences of the Holocaust which was recognised by the Holocaust Educational Trust, and his symbolic capital (the resources available to Zakiah because of his position of surviving the Holocaust) which resulted in these meetings and recognition.

However, it was not always the case that others would recognise the symbolic capital of the survivor. Lili's family did not attach much importance to her being a Holocaust survivor.

> I only became a Holocaust survivor I would say in the 80s which is a very very unusual thing … if I ever I said something about my miserable time

> in the war, my husband, actually my children as well, I have three children, they used to say the thing with the violin [mimes playing the violin], "There goes mother feeling sorry for herself".

This lack of acknowledgement led in some cases to an almost outright denial of survivors' experiences. When she first arrived in the UK, Kitty was met by her uncle, who said,

> Before we go off to Birmingham there's one thing I must make quite clear. On no account are you to talk about any of the things that have happened to you. Not in my house. I do not want my girls upset. And I don't want to know.

Kitty goes on to say that she realised at this point that she would not be able to class herself as 'victim' or 'survivor'.

> Everybody in England would be talking about personal war experiences for months, even years after hostilities had ceased. But we, who had been pursued over Europe by the mutual enemy, and come close to extermination at the hands of that enemy, were not supposed to embarrass people by saying a word.

In failing to recognise Lili and Kitty's symbolic capital as survivors, the response by their families illustrates the problem with such capital. While both women hold significant capital as Holocaust survivors, their families did not recognise this. Lili's family saw her role and status as a mother as more important than her status as a Holocaust survivor. Kitty could not claim the status of either victim or survivor because of the silencing and denial of her status by her uncle and family. Hence, the symbolic capital of a survivor is not transferable to every arena in their lives.

This inability to be heard or to discuss their experiences is something of an anomaly when considering other significant events in history. Events are most discussed shortly after their occurrence, and then they slowly become less important as they move towards the margins of awareness (Novick 2007). For example, the Battle of Passchendaele, which occurred during the First World War, was discussed in the 1920s and 1930s, and the "most-viewed films and the best-selling books about the

Vietnam War almost all appeared within five or ten years of the end of that conflict" (Novick 2007: 1). It was a significant number of years later before there was any real discussion of the Holocaust in everyday society, with Solomon (1995) noting that the distress and experiences of Holocaust survivors went unacknowledged for the first 20 years after the Holocaust. The effects of this silence for Kitty meant that her victimising experiences, and her identity, were denied by wider society.

This denial of experience and identity was not uncommon post-Holocaust, and Stein (2009) suggests that the Holocaust was not only indescribable and unspeakable but also undiscussable. She argues that the Holocaust was without precedent and therefore there was a general inability to understand and comprehend what had happened. Stein goes on to explain that this 'undiscussability' may also derive from audiences being unwilling to confront the information coming from those who had experienced genocide. To face up to this information also meant to confront the behaviours of all people during the genocide, including those who failed to act to save the victimised groups, for instance, the bystanders who were aware of the genocide but did nothing to intervene, such as those who lived close by the camps at Auschwitz camp.

Cohen argues that for survivors the problem is not remembering the story, but locating and making sense of memories that they cannot fully believe (Cohen 2001). Therefore, talking to others about their experiences becomes very difficult when survivors cannot understand them; the questions over how it could be allowed to happen and how a society could engage in planned, organised mass murder is one of the leading concerns regarding life after the genocide. These experiences may challenge an individual's fundamental assumptions of life, such as life being precious and things happening for a reason (Stein 2009). In Janoff-Bulman and Hanson Frieze's discussion of the effects of crime, they argue that experience of victimisation may shatter an individual's cognitive meanings of the world (Janoff-Bulman and Hanson Frieze 1983). Consequently, genocide survivors not only face the issue of making sense of their victimisation but also having other people being unable to comprehend or accept it. This is evident in Kitty's story when considering the actions of her uncle. In the immediate post-war period, everyone had been affected by the war in some way so there was an unwillingness to listen to others' stories of loss when he or she had experienced loss and could not conceive of a horror greater than his or her own. This lack of acknowledgement, however, leads to challenges to survivors' identities as the life-changing events they experience are ignored, downplayed or even denied.

The Bourdieuian field is a field of struggles, which preserve or transform the configuration of the forces of capital. Those within a field either compete to become dominant in that field or attempt to redefine what is essential and the form of cultural capital which is recognised. In Lili and Kitty's situation, it is evident that the people outside the field affect the value of the capital held by those within the field. One of Lili's reasons for not talking about her experiences was that her family did not appear to value her status as a survivor. This was seen most clearly by Lili's daughter, who, when asked if she was a second-generation survivor (i.e. the child of a Holocaust survivor), said no. When Lili asked her why, her daughter replied,

> "Well, Mother, you were not Holocaust survivors … you were never in a camp, you were refugees." So isn't it amazing, a daughter of mine didn't like having the label of Holocaust, and I explained to her what is a Holocaust survivor and we left it at that, we never broached the subject since.

Lili's symbolic capital became devalued by her children, who did not perceive Lili as a valid survivor, in part because of the impact that status would have on them. Dan Bar-On suggests, "Holocaust survivors raised children who became, biologically speaking, the second generation. This may have stigmatising connotations: they bear some hidden 'infection' (like the genetic radiation effects of Hiroshima survivors) transmitted to them by their parents" (Bar-On 1998: 94). Thus, Lili's daughter rejected the idea that Lili was a survivor because the label 'survivor' was stigmatising, and one to avoid at all costs. By not recognising Lili's symbolic capital and limiting her field, Lili's children protected themselves from the perceived stigma of being the child of a survivor.

Lili pinpoints her move into survivorhood as being related to Robert Maxwell, who funded a conference in Oxford in 1988 entitled 'Remembering for the future'. Lili attended this conference and met "people like myself". By this time, Lili's children had grown up and left home, which meant that their restrictive influence on Lili was removed. This lack of influence meant that Lili was able to explore her survivor identity without hindrance from her family.

While Lili's family actively sought to reject her status as a survivor, some survivors such as Julien found meaning and value in their survivor status. For him, being seen as a survivor had positive aspects, in that sometimes children who have heard him speak respond practically:

> Children … like talking to a survivor, the person who has gone through it; they see the person. It does affect them; they come up with a project.

The children that Julien referred to developed a project that funded 15 Rwandan children through school. This project was a positive response to Julien's experiences, rather than Julien as a person. However, there is a suggestion here that Julien accepted his survivor role if some meaning and good came of it, that the pain and trauma which was unearthed when talking was worth it if people learnt something from these experiences.

> It's really encouraging when your … the message you receive from students … encourages you.

Thus, Julien's survivor identity was something which he tolerated because the responses to it often produced good things which improved other survivors' lives. The survivor identity is not one that is taken on without much thought and consideration. The survivors in this research did all see themselves as survivors, but most of them only took on this identity later in life, often years after arriving in the UK. Bourdieu's (1986) concept of the habitus draws attention to this change, illustrating how people 'become' survivors through a slow process of readjustment and redefinition of themselves. Survivors' habitus changes as their understanding of their status changes. For some, this was a relatively quick change; for example, Zakiah was happy to identify himself as a survivor because he had always been in contact with other survivors, known as 'The Boys'. This contact meant that Zakiah had a 'survivor' identity from quite early on in his acculturation and resettlement and this identity allowed him to be part of the group that he saw as family. Conversely, Lili's children did not perceive her as a survivor, and consequently, she only began to identify herself as a survivor once her children had grown up and left home. These two cases illustrate how the habitus works in the context of symbolic capital. For Zakiah and survivors such as Sefik who arrived and lived alongside other genocide survivors, their habitus became that of the genocide survivor, and being a survivor was an accepted part of their identity; their status as survivors reflected in their symbolic capital. For others, such as Lili and Judith, their habitus developed without that 'survivor' aspect of their identity and had to be incorporated later in life, often when the status became acceptable in the eyes of others. Importantly, this is where it is possible to see a more nuanced understanding of the habitus. Despite Bourdieu's argument that the habitus only changes slowly (Bourdieu 1977), what has been discussed here illustrates that the habitus can change quite quickly and without significant upset for some individuals. This appears to be the result of the individual having a viable identity which they can accept: that of a survivor. If that identity is not available, because others deny it or because they do not recognise themselves as such, then the habitus may take longer to change, or the transition becomes especially problematic for the individual. Hence, it is evident that Bourdieu's assumptions regarding the habitus can be further developed and extended here. Rather than the habitus being embodied to the point that it can only change slowly, or with much trauma, it can be argued that the habitus can change quickly, provided there is an 'alternative' habitus that can be adapted and utilised that is acceptable for the individual. The central problem is caused when there is no alternative, or when the alternative is unpalatable to the individual when he/she is unable to see where he/she fits in within their new world. At this point, they recognise their difference and become particularly aware of it, knowing that their experiences mark them out as being unlike the rest of the population. It is this recognition that causes the individual to be aware that their habitus no longer fits with the broader society, reinforcing their difference and separating them from the wider population.

Hierarchy

When talking about their survivor identity, several survivors in this study perceived themselves as having a place in a hierarchy of survivors. Therefore, this section aims to explore the notion of a genocide survivor hierarchy and what purpose such a hierarchy serves. As mentioned previously, survivors can be seen as a field in and of themselves. Therefore the hierarchy within that field can be considered through Bourdieu's (1989) viewpoint, considering what functions the field serves, such as facilitating support for survivors, reassuring survivors that there is 'safety in numbers', and providing a network of people who are similar to them, and how the hierarchy works in practice. Bourdieu (1989) has suggested that capital confers power over the field, and this next section will explore what capital survivors need to be acknowledged as near the top of the hierarchy and therefore as socially and symbolically powerful actors in their field.

As discussed at the beginning of this chapter, for those who experience genocide there is a difference between being a victim and being a survivor. All the participants in this study acknowledged their status as survivors; however, one participant also referred to herself as a victim. In talking about her family, Lili suggested that the reason why some family members were distanced from her was due to her victim status.

> I don't know; maybe they don't want to be descendants of such victims, maybe that's it.

After the war, Jews who migrated to Israel were viewed with suspicion by some of the indigenous population whose perception was that Jews had gone 'like lambs to the slaughter' during the Holocaust and that those who survived must have been deviant in some way to survive (Yablonka 1999). Those who survived the Holocaust were seen as weak and therefore inferior to the Israelis, and such people were viewed as 'victims' and not what the state of Israel should be built on. During the development of the state of Israel, 'New Jews' who were proud and strong were needed, and diaspora Jews were seen as a threat to this, with personalities "distorted by centuries of persecution" (Solomon 1995: 219). It is possible that these attitudes persisted elsewhere, in others who felt that they wanted to be associated with a different definition of being a Jew regarding the new conception of the state of Israel as a (militarily) strong state which was able to defend itself.

Lili also downplayed her survivor experiences when comparing them to other survivors. She viewed her husband as having had a much worse Holocaust experience than she had, even though he never lived under Nazi occupation. She also compared herself to her friends, saying,

> I think I danced through the war even so I've got bad enough stories, but their stories, you just can't compare at all … as far as the Holocaust is concerned I didn't … emotionally I didn't do too badly at all.

Bourdieu (1989) suggests that in any field there are those who are dominant because of the cultural capital they hold and how others perceive it in that field. There are also those who are dominated because of the perceived lower value of their capital. However, those who are dominated sometimes resist the dominant individuals in a field, and in this case, Lili did this by negating and downplaying her experiences and by resisting involvement in this field to a certain extent. She expanded upon this when she discussed her involvement in survivor groups:

> We are a peculiar lot. I mean you put us, you have the Holocaust survivor's centre in Hendon, in no time at all there is a split. So I am amongst the 'kick out' group, John Fransman kick out group, so we were kicked out.

This draws attention to the competition within the survivor 'field', and Bourdieu's (1989) ideas on competition within a field can be used here to focus attention on the struggles for exclusion and inclusion that are played out in the field of genocide survivors. Lili also suggested that she 'became' a survivor in the 1980s, which suggests this was an identity that was either not immediately available to her or one she actively chose to avoid. It is more likely that this identity was not available to her, as very few survivors talked 'officially' in the years immediately after the Holocaust.

However, some survivors do seek to have their status recognised, such as Judith who said that she "was a survivor before it was fashionable" but had her survivor status denied because of her nationality. Her claims for compensation were initially denied because she was Polish and therefore seen as a victim of war, rather than a victim of genocide. Again, the competition for a place in the field is seen here, but rather than moving away and resisting the dominant forces of the field, Judith challenges them by arguing that her experiences should be recognised as much as any other survivor.

> We weren't accepted as being survivors, initially they, it was the camp survivors and which camp you were in and whatnot. It was interesting in that … it's hard to explain, it's not … because we weren't accepted as survivors, in a way, it made our experiences have no validity.

Here the competition and struggles within the field are evident with Judith striving to be recognised as a member of the survivor field but the more dominant members (camp survivors) preventing her recognition. Also, there was also a further lack of recognition because of her nationality, and Judith suggested that the Association of German Jewish Refugees (now the Association of Jewish Refugees) were a gatekeeping organisation and viewed Polish refugees as mentally slow and not worthy of support:

> We were Polish Jews, and in this country, the relief organisations were the German Jews, and there was a lot of antagonism toward the Polish Jews, so we were made to feel that it was our fault. There was an awful lot of that, and it still carries a lot of resentment between the survivors because you still get a German Jew making a really inappropriate remark even when we're amongst ourselves as survivors.

The hierarchy of Holocaust survivors developed initially because of the compensatory scheme that initially focused exclusively on German Jews. The 1953 German indemnification law (known as Bundesentschädigugsgesetz, or BEG) required the German government to engage in the process of 'Weidergutmachung'—making good again by paying reparations (initially) to German Jews. However, many Jews refused to submit claims for compensation, saying that the Jewish blood of those who did not survive would taint any claim and seeing the payment as aggravating an injustice that could not be measured by money (Sicher 1998). To claim any reparation, Jews had to be interviewed by a psychiatrist to establish the veracity of their claim, something that frustrated Judith:

> It was a German Jewish doctor that interviewed my mother, and admittedly they didn't understand post-traumatic stress disorder, but because she was Polish they just looked upon her, and they actually said to my father, "Well, she's mentally retarded and therefore she hasn't suffered". And that was the attitude, absolutely. My mother, she wasn't the most streetwise lady, and she had a very limited education, as women would have, but she spoke, read and wrote six languages. Mind you I suppose being a German he [the doctor] probably spoke seven.

The struggle for dominance within the survivor field is often related to the need to have suffering recognised, either by the world at large or by specific individuals or organisations such as compensatory bodies. If an individual is widely recognised as a survivor, then it is argued that it becomes harder, if not impossible, to deny their experiences. This competition for recognition was still felt keenly by Judith, and the competition within the field earlier in her life has continued to affect her. She finally received compensation for her experiences in 2009, when she was awarded £2500 from the Conference on Jewish Material Claims against Germany. However, Judith indicated that a letter she received still denied her a pension. She reported that the letter said

> that I hadn't been in, under occupation long enough, I was only occupied for two years, and it was a real patronising letter, saying "we do appreciate you've suffered, but not enough"... My mother was refused, but my father actually did get a pension because he had been interned twice, and it was a nominal pension, but it was the ... what was the word ... the fact that his suffering had been accepted, you know, that it wasn't his fault.

Again, the dominant agents in the field, which in this case is the compensatory organisation, could control who accessed resources within the field and therefore controls the positions of others in the field. However, dominant organisations can also facilitate involvement and inclusion in the survivor field where other survivors may disagree. Jack gives regular talks about his experiences as a survivor of the Holocaust to schools and community organisations. Jack is a Hungarian Jew and did not experience life in the concentration camps; the Nazis did not occupy Hungary until March 1944, by which time the programme of mass extermination was in full swing, and so most Jews were sent to immediate death.[1] Despite living through the Holocaust Jack was told,

> I shouldn't be doing this [talking about his experiences] because I wasn't in a concentration camp.

This does not appear to be a one-off incident, and something similar was referred to in Jonathan Freedland's article in the *Observer* magazine, where he visited the Hendon Holocaust survivor's centre and interviewed survivors about the centre.

> Sam Pivnick and I had been talking for only a few minutes when another man wanted to join our conversation, standing over us, interjecting with observations of his own. It turned out he was one of those who had escaped Germany as a child, a baby in fact. Soon Sam's patience snapped. "Who wants to hear about you?" he shouted. "What did you survive? You were in your mother's womb!" (Freedland 2011)

Again, the struggle for recognition within the survivor field is illustrated here, with both Pivnick and the other man wanting to have their status as survivors recognised, but Pivnick appearing to be the dominant agent when considering recognition of that status.

Other survivors appear to have managed to develop a dominant position in the survivor field. As mentioned previously, Zakiah argued that he

---

[1] Around 70% of Hungarian Jews were murdered during the Holocaust. Jack lived in Budapest and, benefited from Raoul Wallenberg's protective passport scheme. Wallenberg was a Swedish diplomat and served as Sweden's special envoy in Budapest for the last half of 1944. During that time, Wallenberg issued around 9000 passports. Jack's family were part of a further 10,000 people who were housed in properties that Wallenberg had designated Swedish territory and hence were protected by diplomatic immunity.

was known as just Zakiah, rather than Zakiah the survivor; but then went on to discuss how the recognition of his life had been in terms of his life as a successful Holocaust survivor. Zakiah appeared to be the archetypal Holocaust survivor because of experiencing life in Auschwitz and the loss of his family there. Post-Holocaust, Zakiah built up a successful business, as well as volunteering his time to talk about his experiences in schools and communities, again through the Holocaust Educational Trust. Thus, Zakiah holds a dominant position in the survivor field because of his experiences aligning with the overall expected narrative of survival, such as triumph over extreme adversity and being a survivor of a famous camp, resulting in Zakiah holding a significant amount of symbolic capital. Other survivors who acknowledge the survivor's 'expertise' in the field and recognise their cultural capital can sometimes reinforce these dominant positions. Julien, a survivor from Rwanda, talks about meeting with Holocaust survivors as part of a support network.

> I've initiated the so-called 'mutual support groups' so they are talking to Holocaust survivors, they have a centre near Hendon. So I've been going there several times to see how they came up with projects.

In this case, Julien acknowledges the dominance of specific survivor groups by seeking guidance from them to support Rwandan survivors. Therefore, it seems there is a temporal dimension to the survivor field, with the dominant members being the ones who have lived longest and have spent more time recovering from their experiences. Those who have more recently become survivors, such as those from Rwanda and other genocides, are often 'dominated' in that they seek guidance from the dominant group and have not achieved the success either in the role of 'survivor' or in life generally that other survivors such as Zakiah have as yet.

One way a survivor can establish their status in the survivor hierarchy is through their language, and one survivor sought to establish his survivor credentials throughout the interview. All other survivors began their interviews by talking about their life after the genocide, but Vincent spent a significant portion of the interview talking about his genocide experiences, mentioning the camps he had been in and how he managed to survive life in several camps. Throughout this, Vincent used language and talked in a way that was consistent with a range of Holocaust testimony. For example, he began his talk by explaining what life was like before the genocide; then when he arrived at Auschwitz, he talked of people being chosen to live or die by "the flick of a thumb" and made regular reference to 'luck' and survival being a matter of luck, rather than judgement. These are all common markers of a 'standard' Holocaust testimony, along with a representation of the group experience. For example, in the documentary *Britain's Holocaust Survivors* (2013), Freddie Knoller started his testimony with the phrase "My story is the story of the six million". Vincent also gave this impression in his interview, saying,

> When we talk about the Holocaust, the Shoah, we speak about the greatest tragedy.

Later in his interview for the current project, Vincent did discuss his life afterwards and continued to use "we" rather than "I".

> Most of us … who remain here, we try to put the past aside and try to make our way in life, to be successful, and I can tell you that most of us managed to do that. Some of us continued with studies, and they went to university, and we even produced three university lecturers and some dentists and doctors. We all became successful; we managed to get on in life, find wives and bring up families.

This illustrates that for Vincent the survival experience was a group one, rather than a varied, singular experience. As a result, Vincent established his right to be included in that field by discussing his concentration camp experiences but locating them in the group experience.

However, some survivors such as Sarah actively resisted the status and label of 'survivor' in her day-to-day life.

> I want to be just me, not a survivor… to friends. Yes, I've had that experience, but I'm also somebody else too, I haven't been stuck in that frame … I don't see myself as a survivor … I've done quite a lot of things that removed me from that survivor mentality.

Despite this, Sarah is still a part of the genocide survivor field, giving regular talks about her experiences to schools and community groups. However, Sarah appeared to reject the notion of being dominant in that field, arguing instead that she had moved on from that role and mentality. Sarah was liberated from Bergen-Belsen, having survived a slave labour camp and also spent some time in Auschwitz. These 'survivor credentials' meant that if she wanted she could have claimed a dominant place in the survivor field. Instead, she chose to resist that role, instead preferring a lesser space in the survivor field instead. Allied to this is the development of a survivor hierarchy that is particularly related to Holocaust survivors. This hierarchy, while sometimes serving as a unifying force for survivors who needed to feel part of a larger group, it also served to exclude some survivors because they lacked the 'required' experiences (i.e. having experienced life in a camp, especially Auschwitz). Again, this illustrates the linguistic habitus in action. Some survivors' talk was recognised as being 'valid' by other survivors and the wider society, and this speech was able to set agendas and narratives resulting in metanarratives relating to the genocides they experienced. Conversely, those whose talk was not recognised found that they had less ability to set agendas and structure narratives, finding that they had 'less' symbolic capital to draw on than others. For example, Jack mentioned that other survivors had said to him that he should not be speaking as a Holocaust survivor because he had not experienced life in a camp. Survivors of the Holocaust who had the most symbolic capital were those who had experienced life in a well-known camp such as Auschwitz, as well as experiencing the deprivations of ghetto life and then the 'death marches' following liberation. These survivors could be seen as being linguistically competent in Bourdieuian terms. This is about producing the right talk for the right situation and the capacity to make oneself heard and believed. Some ways of talking are a way of participating or acting in a ritual, the conditions of which are defined by an institution and the power that speech acts have come from the social structure of which the speech is a part. Those forms of expression which hold the highest value and secure the most significant profit for the speaker are those which are most unequally distributed, regarding both the expressions themselves being rare and the conditions in which to acquire those forms of expression being rare or restricted. For genocide survivors, the forms of expression that hold or receive the greatest value are those which have several markers of the archetypal survivor experience: life in Auschwitz, being selected for work, and the loss of a large section of a family. These are experiences that together are relatively rare and indicate a dominant place in the survivor hierarchy. Because of this dominance, they are seen to speak for survivors as a group.

In excluding some survivors, this hierarchy serves to limit the field of genocide survivors by preventing them from accessing groups of individuals who could aid the development of social capital and equally prevent survivors from accessing peer support from other survivors. For those survivors who are perceived to be near the top of the hierarchy, their views are sought out more, and they are often more in demand when it comes to speaking about their experiences in educational settings. They are, in Bourdieuian terms, the 'noble of the group', and for Bourdieu, "the noble is the group personified. He bears the name of the group to which he gives his name" (Bourdieu 1986: 252). Essentially, Bourdieu argues that the elite set the rules and limits of the field. Fields allow one form of capital to be 'cashed in' or converted into another. Where there are sites of struggles, individuals seek to maintain or alter the distribution of the forms of capital specific to that field. Individuals within the struggle have different aims; some wish to preserve the status quo, and others wish to change it, with differing chances of success. Despite this struggle, all individuals in a field share common presuppositions; they believe in the 'game' they are playing, and believe in the value of what is at stake in the struggles they are waging. Because of this, if survivors do not believe in the game, or value the game within a field, they withdraw from the field. Some survivors are the genocide survivor group personified. They are the elite, the ones who have the sought-after stories, and they bear the name of the group; they are survivors. However, other survivors do not have the relevant linguistic habitus, and they can either contest the legitimacy of the dominant language by refusing to recognise it or try to fit in and euphemise expressions by putting them into forms that are acceptable to the market (Topper 2001). In this project, both these approaches are evident, with survivors such as Vincent ensuring that their narrative matches the accepted narrative of the Holocaust survivor and reinforcing the 'group' nature of his experiences throughout the interview.

Other survivors such as Lili and Tabitha contested the legitimacy of the initial silence of Holocaust survivors by talking about their experiences to their families and, in Tabitha's experience, to other community groups too. Thus, individuals found space in private life where their illegitimate linguistic products became legitimate. However, the formal linguistic law reimposed itself upon individuals once they left that unregulated area. For example, while survivors talked about their experiences within their families, their talk, and thus symbolic capital, was not recognised beyond the confines of the family. For discourse to exist, it has to be socially acceptable, meaning that it is heard and believed within a given state of relations. Thus, some survivors' discourse and resulting linguistic product become affected by the anticipation of sanctions from the wider field; that is, survivors modify their speech in anticipation of its likely reception. This is most clearly seen in Tabitha's experiences, wherein she initially began talking about her experiences to the local population but found that they were not recognised, so she modified and, in several instances, silenced herself because of her perceptions of how she would be received. Tabitha and survivors like her did this to be seen as part of the 'normal' population, to fit in and re-establish themselves with the minimum of upheaval. Thus, Tabitha's experiences show that those who do not believe in the game or value the game within a field may withdraw from the field. This can also be seen when considering that there are a significant number of genocide survivors in the UK, yet proportionally very few of them speak in public about their experiences. Many do not believe in the 'survivor talk' game that others are involved in. Others may accept and believe in the game and value what is at stake, but be unable to achieve dominance in that field because their experiences do not 'qualify' them to be a member of that field.

The survivors' inability to talk when they first arrived in the UK, and, conversely, being expected to talk as soon as they arrived, can be seen as an act of 'symbolic violence'. Bourdieu and Wacquant (1992) coined this term to refer to acts that lead to the misrecognition of reality or a distortion of underlying power relations. Through acts of symbolic violence being committed by those who have symbolic power, a misrecognised vision of the social world is legitimated, one that reproduces a stratified social order. Some Holocaust survivors in this study indicated that they did not talk officially for a long period following their arrival in the UK, and Bourdieu's concept of symbolic violence aids the understanding of why this was so. The overall, dominant narrative after the war was one of 'moving on' and leaving the past behind. As already mentioned earlier, 'everyone' had a war story, so survivors were perceived as nothing different to the larger population. In addition to this, official recognition of the survivors by the government would have led to further questions about the UK's lack of involvement and reluctance to rescue more Jews. This failure to recognise the extreme nature of Holocaust survivors' experiences can be understood as an act of symbolic violence by the government and wider society and resulted in a misrecognised social world wherein survivors were merely migrants with the same experiences as those who had not been targeted; everyone was simply a victim of war. It was only when those in powerful positions, such as Stephen Spielberg and the UK government, began acknowledging Holocaust survivors' experiences as 'different' that they became more widespread and Holocaust survivors became in high demand. Survivor practices, like all practices, are the result of the encounter between a habitus and a field. Initially, for Holocaust survivors, the habitus involved talking about their experiences because everybody was doing that, but those in their field did not wish to listen. This resulted in a lack of congruence between the habitus and the field, and as a result, survivors chose not to speak 'officially' or in public. Later, as seen above, the conditions of the field change, and as a result, there is a greater congruence between the habitus and field, which facilitates survivor talk.

Nationality and Alienation

Alienation, the idea that one finds oneself separate from society, highly isolated and with low integration, was a very clear thread throughout the life stories, and Kitty in particular found it very difficult to fit into the 'accepted' way of life when she was training to be a nurse in the UK.

> From their point of view I must have seemed an alien creature. It was difficult for me to be polite and deferential. In the world of the concentration

> camp there had been no courtesies … From a world of ceaseless bullying and shouting, of beatings and hunger and hatred, it was hard to adjust to artificial politeness, manners and mannerisms.

As well as the sense of alienation survivors feel as a result of the genocide, they are often subjected to further alienation due to the migration experience, with immigrants being "regarded as outsiders, as different, marginal to the mainstream of English society" (Holdaway 2003: 140). Halima experienced exactly this and struggled to understand everyday life in England. She found London a strange place.

> No one ever said 'hello'. People didn't even seem to speak with their neighbours. They just went around with a face like a closed mask. There was none of the spontaneous warmth that I was used to in my village.

These experiences served to alienate her from her new host society. Halima could not be part of her birth society, but neither could she feel fully engaged in her new country. This is something which was also common during the Second World War, as Laqueur observed that those who came to the UK as refugees say that they do not truly feel at home in Britain, but feel even less at home elsewhere (Laqueur 2004). He goes on to cite the comment of one refugee who indicated he felt that the British are one of the nicest people on earth, but "one will forever remain an alien for them unless one was born among them" (Laqueur 2004: 198). There is a gap between the migrant and host society that appears to be unbridgeable, with refugees forever seen as "foreigners with British passports" (Laqueur 2004: 195).

As well as the survivor identity, nationality is also an essential factor for survivors. Laqueur's suggestion of a gap between the migrant and the host society leads to a consideration of how those who experience genocide and migrate to the UK resettle and re-establish their lives. In particular, it drives the question of whether migrants ever consider themselves British, or how well they feel they have integrated into British society. Generally, migrants have the problem of not knowing where they belong, often seeming not to belong to the country of origin, or the host country. This can often be in a legal sense in that they may not have citizenship in either country; this was exemplified by Trude, who spent 12 years stateless after the war had ended. However, this gap can also be an emotional one, with some migrants feeling little or no emotional connection with their host country. Krzyzanowski and Wodak suggest that "migration implies constant mobility and instability, an often endless search for belonging to the constantly changing other, as well as having to cope with constantly shifting legal and bureaucratic requirements for social acceptance and divergent parameters for recognition" (2007, 97). Hence, migration alone brings with it difficulties of knowing where to fit in and a recurrent instability in an already-unstable life. The added experience of genocide, where individuals have been targeted because of who they are, adds a further layer of confusion to individuals' understandings of their identity, with the violence violating understandings of identity and relations with community as well as the individual violation (Veale 2000). Trude referred to this at the end of her account when she discussed her son's suicide.

> I blame Hitler for his death. Because of the Holocaust, Ilan [Trude's son] lacked the support which grandparents and an extended family normally provide. Even from me he was constantly separated through all the predicaments. I am convinced that if I had been able to give him more security and a feeling of belonging, he would not have been driven to an early death.

The genocide and subsequent forced migration had left Trude feeling unable to imbue her family with a sense of belonging—a sense of who they were in the world. This, she felt, was a direct result of the Holocaust. Illuminée, however, identified what she should have been, rather than what she was, saying, "I should be a traditional Rwandan mum surrounded by a noisy brood of children." Interestingly, however, she also embraced her new nationality, stating, "When I went to Brussels in 2006, I was asked my nationality. I was proud to say I am British." Illuminée did not indicate what being 'British' meant to her, and whether it was merely a statement of nationality or a deeper understanding of citizenship which involved a recreation of identity in line with the characteristics, values and beliefs of the British national identity. Nonetheless, the identity was positive. There was no single pattern to the methods and experiences of adaptation regarding nationality, and consequently, the experiences of the survivors in this research are quite individualistic. While all survivors discussed changes in their identity and nationality, the changes themselves varied depending upon survivors' genocide and migration experiences. Several Holocaust survivors rejected their birth nationality, not wishing to be identified with that nationality because of their previous experiences. For example, when asked about her nationality, Tabitha immediately replied,

> Hungarian I definitely never felt, because they treated me so abominably so that I said I don't want to go back.

Tabitha remained stateless for some years before she eventually gained British citizenship. One other participant in this research indicated they had become stateless following the war. Rebecca indicated that

> after the war, without nationality, you couldn't get a passport and I had to travel with an A4-sized sheet of paper with 'person of no nationality' written across the top which I bitterly resented. It makes you feel so inferior when everybody else takes a shiny passport out of their pocket.

Others, like Jack, rejected their previous nationality because of the country's actions both at the time of the genocide and more recently.

> Hungary has taken a turn right politically in the last couple of years in a particularly bad way. I mean I am proud of the culture of Hungary, the music of Hungary, but I wouldn't like to go around saying 'I'm really Hungarian'. But I'm very happy to say I'm European.

Unlike Jack and Tabitha, Henry was happy to remain Austrian initially.

> When the war was over, and Austria became an independent country, I got myself an Austrian passport, because I was an Austrian citizen and entitled to one … in 1949 I applied for naturalisation [in the UK], and I swore my allegiance to the King.

When asked whether he now saw himself as British, Henry replied,

> Oh, 100%, 100%. Except for my love of Viennese music, which hasn't gone away.

It is interesting that Henry sees a love of Austrian music as being 'non-British' and this seems to be his link with his previous 'Austrian' habitus; he has become wholly British except for this love of Viennese music, and this enables him to recognise his heritage and live his current life at the same time.

Lili still saw herself as Polish, despite having lived in the UK for over 50 years. She asked herself the question "what are you?" and worked out what she is not, as a way of narrowing down her ideas about her nationality:

> I said French, I thought it was ridiculous, I've got a French passport, there's nothing, I mean I'm not really French. I speak the language but no accent, but I'm not French. So they say what are you, so you're Polish, but I'm not a Polish, like this Christopher (holds up St Christopher pendant), basically, as a Polish Christian we have the language, that was my language, but we were different people. We were as different in Poland as maybe if you were black here.

When asked if she felt British, her response was very emphatic:

> Not at all! Absolutely not at all! I mean basically what I am is a Polish Jew. I'm 74; it really doesn't matter. I decided many years ago that people … it's an opening of a conversation 'where do you come from?' and it's only an opening; basically, it just doesn't really matter.

Despite her assertion that nationality does not matter, in drawing out the differences between Polish Christians and Polish Jews, Lili presents herself as being in a niche; she is not merely Polish, she is a Polish Jew, and that is different to being 'just' Polish.

Other survivors felt wholly British and reflected upon that status, with Sarah saying,

> I'm British. I hold the good British values, the fairness, the decency, the kindness. I've seen a lot of kindness, goodness, so in that way, yes I am first and foremost British.

Vincent observed,

> I feel very British. I became British in 19 … late 1940s actually. I'm very loyal to Britain. I owe Britain a lot, because I've had every opportunity, had a very good life and freedom to live my life.

Both Sarah and Vincent tied their Britishness to the kindness and opportunities that being in Britain brought, making a choice to be British because Britain provided them with opportunity and safety, so their adoption of British nationality is an acknowledgement of the role the UK played in their survival. Zakiah also said his Britishness was a choice and explained that he supported England in football. When he is questioned about his loyalties by other people, Zakiah said that he replies by saying,

> "I am more British than you are," and they look at me as though I have gone completely off my head. I said, "Look, it's a simple thing. I'm here because I wanted to be here. I came here, and I wanted to be here. You are here because your mother happened to drop you here … I am so British that I go mad, even at cricket which most of my friends don't understand!"

In both these cases, the survivors saw their nationality both as a choice and as a reflection of their values. Zakiah emphasised his Britishness by talking of 'going mad for cricket', seeing cricket as a key identifier of Britishness. As discussed in Chap. 4, Henry also saw cricket as a very British pastime, but one which he never mastered. For Zakiah and Henry, cricket was a marker of Britishness, in terms of either Zakiah enjoying it or Henry being confused by it. This serves to illustrate the role of habitus; for Henry, his habitus did not initially 'fit' with the host society's way of being, and his experience of cricket brought this difference to the fore. Zakiah showed how his habitus developed and adapted over a number of years by mastering the rules of cricket. Henry never understood the game of cricket, and instead sought out other sporting and cultural opportunities such as swimming and concerts that were more familiar to his life in Austria. These activities aided his acculturation and adaptation in the UK.

For those who experienced the genocide in the former Yugoslavia and in Rwanda, nationality and identity became a much more complicated issue. Returning to their home country is still an option that is open to survivors, and not enough time has passed for some survivors to acculturate to their new country and nationality fully. Sefik regularly returns to Bosnia on holiday, but when asked about whether he still saw Bosnia as home, he said,

> I don't know … To be honest, most of my life I've spent living in the UK, here in England, so … I don't know, to be honest.

When asked what nationality he saw himself, Sefik replied,

> I am a British citizen now. I was born, obviously I was born back in Bosnia, but I've been a British citizen now for, I don't know, eight, nine years. I have a British passport… There's still part of me that likes to call Bosnia home, and I think that will always remain, I don't think it will ever change, but most things that I have done in life I have done here now … I think my home is here now and I think that's going to remain for quite a few years.

Sefik's point here illustrates the difficulties that the more recent survivors have; they still have ties to their 'home' country but recognise that their life is now based in the host country. Julien also struggled to explain his nationality,

> I don't know who I am. To be Rwandan … to be honest, I don't know. Rwandan, of course, I'm Rwandan, that's where I came from but … what can I say, I don't have a big family there, I don't know.

For Julien, it seems that his Rwandan identity was his previous identity ("that's where I came from"), which is similar to Sefik's acknowledgement of Bosnia as where he was born. However, Julien had not as yet identified his current nationality or identity as he was still in transition. The lack of a family in Rwanda is one aspect that resulted in Julien not seeing himself as Rwandan; this illustrates the effect of the genocide beyond the conventional narratives. It is not just about the loss of a family but the impact of that in terms of the perception of the self. Julien indicated that having a large family in Rwanda would mean that he would be more likely to see himself as a Rwandan. Thus the genocide, as well as targeting him specifically for being a Tutsi, has also had an impact on his identity as a Rwandan because of the killing of his family. This is the same for Sefik, who has no close family left in Bosnia.

> Most of my family are still here [in the UK], that includes my mum, my sisters ... my brother still lives here ... I have relatives who live back home, in Bosnia but not what I would call immediate or close family.

Both survivors show that having family around can have an impact on how they see his/her self in terms of nationality. Furthermore, these two cases illustrate how the genocide has an impact beyond the immediate loss of family in terms of being able to identify with a nationality. Hence, the inclusion of survivors from more recent genocides has been invaluable, as it shows the temporal effects of migration; both Julien and Sefik were still unsure of their nationality, and in particular, where 'home' was.

Nationality for survivors is complicated. Some, such as Jack and Sarah, chose their identity because of their reaction to the actions and behaviours of their 'home' country. Lili was the only survivor who specifically said that they were happy to retain the nationality of their birth, which was, in Lili's case, a Polish Jew. Most survivors saw themselves as British; however, more recent survivors' identities still appear to be in a state of flux, with nationality being moveable as the survivor changes their own self-perception. Of course, it must be pointed out at this juncture that the majority of survivors in this project have lived in the UK for a considerable amount of time, with the Holocaust happening almost 70 years ago. This means that those survivors have had a significant amount of time in order to come to terms with the events and their nationality. Survivors of the later genocides may still view themselves as Rwandan or Bosnian simply because they have not lived in the UK long enough to see themselves as British. Furthermore, changes in the home countries of survivors may also have had an impact on their perception of their nationality. Rwanda and Bosnia are still in a state of flux, 20 years after the genocides occurred, and importantly, the governments of those countries are still managing the after-effects of the genocide in terms of the criminal culpability of the perpetrators. With respect to the Holocaust, whilst there have been recent trials (such as the case of John Demjanjuk, a Ukranian who was convicted in 2011 of being an accessory to war crimes during the Holocaust, or Reinhold Hanning, convicted in 2016 for facilitating the killing of at least 170,000 people), the perpetrators have, in the vast majority of cases, been identified and faced justice in some form. Hence, nationality is a complex phenomenon that cannot be simply explained by one single factor. What is important is that Bourdieu's ideas highlight the structures that influence a survivor's status in terms of their nationality. As has been seen, several of the survivors in this study rejected their birth nationality because of the behaviour of their country during the genocide, instead taking on the identity of the host country, in this case the UK. For these survivors, this was a conscious decision in order to reject their previous identity and begin to reconstruct themselves in the new country. This reconstruction is enabled by the habitus, the unconscious way of doing things. As survivors arrive in a new country, they often become aware that their habitus does not conform to the host country's general norms and there are subtle differences in the way that they do things such as the food they eat or the clothes they wear. For those who consciously take on the host country's nationality, the change in habitus becomes less disruptive as they are positively and actively seeking to acculturate and become similar to the general population of the host country. Other survivors, particularly those who do not expect to settle permanently in the UK, find the disruption in the habitus more challenging and often struggle to engage with the wider population.

The field of genocide survivors is a complex one that is, as Bourdieu (1989) suggests, a site of struggles over positions and capital as well as a slow redefining of identity in most cases. Nationality and the self-perception of nationality produced challenges, which the survivors in this study managed in different ways. This chapter will now move to consider how survivors come to talk about their experiences and how their field and habitus influence the construction of their narratives.

Talking

Schwartz Lee (1988) and Meierhenrich (2007) both note the impact of cultural trauma, which is where the emphasis is on the collective experience of trauma rather than the psychological impact. This section explores this cultural form of trauma, highlighting the distinction between individual and collective suffering and how cultural trauma is socially constructed in the aftermath of genocide.

Holocaust survivors were not initially expected to talk about their experiences in detail, and for many, their experiences were not acknowledged as valid even if they did talk about them. Often, survivors such as Kitty who arrived in the UK soon after the war were told that they should not talk about their experiences because they should not upset people. Others like Tabitha were just not believed. Many who came to the UK in the late 1940s found that their experiences were not perceived to be anything different to the deprivations experienced in the UK. For example, Jack explained his Holocaust experiences in Hungary to a man in the UK, who said, "You know things were difficult here, we sometimes couldn't get any cigarettes for weeks". This experience was not limited to this study, and several survivors have commented on it (Frankenthal 2002; Goldenberg 2009). Furthermore, this experience was not limited to the UK. In the setting up of the Auschwitz state museum in Poland in the late 1940s, it was decided to emphasise the mass victimhood of the Holocaust, rather than focusing on individual stories. This was because those who visited the camp just after the war had experienced war first-hand and had lived through it, "so the story of a single death did not necessarily move them, because they had seen so much death, in their families and in the streets, whereas the scale at Auschwitz was shocking" (Mrek Zajac interviewed in Kimmelman 2011: n.p.). This is in contrast to today where those in the UK are mostly unfamiliar with mass death through war and, hence, are much more receptive to individual stories, as evidenced by the popularity of biographies in the 'tragic life stories' vein.

When survivors in large numbers began speaking of their experiences, they had no point of reference to aid their understanding, so they modelled their testimonies on the few that had gone before them (Stern

1992). Survivors did not fully understand how to tell their stories, or whom to tell them to. At this point in time, there was not an event called 'The Holocaust' that they could situate themselves in (Stein 2009), and there was also a lack of a meaningful paradigm in order to evaluate the massacre of the Jews (Dubiel 2003). This meant that not only did survivors lack a framework on which to 'hang' their stories, but the listeners also lacked the conceptual understanding to appreciate the events of the Holocaust. One of the other problems that faced the early writers of testimonies is that people are used to stories with a moral and most Holocaust testimonies do not have a moral or at least a positive one. Whilst a survivor may have managed to survive, they usually had lost a significant amount of family and had to flee, leaving their possessions behind them. There was very little to be proud of, mainly as the majority of people viewed survivors with suspicion. Moreover, as Engelking-Boni and Paulsson (2001: 307) point out, "The end of all stories, irrespective of whether they are fairy tales or descriptors of certain events, usually have a moral, a point, a lesson which is why the story was told … A moral of this kind only achieves its intended goal if the story, event, recounted has a beginning and an end: it is only then that you can comprehend it and evaluate it". For survivors, their story does not have an end; they are still living it. Their testimony will forever be incomplete, and a collective understanding of the messages of the Holocaust needed to be constructed to allow these stories to be told. Felman and Laub (1992) concur, and suggest that as the genocide did not proceed through to completion, survivors live with an event that has no closure and therefore continues into the present. In order to recover from this trauma, survivors have to re-externalise the event by articulating and transmitting their story.

Sajjad (2009: 223) suggests that when a collective trauma is embedded in the social fabric of a group of people, there is a "central and paradoxical dialectic [consisting of] a desire to repress or deny what happened, as well as a perceived necessity to proclaim or speak loudly about the terrible events that occurred". Wajnryb (2001) suggests that literature on survivor testimonies says that either survivors talk all the time about the experiences or there is a total silence. In disagreeing with this, Wajnryb argues that there is a continuum of testimony speech in that there are times for talking and there are versions of talking. Moreover, the speaker may also choose to talk or not to talk based on the likely receptivity of the listener; "people will tell if the telling is allowed" (Wajnryb 2001: 173). Solomon (1995) found that in Israel immediately after the war, the reaction to Holocaust survivors was of indifference and repression. These attitudes resulted in survivors, who already felt abandoned and alienated, to choose to not speak about their experiences.

Therefore, survivors experience an inner conflict: to speak about their experience or to stay quiet. This choice is often influenced by the broader societal reaction to the event. If there is indifference to the situation, then stifling grief becomes both a group norm and a societal conspiracy (Goldenberg 2009), which Danieli (1981) described as 'a conspiracy of silence' which arose between and around survivors. Many survivors have never been asked about their experiences, even by members of their family. Others tried to talk but were not listened to by the wider community (Freedland 2011). For survivors, this inability to speak is compounded if the survivor has experienced sexual violence during the genocide due to the shame and secrecy that persists around those acts. Dan Bar-On (1998) suggests that in reality there were plenty of potential storytellers but few audiences ready to hear their stories. Indeed, Solomon (1995) argues that sharing Holocaust experiences was the only way individuals could bridge the gulf between the Holocaust world they had existed in and the society they were rejoining.

However, others argue that people do not talk about their experiences of genocide because they are focused on the necessary rebuilding of life: the recreation of family and the securing of a stable place to live. Many survivors busied themselves with having children, gaining employment, and generally building a healthy life (Freedland 2011). In addition, the realisation of the effects and losses of the genocide is gradual, and consequently, talking of such losses can only be done once they have been thoroughly understood (Goldenberg 2009).

When survivors do talk, many tell the same story several times over. Those who tell their stories to schools or community groups devise a speech that is rehearsed and practised, rather than an off-the-cuff telling of a life experience. Wajnryb (2001) argues that survivors only tell the stories that they have mastered the telling of, the ones that are in their comfort zones or, at least, only produce a manageable level of discomfort. What is heard when survivors give their testimony in this way is a prepackaged refrain of a shared story. "Given that this pattern is so widespread among the survivors one might conclude that the only way the accounts could happen is through being managed" (Wajnryb 2001: 197). Thus, Wajnryb argues here that survivors have to tell the collective story of the Holocaust because the personal story is too painful to recollect in full detail. Collectivising the story, and telling the 'story of the story', is the way that trauma survivors bridge the gap between the pain of their own experiences and the need to tell others of their experiences and of the experiences of those who died. Furthermore, the collectivisation of testimony is also a way that survivors convince others of the truthfulness of their own testimonies, there being strength in numbers. One story may be disbelieved, but a hundred people saying the same thing is harder to disbelieve.

The majority of Holocaust survivors in this research indicated that the reasons they did not initially talk about their experiences were due to a fear of not being believed.

> There are many reasons why we didn't talk … when we were 15, 16, if we had, have told people that 6 million Jews died, so many Poles died, 60% of the gypsy population … first of all we didn't know all this. But if we had said, even 10 million or 1 million I think people would have said "Well, he's 15, 16 years old, he is … exaggerating it".

Henry's experiences bore out Zakiah's reticence in talking.

> When we told people in company … our experiences so far, that we were thrown out of our schools and so on, they gave us the impression that they thought this was the imagination of the children, it can't really be happening.

Tabitha found that other Jews who had escaped the Kishinev pogrom in 1903 did not believe her.

> I told them what I knew at that point, and when I finished they clapped, and then one woman came up to me and said, "You know, my dear, you

> told us lots of things, I am sure half of it is true"… And that stopped me talking … because I thought, well, if these women and these were women who were survivors themselves, came after the Kishinev … the pogroms in Kishinev. That they went through something themselves and they didn't believe me. They didn't want to believe me. They were all the daughters of people who came from Kishinev, and they couldn't believe me.

Judith acknowledged that she did not believe her father, let alone anyone else:

> My father told us he had been interned in a camp near Anasee … When he told me as a child, things would come up; I just thought it was fantasy. He told us he'd bribed the guards, it all sounded complete fantasy.

This is perhaps surprising, but Judith was very young when her parents fled Belgium via Vichy France and Spain and finally to the US. Because of this, Judith had very few memories of life before living in the US, so her father's stories must have appeared very fanciful to her as a teenager, primarily as there was not a common knowledge of what had occurred during the genocide at that time. This illustrates a particular form of habitus, the linguistic habitus. This form of habitus is centred upon how individuals speak and what is said and is the embodiment of cultural capital. Hence, the linguistic habitus is a set of dispositions that are acquired as speech is learnt within particular contexts (Bourdieu 1991).

The linguistic habitus operates within a market and becomes apparent when individuals either speak in a way that is different to the norm or talk of things which challenge 'official' or 'accepted' narratives around an event. For the survivors in this research, their speech was not valued, and their linguistic habitus resulted in their stories either not being heard at all or not taken 'seriously' by society in general.

Lili said, "I've never had a problem talking about my time in the war," which initially gave the impression that she had been talking about her experiences since they happened, but in reality, she talked to her family rather than anyone else. Tabitha's experiences also reflected this, and she separated out 'talking' and 'talking officially'.

> I found that people didn't want to know, and didn't believe me anyway. Then I stopped talking … I suppose I never really stopped talking, but I stopped talking officially.

By talking officially, it seems that Tabitha meant talking in public, to groups of people, because later she spoke of how she began to talk at conferences in the 1980s. Tabitha's linguistic habitus was initially not accepted by the wider community. However, due to wider structural changes in society such as the trial of Adolf Eichmann (one of the principal Nazi architects of the Holocaust) in Israel in the early 1960s and the inclusion of the study of the Holocaust as a compulsory topic in the National Curriculum for England and Wales, she and her testimony were then increasingly accepted, especially in education.

> Then *Schindler's List* came. The schools did not open to us before *Schindler's List*, so when *Schindler's List* came the doors were opened, and I started speaking really in very many places, and since then I haven't stopped.

The Eichmann trial is recognised as being a turning point in the recognition of survivor experiences. During the trial, the testimony of survivors was broadcast in minute detail across Israel and the wider world. The US Holocaust Memorial Museum and *Schindler's List* both opened in 1993. Following the opening of the museum, there were questions around why the suffering of the Jews was being privileged over the experiences of Africans and the Native Americans. This again highlights the notion of a victim hierarchy, but this time with the victims of different groups arguing that they should be recognised. Despite these issues, the Hollywood transformation of Thomas Keneally's (1982) book, *Schindler's Ark* into the film *Schindler's List* radically changed the survivor speaking landscape. The film grossed over $300 million worldwide and won seven Oscars. The number of talks given by survivors has increased notably over the past 20 years, with 700 schools booking a survivor talk through the Holocaust Educational Trust in 2015–2016. Zakiah saw the work of this organisation as particularly important.

> One thing led to another; there were exhibitions. Would you like to man the exhibition? We said, "Yes, we'll come once a week or twice a week." And then the synagogues asked, not many because even today they don't, synagogues as such. But the most important thing, which is already 20 years, the Holocaust Educational Trust started.

Thus the survivors' linguistic habitus became increasingly accepted, and survivors are now sought out as an important source of information on the Holocaust. Bourdieu argued: "A language is worth what those who speak it are worth" (1977: 652), and this can be seen here as the value of genocide survivors' testimony increases as the wider population express a desire to hear their narratives. Survivors soon became more in demand, and as a result, the value of their stories increased, and they held more symbolic capital. The value of Holocaust survivors' testimony is now at a point where survivors and their testimony are seen as honourable and distinguished. For example, Elie Wiesel, a well-known Holocaust survivor who has published several autobiographical books about his survival, was in 2013 awarded Israel's highest civilian honour for his contribution to Holocaust memorialisation. Genocide survivors' testimonies are seen as 'inspirational' or 'powerful', with survivors being perceived by the wider society as 'remarkable' or 'indomitable'. This change in attitudes shows how the value of genocide survivors' testimony has increased significantly, and subsequently some survivors hold a significant level of symbolic capital.

However, survivors also indicated that the reasons they did not talk were sometimes practical, as Zakiah outlined:

> We started work, and then we started bringing up a family, so we had no time to do … And there was nowhere really you could go to talk because schools didn't teach the Holocaust. So we didn't speak, and then, of course, the children were born. "Can we talk about it?" "No, too young."

As noted previously, survivors initially focused on re-establishing their lives—finding homes, gaining employment and providing for their families—rather than talking about their experiences. This is unsurprising and is clearly illustrated by Maslow's hierarchy of needs. Maslow argued that individuals are motivated to achieve specific needs, with basic needs such as biological and physiological needs taking priority over self-esteem, acceptance of facts and creativity (Maslow 1970). Only when these basic physiological and biological needs are satisfied are individuals motivated to achieve other needs, such as independence and personal growth. Here, survivors only began to talk about their experiences once they had achieved their basic needs of security and stability.

Jack recalls a conversation he had with a historian:

> Now we have a sort of Holocaust industry … we have school visits, we have visits to Auschwitz, we have plaques, and we have films, and we have radio … There was nothing in the '50s, or in the '60s or even the '70s … why not? And he said, "Well, it's due to people like you. All the survivors came to England and all they wanted to do was to leave the past behind, build up their lives, get married and have children and grandchildren."

Again, the practicalities of life are a justification for not talking about their experiences immediately after the genocide. However, two survivors from this study, Tabitha and Lili, indicated that they carried on talking, just not 'officially', so it is suggested that survivors felt they had to leave the past behind because their narratives were not being recognised in most circles and this caused problems for their recovery. Nutkiewicz's (2003) argument that some survivors do not bury their past but silence themselves can also illustrate the issue here. Therefore, for these two survivors, the best response was to cease talking officially in order to prevent the challenges to their linguistic habitus that could cause problems for the re-establishment of their lives and their identities. For others, such as Rebecca, there was no conscious choice not to talk, but a public silence meant that the genocide just was not discussed.

> We weren't able to talk after the war; this is very well known and documented. Parents and children, even adults, were not able to talk about the past. The past was taboo.

There was a presumption that individuals could not talk about the past because they were too traumatised. However, Rebecca's phrase "the past was taboo" seems to suggest that rather than people unable to talk because they could not find the words, people did not talk because they were not expected to talk. Judith also suggested this when talking about the school she attended after the war:

> The school I went to was a Jewish school … The school was very orthodox, and a lot of the teachers were refugees. But it was like a communal silence. No one spoke about it.

This collective silence appeared to be mainly focused on children, as Judith observed:

> You know as children you haven't suffered, that was the attitude. "You survived, be grateful, shut up, get on with it." Actually, I thought I was the only person that had gone through this because it just wasn't spoken about or anything.

Thus, for some child survivors like Judith, the public silence following the genocide served to isolate them even further than they already felt as new migrants. Equally, when survivors' experiences are not recognised because talk is prevented, they are unable to see themselves as part of a wider group, and the identity of 'survivor' may not be accessible for them. Talk aids resettlement because individuals understand they are not alone; they are part of a community who have similar experiences. Yet, the experiences of survivors of more recent genocides such as Rwanda are still quite overwhelming. Julien runs a support group for Rwandan survivors and felt that Rwandan survivors were different to Holocaust survivors.

> It's very difficult because we … erm … in general, survivors we are … opened … we are not there yet. When you talk to Holocaust survivors, they start talking … they only have a few left, so just start talking about what happened, even the second generation is doing that the whole thing. It's hard for [Rwandan] survivors to come forward; it's very difficult at the moment to find survivors who are involved in schools and communities.

As Julien suggests above, Rwandans have not had the time or space to begin to assimilate and understand their experiences fully. In contrast, Lili suggested that whilst telling the story can be draining and upsetting, it is possible to get past this, and for some survivors like Lili "it becomes the story of the story of the story, it's their way of living". It seems that the 'story of the story' is something that develops the more the story is told; therefore it is only something that comes after an extended period of time and individuals are able to detach themselves from their experiences. For survivors of more recent genocides, this is difficult as they are expected to talk about their experiences almost as soon as they have arrived in the UK, either to Border Agency officials in order to gain refugee status or because the wider society expects to hear about these events from those who were there, that is, the eyewitness accounts. Therefore, Holocaust survivors talking about their experiences was a gradual development, aided by changing societal attitudes and a realisation that survivors were growing older and there was a need to hear their stories before there were no survivors left. Survivors of previous genocides have had much more time to process and understand their experience than survivors from later genocides such as Rwanda or Bosnia.

Julien's experience is particularly interesting because whilst he was working to support other survivors when asked about his own needs, he was less forthcoming:

> I was talking to a friend of mine from, the director of the Medical Foundation. We always send people to him, and he said, "You know, I never know about your story," and I said—his name is Alex—"Alex, what do you mean by that?" "I've never known your story." "Alex, I'm fine, don't worry about me."

Julien married his wife, also a survivor, five years after he arrived in the UK. Despite both of them having experienced the genocide, they have not talked about it with each other.

> Me and my wife haven't talked about it, so we have these holes … I don't like to ask her about her experience. But if she asks, I can tell her.

Julien's last point, "If she asks, I can tell her", is particularly puzzling, especially given other survivors in this study indicated that even when they had stopped talking in public, they still talked about their experiences with their families. As both Julien and his wife are survivors, it may be that they are both aware of the impact of the genocide and therefore do not need to know the specific details of what happened to their spouse.

For Zakiah, talking is also a way of repaying the debt of being alive.

> I am happy that I started because I feel I owe so much. I survived, others didn't. I mean so many people have got nobody to talk about them, about their stories, because their whole family was wiped out and there's nobody there … So far, I am able [to talk] so … I feel I am giving something back for being lucky to survive.

Here, Zakiah's debt to those who died is repaid by talking about their experiences and hence there is a moral obligation to tell others of their experiences. Sarah also talked because of this moral obligation:

> I think it's some sort of moral duty perhaps, as a survivor, to do it. I feel that it is … I've been granted life which I cherish … It's difficult, it's a moral obligation, but at the same time I've got to think about.

The tension between leaving the past behind and talking about the past is particularly evident in Sarah's view. On the one hand, she felt honour-bound to discuss her experiences and tell others of what happened. On the other, she felt that it was time to move on and that talking was having an adverse effect on her as she grew older. Like Sarah, Tabitha also talked about the challenges of continuing to talk about her experiences whilst facing the realities of ageing.

> I can distance myself [emotionally] in a way, but it's physically I just can't do it anymore. It's happened to me twice this year, where I was about to tell my story when I suddenly went completely blank, I had no idea where I was, what I was talking about and I had to cut out … But I still don't want to give up, quite give up.

The retelling of the story induces a physical toll on individuals; it drains them and adds stress to other physical impairments. The pressure to talk draws on the nature of the collectivity of genocide survivors, wherein survivors feel they have a duty to represent the group of survivors when they are talking. However, alongside talking, other significant issues may affect how survivor identities adapt. The recognition of the survivor status is dependent upon survivors being permitted to talk about their experiences so that the broader society becomes aware of what happened during the genocide and how it affected individuals. Bourdieu argues that all linguistic exchanges between individuals are imbued with socially structured resources and competencies (Bourdieu 1991). This means that every conversation and speech 'event' bears traces of the social structure it expresses and helps to reproduce. This chapter has found that whether an individual is allowed to talk about their experiences and whether they are heard in an appropriate way is underpinned by Bourdieu's concepts of the linguistic habitus and symbolic capital. When survivors talk about their experiences, they express and reproduce the social structure which 'governs' survivor talk. In speaking of their experiences, survivors unconsciously reproduce the conventional narrative and reinforce the conditions and expectations of survivor talk. Many survivors attempted to speak of their experiences as soon as the genocide had finished, but found that their speech was not recognised. For those who experienced the Holocaust, this was often because 'everyone had a war story' and therefore the survivors' stories were perceived to be no different from the 'usual' war stories which everyone throughout Europe had, and therefore, the survivor held no distinctive symbolic capital which could mark them out as remarkable. Thus, survivors themselves were unable to have their survivor status recognised, resulting in most survivors in the current study ceasing their attempts to talk for a number of years. As times changed and cultural 'events' happened, such as the reunification of Germany and the release of the film *Schindler's List*, some survivors found that their linguistic habitus became acceptable to, and even desired by, the wider society, who were ready to listen to the survivors' experiences. Hence, their symbolic capital began to develop, and certain survivors became well known as genocide survivors. As survivor testimony is rooted in early forms of testimony alongside current structural barriers, any consideration of testimony needs to bear this in mind and avoid the illusion of 'linguistic communism'. The concept of linguistic communism results when an individual takes a particular set of linguistic practices as the normative model, producing the illusion of a common language and ignoring the socio-historical conditions which have established a particular set of linguistic practices as dominant and legitimate. It is here where it can be understood how talk aids resettlement. By having their experiences taken seriously and recognised allows the survivor to be seen as 'valid'. When talk is not accepted or believed, the survivor's identity is challenged and disrupted. When survivors are unable to talk about their experiences, their disrupted habitus becomes evident as there is a break between who the survivor was and whom they need to be. As discussed earlier, denial of a survivor status by authorities such as the Border Agency or compensatory authorities means that individual feels that their experiences during the genocide have no validity, and hence their entire identity becomes problematic. This is because they have to work out a new identity that does not involve their genocide experiences.

Genocide survivors often find meaning in their status as a survivor, and those who hold a significant amount of symbolic capital find that their survivor status can be used to good effect in terms of talking about their experiences to large groups of people. There is often a particular point at which the survivors' linguistic habitus becomes acceptable to wider society, and their symbolic capital increases.

The hierarchy of Holocaust survivors often proves exclusionary, and whilst it is a way for some survivors to receive acknowledgement that they have experienced suffering, others do not receive that recognition because they do not hold the symbolic capital (through their experiences) which would facilitate this recognition. Survivors are often expected to fit a particular framework and those who do not fit often appear 'lesser' in some way, wherein they are told they should not be representing the survivor community. This again limits their speech and controls who hears their story. The competition within the survivor field is one of competition for resources, the resources being audiences who will hear their story and take their 'message' out to other people.

It is evident that survivors need to be allowed to talk about their experiences, but in their own time and at their own pace. Enforced silence or enforced talking is unhelpful for survivors who feel forced into an identity that may not reflect their current status. This is particularly important for the survivors from Rwanda, as the means and ends of counselling for Rwandan survivors may well differ from the expectations of Western counsellors and their focus on individualist approaches, focusing on cognitive modification, which emphasises independence. Instead, they may require a more 'community'-based approach that is more appropriate and reflective of Rwandan traditions and culture.

Finally, genocide survivors' understanding of justice and forgiveness is primarily tied to the acceptance of events by the wider society. When events are not recognised by the powerful in society, this produces acts of symbolic violence that further results in the distortion of the events and reproduce the stratified social order in which some survivors are at the bottom, with their experiences having no validity. This results in some survivors not being recognised, and they, therefore, lack the symbolic capital that others hold and as a result are unable to impose their version of the social world upon the wider society.

References

Bar-On, D. (1998). Transgenerational Aftereffects of the Holocaust in Israel. In E. Sicher (Ed.), *Breaking Crystal: Writing and Memory After Auschwitz*. Illinois: University of Illinois Press.

Bourdieu, P. (1977). Economics of Linguistic Exchanges. *Social Science Information, 16*(6), 645–668.

Bourdieu, P. (1984). *Distinction: A Social Critique of the Judgement of Taste*. USA: Harvard University Press.

Bourdieu, P. (1986). The Forms of Capital. In J. G. Richardson (Ed.), *Handbook of Theory and Research for the Sociology of Education* (pp. 241–258). London: Greenwood Press.

Bourdieu, P. (1989). Social Space and Symbolic Power. *Sociological Theory, 7*(1), 14–25.

Bourdieu, P. (1991). *Language and Symbolic Power* (J. B. Thompson, Ed.). Cambridge: Polity Press.

Bourdieu, P., & Wacquant, L. (1992). *An Invitation to Reflexive Sociology*. Cambridge: Polity Press.

Britain's Holocaust Survivors. (2013). *Directed by Daisy Asquith*. London; Channel 4 27th January, 9pm 2013. Retrieved from https://vimeo.com/106264980.

Cohen, S. (2001). *States of Denial: Knowing About Atrocities and Suffering*. Cambridge: Polity Press.
Colic-Piesker, V., & Walker, I. (2003). Human Capital, Acculturation and Social Identity: Bosnian Refugees in Australia. *Journal of Community and Applied Social Psychology, 13*(5), 337–360.
Danieli, Y. (1981, Sept–Oct). Differing Adaptational Styles in Families of Survivors of the Nazi Holocaust. *Child Today, 10*(5), 6–10.
Dubiel, H. (2003). The Remembrance of the Holocaust as a Catalyst for a Transnational Ethic. *New German Critique, 90*(Autumn), 59–70.
Engelking-Boni, B., & Paulsson, G. S. (2001). *Holocaust and Memory: The Experience of Holocaust and Its Consequences. An Investigation Based on Personal Narratives*. Leicester: Leicester University Press.
Fackenheim, E., & Huttenbach, H. R. (1999). Who Is a Survivor? *Journal of Genocide Research, 1*(3), 463–464.
Felman, S., & Laub, D. (1992). *Testimony: Crises of Witnessing in Literature, Psychoanalysis, and History*. New York: Routledge.
Foxton, W. (2013, March 26). The Farce of UK Immigration Policy: Letting in Parasites, Turning Away Entrepreneurs. *The Telegraph*.
Frank, A. (1997). *The Wounded Storyteller*. Chicago: University of Chicago Press.
Frankenthal, H. (2002). *The Unwelcome One: Returning Home from Auschwitz*. Illinois: NW University Press.
Freedland, J. (2011, May 14). Safe House. *The Guardian*.
Goldenberg, J. (2009). "I Had No Family But I Made Family" Immediate Post War Coping Strategies of Adolescent Survivors of the Holocaust. *Counselling and Psychotherapy Research, 9*(1), 18–26.
Holdaway, S. (2003). Victimisation Within Constabularies in England and Wales: The Legacy of Immigration. *International Review of Victimology, 10*(2), 137–159.
Janoff-Bulman, R., & Hanson Frieze, I. (1983). A Theoretical Perspective for Understanding Reactions to Victimisation. *Journal of Social Issues, 39*(2), 1–17.
Keneally, T. (1982). *Schindler's Ark*. Sydney: Hodder and Stoughton.
Kimmelman, M. (2011). Auschwitz Shifts from Memorialising to Teaching. *New York Times* [Online]. Retrieved December 27, 2018, from http://www.nytimes.com/2011/02/19/arts/19auschwitz.html?pagewanted=all&_r=0.
Klocker, N., & Dunn, K. (2003, November). Who's Driving the Asylum Debate? Newspaper and Government Representations of Asylum Seekers. *Media International Australia, 109*, 71–92. Retrieved October 28, 2018, from http://www.uws.edu.au/__data/assets/pdf_file/0010/26956/A17.pdf.

Krzyzanowski, M., & Wodak, R. (2007). Multiple Identities, Migration and Belonging: "Voices of Migrants". In C. Caldas-Coulthard & R. Iedema (Eds.), *Identity Trouble: Critical Discourse and Contested Identities* (pp. 95–115). London: Palgrave Macmillan.

Laqueur, W. (2004). *Generation Exodus: The Fate of Young Jewish Refugees from Nazi Germany*. London: IB Tauris & Co. Ltd.

Maslow, A. H. (1970). *Motivation and Personality*. New York: Harper and Row.

Meierhenrich, J. (2007). The Trauma of Genocide. *Journal of Genocide Research, 9*(4), 549–573.

Novick, P. (2007). Theoretical Perspectives on Victimisation. In S. Walklate (Ed.), *Handbook of Victims and Victimology*. Cullompton: Willan Publishers.

Nutkiewicz, M. (2003). Shame, Guilt and Anguish in Holocaust Survivor Testimony. *Oral History Review, 30*(1), 1–22.

Sajjad, T. (2009). The Post-Genocidal Period and Its Impact on Women. In S. Totten (Ed.), *Plight and Fate of Women During and Following Genocide* (pp. 219–230). New Jersey: Transaction Publishers.

Schwartz Lee, B. (1988). Holocaust Survivors and Internal Strengths. *Journal of Humanistic Psychology, 28*(1), 67–96.

Shephard, B. (2010). *The Long Road Home*. London: Bodley Head.

Sicher, E. (1998). *Breaking Crystal: Writing and Memory After Auschwitz*. Illinois: Urbana.

Skjelsbaek, I. (2006). Victim and Survivor: Narrated Social Identities of Women Who Experienced Rape During the War in Bosnia-Herzegovina. *Feminism & Psychology, 16*(4), 373–403.

Solomon, Z. (1995). From Denial to Recognition: Attitudes Toward Holocaust Survivors from World War II to the Present. *Journal of Traumatic Stress, 8*(2), 215–228.

Spalek, B. (2006). *Crime Victims: Theory, Policy & Practice*. Hampshire: Palgrave Macmillan.

Stein, A. (2009). As Far as They Knew I Came from France. *Symbolic Interaction, 32*(1), 44–60.

Stern, F. (1992). *The Whitewashing of the Yellow Badge: Antisemitism and Philo-Semitism in Postwar Germany*. New York: Pergamon.

Syal, R. (2014, October 26). British Towns Being "Swamped" by Immigrants, Says Michael Fallon. *The Guardian* [Online]. Retrieved January 19, 2019, from https://www.theguardian.com/uk-news/2014/oct/26/british-towns-swamped-immigrants-michael-fallon-eu.

Timotijevic, L., & Breakwell, G. M. (2000). Migration and Threat to Identity. *Journal of Community & Applied Social Psychology, 10*, 355–372.

Topper, K. (2001). Not So Trifling Nuances: Pierre Bourdieu, Symbolic Violence and the Perversions of Democracy. *Constellations, 8*(1), 30–56.

UN General Assembly. (1948). Convention on the Prevention and Punishment of the Crime of Genocide, 9 December 1948. *United Nations, Treaty Series, 78*, 277.

Veale, A. M. (2000). Dilemmas of Community in Post-Emergency Rwanda. *Community, Work & Family, 3*(3), 233–239.

Wajnryb, R. (2001). *Silence: How Tragedy Shapes Talk*. New South Wales: Allen and Unwin.

Yablonka, H. (1999). *Survivors of the Holocaust: Israel After the War*. New York: New York University Press.

7

Conclusion

Concluding Thoughts

The existing social capital of a genocide survivor undoubtedly aids resettlement for survivors and provides a basis from which survivors can build. However, in cases where individuals were not able to utilise their capital, survivors have tended to innovate and, where possible, subvert the 'normal' methods of resettlement, sometimes through illegal means or exploiting loopholes. Alongside this, cultural buffers such as family or individuals with similar experiences can assist in this shift of habitus. Where individuals do not have these buffers, acculturation and resettlement become more difficult because there is no link to a past identity which gives the survivor some sense of who they were, even if they are not sure who they are at the moment or will be in the future.

Unsurprisingly, education and employment also aid acculturation and the re-establishment of life, especially in terms of younger survivors accessing school; this aids language acquisition as well as helping survivors in building a social network. However, support from others who had been through similar experiences particularly aids survivors' resettlement and acculturation. Those survivors who had access to a group of people

L. Asquith, *Rebuilding Lives After Genocide*, Palgrave Studies in Compromise after Conflict, https://doi.org/10.1007/978-3-030-14074-8_7

who had had similar experiences found contact with that group enabling, with some survivors maintaining that friendship throughout their lives. Thus, survivors are best supported when they have access to a wide range of support services that include access to other survivors. This is important because the survivors in this project often found they did not have to explain their behaviours or feelings to this group, helping them to feel more 'at home' and 'normal'. Ager and Strang's 'Indicators of Integration' (2004) also supports this in terms of the domain of 'social connections', which emphasises bridges between the migrant and the community, but also the links between the migrant and the macrostructures of society as well as bonds between co-nationals or co-ethnics. Hence, migrants, especially survivors, need links with a range of groups and individuals, but in particular, need that familiar cultural link with co-ethnics or co-nationals who have experienced similar events in their home countries.

The notion of being a survivor is a complicated one, and for some people this status *did* aid their initial resettlement, in that it facilitated their migration into the UK. Those people, such as the Kindertransportees and some more recent survivors, found that the status of the survivor, if recognised, allowed them to begin building a life in the UK. It did this by validating their presence in the country and providing a concrete reason to be in the UK. Being perceived and recognised as a survivor meant that they had a valid reason for being in the UK that was generally widely recognised and accepted. However, if this status was denied, this added to the stress and general instability of life as was seen in Halima's case. Equally, for others such as Sarah whose status as a survivor was denied by the denial of her claim for compensation, it was found that this denial of status resulted in feeling that they were seen as 'lesser' people because they had not 'suffered enough' for their survivorhood to be recognised. Thus, survivors' suffering and experiences need to be recognised, particularly by those who hold powerful positions such as immigration officials and those who manage compensatory schemes. For these survivors, not to recognise suffering was to deny it, which caused further trauma and upset. When genocide survivors are not recognised as such, this reinforces the perpetrator ideology and narrative that such individuals are worthless and not full members of society.

Talking about their experiences was clearly important for all survivors because their experiences could be validated by the broader society but also as part of the overall recovery and re-establishment process for survivors. For some survivors in this research, this was as simple as being able to talk to family and tell them what had happened to them; for others, it was about accessing counselling which they could use to process and understand the events that had happened.

It is evident that the individuals in this study were all relatively successful in rebuilding and re-establishing their lives, and social capital did play some part in this. In addition, the *concept* of social capital aided the understanding of the mechanisms of resettlement, by foregrounding the processes by which survivors accessed help and support. However, how survivors developed and utilised social capital was quite varied. Some survivors were able to use the social capital of their family in order to escape and rebuild a new life; others developed social capital through the joining of clubs or social groups. Consequently, survivors used a range of methods in order to develop social capital in order to resettle and begin rebuilding their lives.

For many, employment and education aided the development of capital as well as aiding acculturation and adaptation. Those survivors who were young enough to attend school such as Henry and Sefik found that education aided them socially, as well as intellectually. They were able to broaden their field and learn how to speak English, not only the mechanics of the spoken language but also the relevant inflexions and intonations for the class background of the area. Ager and Strang's (2004) model highlights how these are the 'means and markers' of integration, in that employment and education are a means of integration, but also a marker of integration. Hence, access to education and employment is essential for survivors, not least because it builds links with the host community and allows the host community to become 'used' to the survivors' presence.

However, all survivors need the *opportunity* to utilise their social capital, by being given opportunities that allowed them to evidence their skills, such as taking part in sports and cultural activities. These activities provided opportunities that evidenced the survivors' skills and abilities and facilitated acceptance into the host community. Thus, social capital plays a valuable role in aiding the resettlement of genocide survivors and the re-establishment of their lives, but it is not a panacea. Providing people with opportunities or links with their communities, whilst helpful, will not provide all survivors with everything they need to resettle effectively.

An individual's habitus, their way of being, has a significant impact upon their ability to resettle and re-establish themselves, and despite having very little economic capital, most survivors managed to make links and develop their fields in order to maximise their resettlement opportunities. However, there were aspects of resettlement that Bourdieu's (1986) theory could not easily explain or illuminate.

Those who arrived in the UK as refugees, asylum seekers and migrants managed to move away from the class of 'forced migrant' relatively rapidly. Forced migrants can be seen as a class because the structures that surround them such as asylum legislation and associated rules such as welfare and housing force them into particular behaviours, as well as forcing them into particular areas and housing. Such areas are often poor and suffer from a range of factors relating to social exclusion, and the housing that forced migrants are placed in is often substandard (Dwyer and Brown 2008; Phillimore and Goodson 2008). Hence, their abilities to engage in society are inhibited by the wider structures that are in place around them. Alongside this, forced migrants often exist on subsistence-level finances and have their opportunities for employment and education severely limited, if not blocked altogether, by the rules and regulations surrounding asylum seekers and refugees. Furthermore, forced migrants are often perceived as a 'people apart' by the wider population, partly because of the segregation enforced on them by the structures in place. They are seen to be a drain on resources and a problem to be tackled and reduced, rather than being accepted as part of the population (Fekete and Webber 2010).

Moving away from this idea of a 'migrant class' was easier for those who survived the Holocaust, and this seems related to the broader structural issues of the time. Specifically, the immigration regulations appear to have a significant impact on how quickly survivors can re-establish themselves in their 'normal' class. More recent survivors had significant difficulty in doing this because of the legislation surrounding refugees and asylum seekers which prevents asylum seekers from working, and, in turn, prevents them from engaging in their usual 'class' employment.

Bourdieu (1986) argued that families are good sources of social capital, but those that lack capital 'trap' individuals, so they are unable to move out of that particular class (presumably upwards). Whilst families could aid with the development of social capital, in times where they could not or would not, this did not necessarily prevent individuals from accessing capital that could aid their movement to a higher class. Some survivors were able to circumnavigate barriers that would have ordinarily have prevented them from gaining appropriate employment, and several survivors arrived in the UK with very few belongings and no money, yet quite quickly moved into more 'middle class' situations. Thus, social capital and its possession or lack thereof does not on its own restrict genocide survivors to a particular class. Thus, whilst Bourdieu's ideas initially proved useful, there are some aspects of genocide survivors' experiences that cannot be fully explained by a 'face value' reading of Bourdieu's ideas.

Bourdieu argued that the possession of economic capital is the basis of all other capitals. For Bourdieu, cultural and social capital is derived from economic capital, which 'buys' access to education or cultural opportunities that then facilitates an individual's movement in 'higher'-class circles. However, this research found that if the *lack* of economic capital is recognised, this could also aid the development of social capital. Consequently, for many survivors, it is not the lack of economic capital that inhibits the development of social capital, but the *absence* of any recognition of that lack of economic capital. In a complete reversal of Bourdieu's ideas then, this research has shown that a complete lack of economic capital can function for some survivors in the same way that a significant amount of economic capital works for other individuals.

Bourdieu's notion of social capital is underpinned by the concepts of 'field' and 'habitus', and the concept of field has aided this research in understanding how relationships can help or hinder survivors in the re-establishment of their lives. For example, it is known that families can aid the process of resettlement, but this study found that individuals who are not biologically related can function as 'replacement' families and can aid the development of social capital. In addition, survivors are a field in themselves, and this leads to competition within the field. Most notable is the development of a survivor hierarchy, wherein survivors within the field compete through the telling of their experiences, to be recognised as survivors who hold symbolic capital. Those who hold such symbolic capital such as Zakiah and Vincent may be more readily recognised as genocide survivors by wider society and could be seen as the authoritative voice on the genocide experience. Those who have alternative experiences, such as Jack, may not be recognised as authoritative by the wider community; this was seen in Chap. 6 when Jack mentioned that he was told he should not be talking about his experiences as he wasn't in a camp. These assumptions can lead to misrecognition of the nature of genocide, wherein 'consumers' of the narratives of genocide come to expect key events and experiences to be present in all testimonies. This reinforces the symbolic capital of those who have such experiences and denies others who do not, and leads to certain survivors with archetypal stories representing the whole field of survivors; as indicated earlier, one survivor said in a recent documentary, "My story is the story of the six million" (Knoller in *Britain's Holocaust Survivors* 2013).

The individuals in this book engaged in the competition for symbolic capital, and their linguistic habitus was a key part of this competition. In order to be recognised as holding symbolic capital and be seen as a 'proper' genocide survivor, an individual needed to follow certain linguistic 'rules' which they had to follow when they were talking of their experiences. For Holocaust survivors, this involved speaking of the Holocaust in terms of experiencing life in a ghetto and then being transported by train to one of the well-known camps such as Auschwitz or Bergen-Belsen. The survivor then needed to refer to having their head shaved and experiencing perishing cold or extreme heat whilst wearing the thin camp uniform. Mention also needed to be made of food in terms of the starvation rations. Doing this enabled the survivor to be recognised as a Holocaust survivor by the wider society and at the same time reaffirmed the 'master narrative' of the survivor. Thus, survivors who did not exhibit this particular linguistic habitus found that the stories of their experiences were not accepted or seen in the same ways as other survivors who could talk about those experiences.

Furthermore, the disruption caused to the habitus by genocide can have manifest effects on an individual and their ability to acculturate.

What seemed to be of particular importance was the speed at which an individual's habitus had to change. Those individuals whose habitus changed gradually, often as a result of having a relatively stable field, appeared to have a less traumatic time in regard to their adaptation than those who had an unstable field around them. For them, their habitus was subject to a significantly higher level of stress as it was unable to adjust in a clear, logical manner. Survivors appear to 'carry' their class habitus with them from their home country and this did usually aid their acculturation into that particular class. However, for those survivors who arrived in the UK with no family, their class status was not as 'fixed', and as such, they were able to transcend class boundaries, depending upon the environment they found themselves in. In both cases, some survivors were not bound by the class they found themselves in as forced migrants but could draw on their 'home' cultural capital in order to access support and assistance. Survivors can draw on their previous class and culture, but it does not bind them to a particular class. Rather, those who have a middle-/upper-class background in their home country can draw on the cultural capital of that class in order to acculturate, such as professional qualifications or ability to play a particular sport or musical instrument. However, if an individual lacks cultural capital, this does not prevent them from eventually moving into a higher class but does mean that the progression takes longer. Where an individual ends up is more important than their starting point.

Bourdieu's theory of social capital has proved useful in a number of ways. Firstly, in terms of the strategies that individuals use when resettling, Bourdieu's ideas have brought to the fore the importance of opportunities for survivors to access support and cultural activities. Whilst the makeup of these groups can vary, what is important is that they provide a place for survivors to meet with other survivors, or provide a place where survivors can access help and support in terms of their acculturation.

Bourdieu states that education serves to keep individuals in their respective classes through cultural reproduction, arguing that individuals need cultural capital in order to succeed in education. As refugees and/or asylum seekers, the survivors in this study initially had very little cultural capital. They all lacked language skills, and the disconnect between

British and foreign education systems should have resulted in these survivors being unable to access education in a meaningful way which allowed them to retain their original class status. However, this was not the case. All the survivors who accessed education did well and were able to retain, or even move up from, their original class status. This can be explained by the role of the habitus, which Bourdieu suggests needed to be from a 'high class' background in order to succeed in school or university. All survivors in this study succeeded in education despite their initial refugee (and therefore lower-class) status. This was seen to be a result of their 'home' habitus—that is, their way of living prior to the genocide. This transcended their current class status and allowed them to access educational opportunities that were 'appropriate' for their previous class status. Thus, whilst cultural capital is valuable, it is the habitus that is essential in terms of future success for genocide survivors. This may prove to be more problematic for more recent migrants, as the asylum regulations that govern their existence in the UK inhibit their access to employment and education. This can be seen to some extent in Halima's case. In Sudan, she was a well-qualified doctor, but the asylum rules in the UK prevented her from working, and hence accessing her previous class status. Halima is still unable to work because speaking out against the militia has placed her in great danger from those she testified against at the International Criminal Court.

By exploring *how* survivor talk is constructed, this research found that there is a clear hierarchy amongst genocide survivors. By utilising Bourdieu's ideas on the value of speech in this research, it was discovered that survivors engage in the 'game' of narrative telling with some survivors' speech having more value than others, depending on whether their experiences align with the dominant narrative of the genocide. This dominant narrative, entrenched in broader societal structures, has a very practical impact when it comes to issues such as compensation, or recognition as a refugee by the relevant authorities. If a survivor is not recognised as such, compensation may be refused, or an asylum claim may be denied. This was evident in Halima's experiences wherein she was not believed by the Border Agency when she claimed asylum. Equally, this was seen in Judith's experiences where her narrative as a Polish survivor (rather than a German one) meant that her experiences were not seen as valid and hence she was denied compensation.

Moreover, the survivors' linguistic habitus plays an essential role in determining their place in the survivor hierarchy, a hierarchy between and within the different groups of genocide survivors that has a significant impact on how they are seen and how their stories are responded to by wider society. Those who are able to refer to the 'archetypal' markers of a genocide experience, for example by mentioning camps in terms of the Holocaust or being attacked with machetes in terms of the Rwandan genocide, are able to claim a high place in the hierarchy of survivors. Those survivors who do not have those experiences may find that their status is seen as 'lesser' as a result. The hierarchy serves a purpose in relation to survivors' identities, with those who are recognised as near the top of the hierarchy being asked to speak about their experiences at various events. This then reinforces the hierarchy of survivors, as consumers of testimony only hear certain forms of testimony. Thus, Bourdieu's concept of the linguistic habitus has been especially useful in illuminating the structures which encourage or discourage survivor talk and providing a lens through which the mechanisms of talk can be examined and explored in detail.

Bourdieu's ideas have proved to be invaluable in aiding the analysis of genocide survivors' experiences and proved to be flexible enough to highlight a range of issues. Unlike Coleman and Putnam's conceptions of social capital, Bourdieu's ideas have been developed beyond the simple accumulation of social capital to examine the roles of language as well as networks and skills. This proved vitally important when examining survivor acculturation for two key reasons. Firstly, Bourdieu's theory highlights the more common consideration of how survivors learn the language of the host country and begin to acculturate. Secondly, and arguably more importantly, these ideas have shown the strategies that survivors use when talking of their experiences, and how talking has a significant impact on how survivors are seen in society.

Succeeding as a Survivor

It is evident that the individuals in this research were successful in acculturating and re-establishing their lives. There are a number of reasons why this may be, not least the temporal nature of the arrival of the majority of participants. By arriving in the UK at a time when migrants were becoming increasingly common from a range of places; initially post-war migrants, closely followed by commonwealth migrants and others, the majority of survivors in this sample were not viewed as particularly unusual by the host population, and were able to make their way in their new lives with relative freedom. The changes in migratory policy, particularly in terms of the notion of 'asylum seeker', have significantly changed the resettlement landscape, as was seen in Halima's experiences. The increasingly restrictive policy stance towards forced migrants in the UK will have a substantial impact upon those individuals who arrive in the UK seeking safety. In particular, the recent referendum regarding the UK's membership of the European Union (EU) and the subsequent withdrawal of the UK from the EU in March 2019 will have a significant effect upon migrants' experiences, given that immigration was a key driver in the 'leave' campaign leading up to the referendum in June 2016 (Currie 2016). The negative attitudes towards forced migrants may well result in a lack of support for organisations that facilitate survivors' acculturation and adaptation, which further inhibits successful reintegration. In addition, attitudes relating to the 'believability' of migrants' experiences may also undermine their claim to survivor status, as has been seen in the experiences of several survivors in this research. Rosen and Crafter (2018) have noted that there is a bipolar attitude towards migrants, with, on one side, the death of Aylan Kurdi in 2015 provoking significant sympathetic reactions from across the political spectrum and media. Conversely, there are regular references to migrants flooding or swarming into the UK, with those arriving being perceived as a threat, both economically and culturally. Additionally, migrants to the UK are increasingly more visible than those who arrived post-war for a number of reasons. Firstly, they tend to be from non-white countries such as Iran, Pakistan or Iraq (Home Office 2018), hence being visibly different. Furthermore, they are often housed in specific communities, with housing that is easily identifiable as seen in the recent case of G4S (a housing provider for asylum seekers) painting the doors of their properties the same colour, inadvertently marking out which properties housed asylum seekers (Mason et al. 2016). Asylum seekers' inability to work, as already noted in Chap. 5, also marks them out as 'different' and also feeds into the media narratives around 'scroungers' and being a drain on the economy. With this in mind, it can be argued that social capital is essential for migrants to be able to acculturate and establish new lives. Where opportunities to develop social capital are denied or hindered, such as preventing work, survivors are unable to become full members of the society they are joining. Despite the sample in this research not being representative of all experiences, not least because of the relatively small sample size, the findings do highlight some key issues that do relate to the general attitudes of the UK population as a whole, particularly around expectations of migrants once they arrive in the UK and their experiences prior to their arrival.

Policy Implications

There are three key areas of concern in relation to life afterwards. Firstly, when survivors first arrive, they are able to utilise their existing habitus in order to fit in socially. This means that survivors (and more broadly, all forced migrants) need to be able to access a range of support and services that enable that habitus to 'work'. This means that support organisations and communities need access to a range of different activities and need to avoid the assumption that 'one size fits all' when it comes to acculturation activities.

Secondly, resettlement alongside family can aid recovery, but additional support is also needed, particularly in relation to education and employment. It is important to ensure that there is not a presumption that a family can provide all the support needed for genocide survivors newly arrived in the UK. Families can and do provide much-needed support for genocide survivors, but it was found in this study that families can also inhibit survivor resettlement. Consequently, survivor organisations should be aware of the issues which families may be unable to provide such as employment or educational opportunities. Moreover, genocide survivors have very specific needs, and organisations need to be aware that families may not be able to fully support a genocide survivor in terms of their emotional and practical recovery. Several survivors indicated that their family were not prepared to listen to their experiences, for a variety of reasons. Therefore, it is important that survivors are able to access support, which cannot be provided by family elsewhere. Of particular importance is that it is evident that class is influenced by field, and as such, survivors (and forced migrants, more broadly) should be placed in fields that can aid upward social mobility. This is important for those working with survivors and forced migrants in terms of housing options, as it is evident from this research that being placed in hostels, as Halima was, can cause further trauma. Equally, preventing survivors from accessing work and education opportunities also prevents upward social mobility. Therefore, survivors need to be placed into areas with decent housing and employment opportunities for all, and, importantly, not merely dispersed to wherever there is room but housed alongside both host populations and other migrants with similar cultural backgrounds and experiences. This facilitates recovery because survivors are able to talk to others with similar experiences, but also engage in the 'normal' community life of the host population.

Finally, survivors do need to talk about their experiences, but in their own time and at their own pace. Particular attention needs to be paid to survivors from non-Western backgrounds who may have different needs when it comes to counselling. In particular, it must be remembered that immigration officers or other officials cannot enforce talk. Aside from the varying cultural conventions which may inhibit an individual talking about rape or sexual violence, or talking to an officer who is a different gender to the survivor, many survivors may not be able to find the words to explain their experiences. Hence, it must be remembered that just because an individual cannot talk about their experiences does not make them invalid in any way.

Whilst these recommendations are important, it is worth bearing in mind Chamberlain's view that "[t]he very act of telling the story of a previously silenced voice can be enough to both empower socially disadvantaged individuals as well as influence academic thinking and governmental policy-making processes" (Chamberlain 2013: 101). Whilst the survivors in this research were not necessarily silenced prior to this project, what this project has done is draw attention to the situations in which survivors *are* silenced, and what prevents them from doing so. Furthermore, this study supports other research in this field in arguing that those who arrive in the country following forced migration should be placed wherever possible near friends and family (Phillimore 2012) and, at the very least, near those of a similar cultural background. This research has found that Holocaust survivors on the whole acculturated relatively well, and this seems to be because they were allowed the time and space to acculturate at their own speed, rather than being forced to 'fit in' as soon as they arrived. This is most evident when considering when people begin talking about their experiences. Whilst the Holocaust survivors did not initially speak in public of their experiences, most did talk to their families and friends about their lives and, therefore, were able to come to terms with their experiences slowly. More recent migrants are often not accorded this space and are required to talk about their experiences in detail, often to a border official who may be seeking to ensure that the story is true by questioning the migrant in detail about their experiences. Even when survivors are able to answer these questions, their linguistic habitus may result in the questions not being answered in the 'right' way, and therefore their experiences may still not be seen as valid. Moreover, this study has discovered that more recent migrants have to tell the 'right' story in order to have their status recognised, either by immigration officials or by the broader society. Bourdieu's concept of linguistic habitus has allowed us to understand that survivors often have to wait for structural changes in order for their speech to become valid. By placing newly arrived survivors with others from their culture, they are able to engage in survivor talk when they are ready to, rather than being forced to do it in a different language, or being silenced because of the culture of the host country.

Allowing genocide survivors (particularly younger ones) to engage in the usual practices of the host country, such as playing sports and going to school, significantly aids acculturation and resettlement. Sport in particular aids the development of social capital, as seen in the cases of survivors who were able to use their sporting ability to make friends and prove their worth in the hierarchy of the school.

It is evident that sociology has the potential to contribute a significant amount to our understanding of both genocidal events in themselves and the experience of the life afterwards, especially in terms of how and when survivors talk about their experiences. As this book series illustrates, there has been a shift in the intellectual landscape of the approaches to peace and conflict, with sociology taking a much more central role in exploring and analysing this area. This volume contributes to this developing focus by highlighting the value of applying sociological theory to the aftermath of conflict and mass violence. In developing ideas around post-conflict identity, this volume ties in with Jennifer Todd's (2018) work on the importance of identity change in post-conflict Northern Ireland and Sarah Jankowitz (2018) study of victimhood, identities and relationships relating to reconciliation in Northern Ireland. Unlike these two volumes, however, this current book has focused on how sociological approaches can illuminate the post-conflict life following migration. Hence, rather than examining the rebuilding of life from within a post-conflict country, the current volume has instead focused on the impact of migration, and how the dual effects of conflict and migration affect lives. In doing so, this book has identified, through the application of sociological theory, that social capital is not a panacea, and can inhibit resettlement and reacculturation if the social capital is inappropriate or ineffective. In doing so, this argument supports Laura Graham's (2016) argument in her volume of this series, noting that social capital may have negative impacts in some situations. Social capital is extremely valuable to survivors who have migrated to the UK, but only if they can access it and use it in the ways that they need to. Therefore, survivors recover best when they are allowed to acculturate at their own pace, where support is provided, but not imposed, and where survivors can live amongst others who are culturally similar to them.

References

Ager, A., & Strang, A. (2004). *Indicators of Integration*. London: Home Office.

Bourdieu, P. (1986). The Forms of Capital. In J. G. Richardson (Ed.), *Handbook of Theory and Research for the Sociology of Education* (pp. 241–258). London: Greenwood Press.

Chamberlain, J. M. (2013). *Understanding Criminological Research* (1st ed.). London: Sage Publications.

Currie, S. (2016). Reflecting on Brexit: Migration Myths and What Comes Next for EU Migrants to the UK. *Journal of Social Welfare and Family Law, 38*(3), 337–342.

Dwyer, P., & Brown, D. (2008). Accommodating 'Others'? Housing Dispersed, Forced Migrants in the UK. *Journal of Social Welfare and Family Law, 30*(3), 203–218.

Fekete, L., & Webber, F. (2010). Foreign Nationals, Enemy Penology and the Criminal Justice System. *Race and Class, 51*(4), 1–25.

Graham, L. (2016). *Beyond Social Capital: The Role of Leadership, Trust and Government Policy in Northern Ireland's Victim Support Groups*. Basingstoke: Palgrave Macmillan.

Home Office. (2018). *How Many People Do We Grant Asylum or Protection to?* London: Home Office [Online]. Retrieved January 18, 2019, from https://www.gov.uk/government/publications/immigration-statistics-year-ending-march-2018/how-many-people-do-we-grant-asylum-or-protection-to.

Jankowitz, S. (2018). *The Order of Victimhood: Violence, Hierarchy and Building Peace in Northern Ireland*. Basingstoke: Palgrave Macmillan.

Mason, R., Pidd, H., & Khomani, N. (2016). Asylum Seekers in North-East Claim They Are Identifiable by Red Doors. *The Guardian*, 20 January 2016 [Online]. Retrieved January 18, 2018, from https://www.theguardian.com/uk-news/2016/jan/20/asylum-seekers-north-east-claim-identifiable-red-doors-houses.

Phillimore, J. (2012). Implementing Integration in the UK: Lessons for Integration Theory, Policy and Practice. *Policy and Politics, 40*(4), 525–545.

Phillimore, J., & Goodson, L. (2008). Making a Place in the Global City: The Relevance of Indicators of Integration. *Journal of Refugee Studies, 21*(3), 305–325.

Rosen, R., & Crafter, S. (2018). Media Representations of Separated Child Migrants: From Dubs to Doubt. *Migrations and Society: Advances in Research, 1*(1), 68–81.

Todd, J. (2018). *Identity Change After Conflict: Ethnicity, Boundaries and Belonging in the Two Irelands*. Basingstoke: Palgrave Macmillan.

Index[1]

[1] Note: Page numbers followed by 'n' refer to notes.

L. Asquith, *Rebuilding Lives After Genocide*, Palgrave Studies in Compromise after Conflict, https://doi.org/10.1007/978-3-030-14074-8

U

V

W

FSC
www.fsc.org
MIX
Papier | Fördert
gute Waldnutzung
FSC® C083411

Kolibri 360 GmbH
Ferdinand-Jühlke-Straße 7
99095 Erfurt, Deutschland
produktsicherheit@kolibri360.de